POSTED IN PARAGUAY

ELOISE HANNER

ALSO BY ELOISE HANNER

The First Big Ride: A Woman's Journey

Letters from Afghanistan

To my loving sisters,
Linda Leah Carlton and Rita Lynn Tinsley,
who are always there for me.

POSTED IN PARAGUAY
A Peace Corps Writers Book
An imprint of Peace Corps Worldwide

Printed in the United States of America
by Peace Corps Writers of Oakland, California.

For more information, contact peacecorpsworldwide@gmail.com.
Peace Corps Writers and the Peace Corps Writers colophon are
trademarks of PeaceCorpsWorldwide.org.

ISBN 978-1-935925-41-5
Library of Congress Control Number: 2014931811

First Peace Corps Writers Edition, February 2014

POSTED IN PARAGUAY

ELOISE HANNER

A Peace Corps Writers Book

1   The Fateful New Year's Eve

Nobody goes to Paraguay. Even travelers who boast of having been everywhere, haven't been there. It's too costly, too far away and way below the tourist radar. With no famous sites, few paved roads and a visa tax, the incentives to explore the country are few. And for those who like English-speaking destinations, it's almost an impossibility. Outside of the airport and a few hotels in Asunción, no one in the entire country speaks a word of English. For most of the country, the second language is Spanish, the first being a local Indian dialect called Guaraní. Paraguay's population is mostly rural and despite efforts to integrate with the world, it remains a small, isolated country hidden away in the middle of South America. My husband Chuck and I started our journey to this unlikely destination on a chilly New Year's Eve in San Diego several years before we actually got there.

We had decided that the two of us would have our own in-home party that evening, so I sliced some cheese and opened a box of crackers, while Chuck poured us a couple of gin and tonics.

After sitting down on the couch I held up my glass, "To the New Year!" I proposed.

"Yes, but wait a minute." Chuck put down his glass. "There is something I want you to read first."

He ran upstairs then came back with two typed pages, apparently the efforts of his afternoon on the computer. I made myself comfortable and began to read.

The first page contained a series of quotes on change. The first one read:

> There is a certain relief in change, even though it be from bad to worse; as I have found in traveling in a stagecoach, that it is often a comfort to shift one's position and be bruised in a new place. — *Washington Irving (1783–1859)*

It was followed by:

> Every body continues in its state of rest, or of uniform motion in a right line, unless it is compelled to change that state by forces impressed upon it. — *Sir Isaac Newton (1642–1727)*

There were others, and then a quote on work:

> Unchanging work at a uniform task kills the explosive flow of a man's animal spirits, which draw refreshing zest from a simple change of activity. — *Karl Marx (1818–1883).*

At the bottom of the page Chuck had summed it up with his own paragraph that ended with:

> I just don't enjoy my work anymore. There . . . I've said it. I can't believe I said it. I am sick to death of commission sales, at least in the way I am doing it now. So here is the deal. I am resigning on January 1, 1996.

I was stunned. We were both career stockbrokers and the business had been good. We lived in a spacious condo, were members of a golf club and had about everything we wanted. We were still young — late forties and I hadn't expected changes for years. Tears were filling my eyes; I hadn't realized Chuck had been unhappy. My universe, which had seemed so secure, had cracked wide open.

Chuck was true to his word. The next January he had an early retirement party and said good-bye to twenty years of broker-age. He started a business out of the house as a vitamin distributor and seemed happy doing his own thing. But his departure was the pulling of the linchpin. The following year my hopes at higher management were dashed and then I too wanted out. I left exactly two years later, January 1998.

We spent the next six months training for a grand athletic adventure — cycling across the United States. The trip started in mid-June and took seven weeks, making it September before we arrived back home to face the reality of "Now What?" We had vague plans of finding new jobs, but it was harder than we thought. We were willing to work for less, but wanted occupations that didn't require the commute or the stress. Nothing came along. Either the jobs weren't close or they required more education or they didn't pay at all or . . . or . . . something.

We were scanning the Sunday help wanted ads one morning when Chuck suddenly looked up, "You know what I think we should do?" he asked brightly.

"No, what?"

"Rejoin the Peace Corps."

I recall a sudden panicky feeling, reminiscent of very bad news. It took me several seconds before I could reply with a weak, "Now?"

True, we had both been feeling restless. Part of it was that life outside of work was quite a different ballgame. The friends we had worked with were still involved with their careers and we weren't part of that anymore. And we had to admit that they really weren't close friends anyway, just business associates. The more we played golf, the less we liked it, and I found that there were few women at the club with whom I had much in common. Chuck had grown to despise the game. Still, joining the Peace Corps sounded drastic.

We had first joined right after we graduated from college in 1971 and had been sent to Afghanistan as English teachers. We had loved it. When we finished our tour in 1973, we had said something like, "Wouldn't it be fun to do this again someday, at the end of our careers?" At that point in our lives the Peace Corps had been the best and most exciting thing we had ever done. Actually, it was the only thing we had ever done, given that we had left directly out of college and it was our first home, our first job, our first trip abroad and our first two years of married life. At the time, the idea of repeating the experience when we were "old" had a romantic appeal. No matter what the next thirty plus years would dish out for us, we envisioned rewarding ourselves with another wonderful overseas experience before we died. That was the idea. But it was still a shock when Chuck mentioned it. In 1998 I didn't feel old enough. I was forty-nine; Chuck was fifty-one and life had been abundant. True, I did want another job but I wanted it to fit into my framework. I loved our condo in Rancho Bernardo overlooking the 5th fairway of the golf course. I loved being able to pick up the phone and chat with my mother or sisters. I loved renting a movie video and watching it while sipping a gin and tonic. I loved my shiny black Honda Accord with its beige, leather interior. I loved the good life of America and I was spoiled.

I fretted over the matter for a couple of days while Chuck reminded me of all the wonderful experiences we had before: the close friends, the travel, the adventures. Slowly I came around to the thought — perhaps it wouldn't be a bad idea — it would be interesting, and an escape from aspects of American life I didn't like, most notably driving in rush hour freeway traffic. And I reasoned maybe it was better to go now while we were healthy, instead of later when God-knows-what ailments might befall us. We had already lost friends to strange cancers and my own father had died in his fifties.

Going now wouldn't be any harder than going later, as far as tending to household possessions went. That would be an equal task at sixty, maybe even worse. When we applied for the Peace

Corps in 1970, we had no house, no possessions, no money and a junker car that we had bought for $50.00. Now we had a home, furniture and two nice cars. We also had parents. We had parents before, naturally, but being newlyweds off on an adventure, we didn't think or worry about them that much. Now the separation seemed vast and I knew my Mom would be devastated to think of me so far away. In the previous year she had been widowed for the second time and now I called her often. From San Diego I could catch a plane and be at her side in two hours.

For two weeks Chuck and I talked about the Peace Corps incessantly — at mealtimes, on bike rides and on nightly walks around the neighborhood. I finally decided that yes, I wanted to go, but my spirits sank when I thought of my Mom. She'd had a very hard time accepting the news I gave her the year before about riding our bicycles across the United States. This would be worse. My sisters were easier. I knew they would be relaxed and even enthusiastic about it. Although we were very tight-knit siblings, we didn't live close to each other. Linda lived outside of Portland, Oregon and Rita was in Washington D.C. so it wasn't as though we saw each other more than once or twice a year. We decided that they would have to come and visit us.

In 1971 as college seniors, when we had filled out our applications, we had requested to be assigned to the South Pacific — and ended up in Afghanistan. But we didn't much care — it was all an adventure. This time, though, we wanted to serve in a Spanish speaking country as we had been studying Spanish as a hobby for five years, taking numerous vacations to Mexico where we had attended Spanish language schools. We filled out the applications, sent them in November and expected to wait several months for a reply.

Three weeks later we received a call from the Peace Corps to meet with a recruiter. I was staggered at the suddenness of it all. I didn't feel ready, but we agreed to a meeting and went with a list of questions, the biggest of them being — when would we go, where would we go and what exactly would we do? I was skeptical that our twenty years working as stock-brokers would be of much use.

We met with the recruiter at a nearby Denny's, a pretty girl who had served in Africa and was now working for the Peace Corps staff. Over coffee, she assured us that we could be quite useful in the small business programs, helping develop cooperatives for local farmers and small businesses.

"Cooperatives are basically group ownership enterprises," she explained. "Sometimes they act as savings and loans or sometimes they are simply markets for members. Your understanding of businesses, budgets, your organizational skills, all of these would be very useful."

She went on to explain that in the larger towns the cooperatives would be big enough to use both of us.

"Larger towns," I repeated, looking over at Chuck. "That would be good."

Chuck nodded, thinking the same thing. In Afghanistan, we had lived and worked in Kabul, and not only had that been "rustic" enough, it had provided a vast array of services and friends that the Volunteers out in the provinces didn't have.

The recruiter continued, explaining that there were two small business programs in the Western Hemisphere, one in the Caribbean and one in Paraguay. We could go to either one as soon as January

But I wasn't remotely ready for January. In addition to selling or storing all of our possessions, I wanted to finish a book I had started writing about our bicycle ride the previous summer. Chuck was also involved in a business of marketing vitamins and he had to do something with that. It was finally settled we could enter the Paraguayan program in June, giving us five months to prepare.

As I expected, Mother did not take the news well. She thought after our adventure on the bicycles, we might have such foolishness out of our heads and return to the workforce like sensible adults.

I heard later that she cried for hours in her sister's arms, which left me feeling like a heartless scoundrel. My own sisters assured me that it would be OK and they would look after her, but I still felt terrible.

To help ease the absence we bought her a computer and my brother-in-law, Don, gave her basic email lessons. That raised my spirits some, but I continued to fret. Was going worth causing Mom so much anguish? Truly, in my heart, did I want to go? I couldn't answer that. I didn't want to leave Mom though, that was for sure. I promised her that I would return in a year for a visit, so it wouldn't be like Afghanistan, when we were gone for two and a half years. From Afghanistan it had been impossible to come home since we had no money to make the trip and Volunteers were not permitted such travel, but now things were different. We had enough money. I could just fly back and see her. I wasn't sure how Peace Corps would like that, but I didn't care. Surely it could be worked out.

Chuck didn't have these issues; he was 110% ready to go. As far as his Mother was concerned, whatever he wanted to do was just dandy. If Chuck had wanted to go to Tibet and raise yaks, that was fine with her. Chuck enjoyed seeing his brother, Brooke, but they didn't get together often. Brooke was occupied with his own family and business and even though they only lived thirty miles away, we didn't schedule many get-togethers. Mostly just Christmas, Thanksgiving and maybe Mother's Day or a birthday. If we didn't say anything it would be months before Brooke would realize Chuck was gone.

As June approached and I became more apprehensive, Chuck was getting more and more anxious to leave. He re-read everything the Peace Corps had sent us and emailed everyone's friend-of-a-friend who had traveled to South America, but had a hard time finding anyone who had actually been to Paraguay. He finally came across an email address of a Peace Corps Volunteer in country whose main advice was to bring duct tape and long-johns — Paraguayan duct tape, if it could be found, was crap, and we'd freeze in the winter, which for them was July. He said he had never been so cold and

7

he was used to Chicago winters.

"Long-johns? How cold can it be?" I asked Chuck after he read me the email. "Look at the map. It's exactly the same distance from the equator, going south, as La Paz, Mexico is, going north." We had been to La Paz two years before in January and it hadn't been cold at all.

We didn't have any long-johns anyway, so as I laid out what we would take with us I settled instead for a pair of tights for myself, and sweaters and jackets for us both. We carefully weighed our piles as I added our cold weather clothes, hot weather clothes, the recommended duct tape, two needlepoint kits (which had been in my closet for twenty years), our laptop, Chuck's guitar (which he loved, but hadn't played in a decade), two cameras, sleeping bags, backpacks, a pile of my favorite recipes, a framed picture of my Mom and sisters, a calendar, binoculars, flashlights and as a final touch, two swim masks and snorkels.

"For our vacations to Rio," I told Chuck.

The pile for checked baggage teetered at the exact maximum — 140 pounds.

2 The Retreat

By the third week in May we were ready to depart.

My book (now entitled *The First Big Ride — A Woman's Journey*) was finished and I had sent copies to ten publishers who appeared to accept memoirs from authors without agents. I didn't have high hopes. I had read countless stories of writers sending their books to hundreds of publishers and still never getting anywhere, but I thought maybe publishers would send back suggestions or helpful critiques. Chuck had sold his vitamin business to a fellow distributor, and together we had sold the house, the cars, and stored the best of the furniture.

On the 24th of May we flew to Miami for staging in preparation for departure for Paraguay, and made our way to the designated Holiday Inn. There we rendezvoused with the rest of our training group, and checked in with the Peace Corps staff members.

There were seventeen Trainees in our group, most of them under thirty and all of them, except us, single. It was a contrast to our long-ago Afghanistan group where almost everyone was married. In Afghanistan, they had wanted married couples because the dating life for single men was non-existent, and it wasn't considered a safe or culturally acceptable country for single women. In Paraguay it didn't matter. In addition to being married, we were now the "old" ones along with two others: John, a retired lawyer from Portland, Oregon and Doris, who was the oldest at fifty-nine.

We spent the rest of the day going through various exercises for introducing ourselves, sharing our backgrounds and why we had joined the Peace Corps. For most it was adventure, maybe sprinkled with altruism; for others it was the lack of jobs. One exercise had each of us telling the others what worried us the most about going to Paraguay. For some it was snakes or bugs or learning a new language. No one shared my apprehensions: missing Mom and moving from a spacious condo overlooking a golf course to a hovel in a developing country. The idea of the exercise was to get rid of anxieties, but the more I listened, the more anxious I became, hearing new fears I hadn't thought of. We ended the session describing the "stupidest" thing we had packed. I confessed to our diving snorkels.

The next morning we had another quick session and learned that we would spend our first three days in Asunción in a retreat before starting training in earnest. Despite the heat in Miami we were reminded to dress warmly as it would be chilly when we got off the plane in Paraguay, which was now starting its winter season. This made our choice of spending our last stateside afternoon on the beach a bit problematic, but we were able to leave our jackets in the bus and rolled up our jeans to wade in the surf. I wondered how long it would be before I would be swimming again. At five o'clock we gathered in the bus and headed off to the airport for the midnight flight.

It was not like our trips to Mexico where a day of travel was rewarded by margaritas served at sundown on a hotel patio. With a long layover in Brazil we didn't arrive in Asunción until nine o'clock in the morning, with our backs and necks aching from trying to find comfortable sleeping positions on the plane. We were greeted by an authoritative, robust man with snow white hair, who was the Peace

Corps director of training for Paraguay. He whisked us through customs and led us to a bus at the curb where we were greeted by some currently serving Peace Corps Volunteers holding welcome signs. They were a jolly group and told us how much we would enjoy the retreat.

Retreat. For me the word conjured up something modestly swanky, maybe set in the mountains with a stream or lake nearby. During our broker years we had countless Merrill Lynch meetings at plush resorts and while I knew it wouldn't be that fancy, I was thinking along those lines. I knew Paraguay was flat, so I don't know where I was coming up with my illusions of streams or mountains, but thought we might be heading to a little mountain, maybe out in the countryside somewhere.

As we drove into the inner city, however, this possibility grew increasingly dim. It was chilly, as advertised, with a gray, overcast sky and the city equally gray and depressing with few trees or bushes or anything green. We passed modern looking buildings for a block or two, then rows of small, squat, cement ones, with either no paint or painted one color on the top half, and a different one on the bottom, both faded and flaking. With the exception of the occasional new car dealership, everything looked run-down. Streets were lined with small wooden shacks selling everything from automotive parts to ropes of garlic. Litter swirled along the curbs, where there were sidewalks at all, and stray dogs slunk around sniffing piles of garbage. I stared out the window, weary and slightly depressed, but decided not to voice my opinion on my first impressions of the city, which were decidedly negative. My mood didn't improve much as we finally turned down a side street into a compound and stopped. Obviously the location for the retreat. There was a big tree in the middle of a circular dirt drive, with sparse grass and bushes at the edges and some plain barracks scattered about.

"Volunteers always love coming here," a female Volunteer gushed. "It's such a treat."

I wondered what life was going to be like if this place was considered a treat.

As we got off the bus we found that our bags were already in a big heap in the middle of the compound, so after finding ours, we lugged them to our designated building. Chuck and I were assigned to what was called the "honeymoon suite" because this room had only two army cots, while the others had four. The room looked exactly like the barracks of an army training camp, except smaller. The walls were bare, the floor was cement and there was nothing in the room besides the cots and a small wooden table between them. There were folded grayish towels on each bed. The small bathroom was shared — one to a building. I tried to be optimistic.

"Oh well, it's clean," I offered.

"And it's not like this is where we're staying," Chuck added. He could see that I was tired and a bit distressed and gave me a hug, reminding me that it would all work out, and we should, as my golfing friend Patti used to say, "Wait to worry."

We had medical check-ins and I hopefully presented my worn, yellow immunization book that I had kept from Afghanistan, thinking it would spare me a shot or two. I have a total phobia of doctors and needles and can pass out just thinking about them.

The doctor took my book, flipped through it and broke out laughing, "Gamma Gobulin," he chortled, "they used to think that prevented tuberculosis!"

"It doesn't?" I asked.

"Oh no, not at all. Total waste," he said, still chuckling and shaking his head.

That was stunning news, even after thirty years. We had those painful shots every three months and had consoled ourselves with the thought that we were protected.

The doctor then flipped through the rest of the book and just shook his head muttering, "Nope, nope, nope."

The only good one was the hepatitis shot I had gotten in December for the Peace Corps exam. I received three more shots, but warned the nurse I was a fainter so she gave them to me while I was lying down.

The medical lecture came next. We were told to take notes so I had my notebook and pen ready for all information.

Julie, an American nurse, reminded us first that all toilet paper was to go in the baskets next to the toilet, which would be emptied daily. "The smallest square clogs the pipes," she told us sternly, "so PLEASE remember to use the baskets."

We all nodded obediently and scribbled in our notebooks.

"We're all quite lucky to be in such a healthy country," she continued. "One of the few in South American where you can drink the water."

I glanced at Chuck, raising my eyebrows in pleasant surprise, remembering the totally contaminated water in Afghanistan.

"So, we have just a few things to be aware of," she continued. "First and the most irritating are the red ants, called *colorados*. They are literally everywhere and bite like crazy. Their bites leave a pustule which is easily infected and lasts a week no matter what you put on them. So, try to avoid them."

I underlined *avoid*.

"You might also have problems with the *pique*. It's an insect that lays its eggs under your skin, usually on the soles of your feet. It makes a bump that hurts and gets bigger as the larvae grow. You know its *pique* if it has a black dot in the middle. And it doesn't go away. You have to have them dug out," she stated matter-of-factly.

Someone asked if she had ever had them.

"Oh yes," she said nonchalantly, "from time to time — everyone gets them."

I grimaced and underlined *black dot* and *dug out* twice. She went on to describe another under-your-skin seeking bug, this one you could get rid of by covering it with salve and tape which suffocated it.

I felt hot and clammy and needed air. I got up and went for a glass of water at the back of the room. When I returned to my seat Julie was discussing dengue fever.

"It's like malaria, but worse. They say with malaria you think you're going to die, but with dengue, you hope you do!" She chuckled at her joke. "We don't see it too much with Volunteers as it mostly spreads in the capital. You'll get more information later on eliminating mosquitoes from your site." She looked through her notes and added, almost as an afterthought, "Oh, watch out for orange fuzzy caterpillars on the mangoes. Their bite will leave a purple welt and puts a virus in your blood. Then, in some twenty years, long after you've left the Peace Corps, you will find one day that all your organs harden up and cease to function. It's fatal, or course," she added nonchalantly, "but so far we've never had a Volunteer get bitten."

Someone asked, "How did they know?"

"A blood test," she said. "You will all get a blood test upon leaving the country which could confirm if you have been bitten."

John, the retired lawyer, raised his hand, "Can they help you if they find it early?"

"Not at this time."

"Well then, why would you even want to know you had it?"

Julie didn't really have an answer for that. She just smiled and shrugged and added that it was quite difficult to get bitten.

I drew a caterpillar in my notebook, followed by skull and crossbones.

Another Volunteer took over to explain Paraguayan snakes and wildlife.

"There's a little viper," he began, "that the Indians call, the-thir-ty-seconds-and-you're-dead-snake."

Thirty seconds and you're dead? I drew a little snake in my notebook and another skull and crossbones.

"But I don't think you'll find any," he continued optimistically, "they are rare and only in the north. The only snakes I've seen are the garden variety. Well, there was a python once, down in the river, but those aren't common either; too cold here." He paused to think. "Hmmm, tarantulas, but they're harmless. I suppose the most dangerous thing are the watch dogs — never go inside anyone's fence without clapping at the gate; that's the Paraguayan doorbell. And wait to be escorted in, especially at night. And don't

14

cross fenced pastures with bulls — they can turn and be on you in a second."

I drew a dog head with giant fangs and a little Merrill Lynch bull and another skull and cross bones.

"But really, this is a pretty safe place, considering how rural most of you will be. And you will each get one of these," He held up a blue plastic medical kit, opened it and read the inventory. "Bandages, needles, antiseptics, cold remedies, pain pills, thermometer, anti-diarrhea pills, anti-fungus cream, aspirin, sutures — more than you'll need."

I drew a little suitcase and a happy smile.

When we returned to our room after dinner, I sat down on the bed and was about to lie back when a movement caught my eye. Crawling across the pillow were legions of small red ants. I jumped up.

"Oh my God, look Chuck, I bet these are the *colorados* that Julie was talking about. The ones that are everywhere!"

Chuck came over and we both looked at a thick line of them crossing the pillow. I carefully pinched the corner of the pillow and turned it over. The mother lode! Thousands, millions, swarming all over the bottom sheet.

"Oh crap!" I exclaimed to Chuck. "I need a new bed."

I went back to the dining hall, and found one of the trainers still there. I described the ants, trying not to sound like an overly-picky American tourist — like a billion ants in your bed wasn't a particular concern — but did he have, perchance, a large can of bug spray? He followed me back to our barracks, took one look at the bed and said bug spray wouldn't quite do the job. Instead, we could move to the other side of the building, which was empty. We checked our gear to make sure no ants had colonized there, then hefted the backpacks, grabbed the duffels and resettled in a new room. This time I carefully inspected the blankets and sheets and once deciding they were OK, I dug out our toilet kit and asked Chuck if I could be the first one to try out the communal shower.

"Be my guest," he said. After the hot Miami sun from the afternoon before, all night on the plane and a day in Paraguay, I was decidedly grimy.

I left him reading some of the material we had been given during the day, and walked down the hall to the bathroom, shut the door and shed my clothes in a heap. I reached into the shower to crank on the hot water and noticed there was only one handle for water, and it wasn't one of those fancy modern gizmos that twist in all directions. It was a plain round knob, identical to the one we had outside — or used to have — for the garden hose. I turned the knob vigorously and cold water spurted out. I waited, looked at my watch and waited some more. I stood there freezing for five minutes.

"Shit," I said aloud, as I got back in my jeans and shirt and went back to our room to see if Chuck had any suggestions, or would be sweet enough to go outside and see if he could still find a trainer wandering around.

Chuck thought there might be something he could fix. He followed me back to the bathroom, pulled back the tattered shower curtain and ran his hand around the shower head. The top part was covered by an odd-looking plastic ring. On the wall next to the shower was an electrical switch, which I had failed to notice.

"OK, let's try this," he said flipping it up and turning the water on again. Sure enough, after a minute it was feeling warmer and we could see something glowing red inside the ring on the shower head.

"So, I guess that's the heater and the water warms up when it passes through it."

"Doesn't that go against the rule of combining electricity and water?"

"Well yes, but it's separated by the plastic. They can't be electrocuting all the Trainees."

He left as I undressed again and stepped cautiously inside. It was still only tepid so I turned up the water flow, only to discover that it got colder. I quickly reached down and turned the volume almost off, and was rewarded with scalding drops on my neck and back. Obviously, the more water through the ring, the colder it became; the less water, the hotter it became. I fiddled it back and forth and finally achieved a tolerable, warmish dribble. I still had my doubts about its safety, but at that point I was too tired and dirty to care. If it was my fate to be electrocuted my first night in Asunción, so be it.

Our concerns with the showers were shared by others at breakfast and we were assured that it was very safe. Not to worry. One trainer said the only problem was maintaining a constant temperature, which I had already experienced.

We went through language evaluations that morning and with the exception of a girl named Beth, we were way ahead of the others in Spanish fluency. Our feelings of accomplishment evaporated, however, when we were told that most of us wouldn't be speaking much Spanish, but rather the native language of Guaranie. Chuck just rolled his eyes and whispered to me that he was sticking with Spanish. I didn't see how that was going to work, but decided to add that to the "wait-to-worry" list.

We learned about the basic currency, the Guaranie which was 4,420 to the dollar, and discussed basic types of introductions. The Paraguayan standard was a kiss on both cheeks.

Chuck and I decided we would henceforth call ourselves Carlos and Eloisa, since Eloise and Chuck were too difficult to pronounce for Spanish or Guaranie speakers. One gal in our group, named Penny, had to change her name completely since Penny sounded just like *pene*, Spanish for penis.

With our evening free, we walked to a nearby shopping plaza that was quite modern and full of State-side brand stores. The teachers at the compound had told us it was "*chu-chee*" a word they used for excessive, expensive things that we could never buy on our Peace Corps salaries nor need in our Peace Corps lives.

It was odd to think that for years, working for Merrill, I went to such malls, bought expensive clothes and never thought about it. Now I was "poor" and could only look in the windows. I felt out of place there, wearing jeans, heavy boots and my warmest jacket, as rich Paraguayan women passed us in tight designer jeans and high heels.

We did make it to an Internet café though, and I sent a quick note out to my sisters and Mother. *We are well*, I typed, *everything is going smoothly*. I decided not to enumerate all of my anxieties.

3 Poorest of the Poor

During training in Afghanistan thirty years ago, we were housed with another married-couple from our training group — the Hohls — and were taken care of by a part-time servant who made sure we were fed. Now, for better cultural immersion, we would all live with local families for the next two and a half months. It probably was a better system, but left us a little anxious, wondering what kind of family we would get, and how we would adjust to living with anyone after thirty years of living by ourselves.

After three days at the retreat, we embarked on a bus to Pindolo, just outside of Asunción, where our families lived. Accompanying us was our trainer, Mark, a former Volunteer in Paraguay who was now on the Peace Corps staff. He referred to Pindolo as a suburb of Asunción, so I was still looking for a little town when we stopped at a lonely crossing of dirt roads and a couple of houses. A cluster of women and children on one corner indicated, that yes, this was Pindolo.

One by one, our names were read off, paired with the name of the assigned family.

We were some of the last ones still on the bus when Mark finally called, "Carlos y Eloisa Hanner, meet Digna Dominguez."

A pretty woman with a warm smile stepped forward with a small boy and a teen-aged girl who hung behind her. We were all set for the double cheek kissing, but the hosts had obviously been tutored in *Norte Americano* greetings so Digna stuck out her arm and vigorously shook our hands. She nudged her children forward and the little boy bravely stepped towards Chuck, looked up at him and squeaked out, "Victor," while cautiously extending his hand.

Chuck took his small hand, shook it and said "*Soy Carlos, el gigante.* [I am Carlos, the giant.]"

That brought a big smile from Victor. The daughter then followed suit, introducing herself shyly as Diana.

We followed them down the main road, then off on a smaller road to their home, a small white house with an area of grass in front and a sizable shade tree.

By the time a Peace Corps staff member brought the truck around with our bags we had acquainted ourselves with the small family and an outdoor guard dog — a mangy, white animal named Lupo, that we were warned to steer clear of because *de vez en cuando* [once in a while] he bit someone. Victor nodded solemnly adding, "*Si, la semana pasada.* [Yes, last week.]" I didn't need to be told more than once.

The father, Victor Senior, wouldn't be around much as he was a truck driver and was rarely home. When he did come home, Digna said he came in late and left about five a.m. so there was a chance we would never even meet him. It was one of the reasons she had signed up for the program, she explained. They had only lived in Pindolo a couple of years and she had few friends. *Norte Americanos* in the house sounded fun.

She showed us our room and stood back, anxious that we would find everything OK. And actually, it was quite nice. There was a double bed, a small plastic table and chair in one corner and in the other was an improvised clothes rack about three feet wide with two shelves on the bottom.

Chuck and I entered the room, looked around and turned to her with enthusiasm and thanks, both of us exclaiming, "*Que bueno,*" and "*Esto es perfecto!*" and "*Muchas gracias.*" I could see happy relief on her face. The bed was covered with a warm looking blanket, and it had a headboard with several locking compartments, the keys were placed in the locks.

Digna explained that no one would be allowed in our room, but we could lock anything important in there. I couldn't think of anything important except maybe our passports and some extra dollars. There was a window to the side with opaque amber panes and bars mounted on the outside. Digna said crime was a problem, but when we asked if there were many robberies, she replied there were none because of the bars on the windows. And of course, they had Lupo. She said to always lock the windows before we left for the day, and to lock our door with the key she gave us. It seemed a little excessive to me, given the rural atmosphere, but I reasoned that living alone most of the time might have heightened her feelings of vulnerability.

The house had two other bedrooms, a small front living room, a tiny dark kitchen and a wide passage way which accommodated a dining table and chairs. The bathroom wasn't exactly attached to the house, but was just on the other side of the back porch. It did have a flush toilet, with the omnipresent basket and most surprisingly, a hot water heater. Digna pointed it out with pride, saying it was a real *lujo* [luxury], and that they had bought it on credit. She believed they were one of the few families in Pindolo that had one.

While I began to do some unpacking, Chuck played with little Victor in the living room. Victor seemed to find Chuck a combination of a long-lost-uncle and a jungle gym and was crawling all over him. Normally, I would have worried that something might be knocked over, but there was nothing in the living room to knock over. A simple couch and two chairs, both covered with sheets carefully tucked in around the edges, was the extent of the furnishings.

I hung up and put away some clothes I thought we would use the next few days, took our toiletries and put them out on the table and stacked the rest of the bags against the wall. Digna, meanwhile had set the table with an ample lunch of baked chicken, rice, sliced tomatoes and green peppers. It could have been a State-side lunch except that in the place of bread, there was a bowl of cold sliced Yucca root, called *mandioca*, which Digna said was Paraguayan bread. I took a slice, tasted it and found it totally bland and a little stringy. I also noticed there were two cloth napkins, one the family shared and one obviously for Chuck and me.

After lunch we were at loose ends, having exhausted our brains with our Spanish conversations so we took a walk around the so-called suburb. We spotted another Trainee, Shon, who was out in a yard down the street, and he joined us on our stroll. The three of us discovered two more Trainees' houses, and were invited to take peeks inside. From a quick glance, it appeared our place was nicer and in the case of one house, definitely cleaner. Maybe it was lucky that we were a "twosome" as it necessitated the bigger space, bigger house and maybe a more well-to-do family, although the term was relative.

After an hour or two, it became quite cold and a brisk wind blew from the south, which of course, was now the cold Antarctic. Even with my sturdy hiking boots and thick socks, my feet were cold. We returned to Digna's, but I didn't warm up, as the house, like all others, didn't have heating.

"*No es frio mucho* [it's not cold much]," Digna had explained. "*Solamente julio y agusto.* [Only in July and August.]"

It was May 30th, and I wondered how cold it had to get to be considered cold.

With our coats still on, we stood around the dining table nibbling on a light snack of some small *empañadas* of onions and beef, and discussed our morning schedule. Our training classes would start in a neighboring town at 7:45 a.m. so Digna would wake us at 6:00 a.m., which was to be our shower time. That would be followed by breakfast and the local coffee, which wasn't really coffee, but contained *matine*, that supposedly had the same effects as caffeine. We chatted politely a bit longer then Digna and the kids retired to her room and we went to ours. She had a small black and white television in her room and apparently they all got under the covers to get warm and watched TV.

Under the covers sounded like a great idea to me since my feet were like ice, so Chuck and I gave our *"buenos noches"* and went to our room.

"It's closer to Antarctica," I suddenly said aloud, the geography of South America finally dawning on me. "I forgot about that."

Chuck just nodded and decided that the blanket on top of the bed wasn't going to be enough so he unzipped his sleeping bag to put it over the top. We checked quickly for nesting *colorados*, then dove under the covers. I snuggled up to Chuck for warmth and ignored his yelps as my cold feet touched his legs.

The Paraguayan breakfast was limited. We gnawed on small, rock-hard, round rolls, about the size of walnuts, dunking them in a caramel sauce called *dulce leche* [sweet milk]. I couldn't decide if the rolls came rock-hard or these were particularly old, but the dipping sauce was fabulous and could have been eaten with a spoon. We drank our "almost" coffee, thanked Digna and were out the door to meet our compatriots at the main highway. Together we waited for the bus, and we all described our experiences from the first night. Everyone was upbeat, happy with their houses and families, but in listening to the others I did feel we had lucked out with Digna.

We got off in the neighboring town of Aregua and, following the directions that had been provided, made our way through town to a large, dilapidated house, where the training classes were to be held. It was a wonderful old mansion that had fallen into disrepair and had a shabby comfortableness about it. The largest room, probably the old salon, now served as the principal class room. We took our seats, and the same austere, white-haired gentleman who had met us at the airport introduced himself as the Director of Training.

After welcoming us, he began with the mission statement and our goals in Paraguay. A great deal of emphasis was put on the fact that our purpose was to help the poor. And not just the poor, the poorest of the poor: the farmers out in the most rural areas, the children without medical care, the downtrodden. The more I heard the more I felt like a college student who had wandered into the wrong classroom. I kept listening for mention of larger cities and cooperatives and finally did hear the words "the small business programs" that was followed by lengthy descriptions of small chicken farms, pig farms or bee-keeping. My spirits were steadily sinking as the director went on to explain that growing a good garden was a high priority and one of our first tasks was to learn how to make good compost, the foundation of good gardens. For experience we would have a hands-on class, making a compost heap together. I shot a look at Chuck and knew he was thinking the same thing I was.

"Poorest of poor? Compost?" I whispered. "What happened to being Business Volunteers in a city?"

He shrugged his shoulders and mouthed the words "Wait to worry." I glumly nodded back.

We finished the morning doing all sorts of training exercises to let us discover what kind of thinkers we were. I turned out be analytical and Chuck was "hands-on." I wasn't sure how that related to anything, and was annoyed at the time spent, thinking it could have been better used, but the younger Trainees seemed to enjoy it. Only Chuck and John and I were rolling our eyes.

We finally got to Spanish class and it was a relief to be doing something that I thought was useful, but it turned out it would be short-lived. We were told that only a few weeks would be spent on Spanish and then we would all switch to Guaranie studies. I was distressed to think of starting all over with another language after the years we had dedicated to Spanish, especially given that Guaranie was a language we would never use again. I thought back to all the work we had put in learning Farsi in Afghanistan, only to have it disappear from our memories with lack of use. I sighed and realized I was not in the right frame of mind. This wasn't about what was useful to me, I told myself, but what was useful for Paraguayans.

It was still depressing. I confessed my disappointments to Chuck at lunch, but he remained hopeful that our situation would turn out like our stay at Digna's, where she preferred speaking Spanish.

After lunch, Mark told us it was time to get acquainted with *yerba mate*, usually just called *mate* (pronounced maw-tay), the life blood of every Paraguayan.

"Everyone drinks it; most Volunteers find they like it too. And they say it's good for you." He picked up a brochure and read, "*Yerba mate* can be used to boost immunity, cleanse and detoxify the blood, tone the nervous system, restore youthful hair color, retard aging, combat fatigue, stimulate the mind, control the appetite, reduce effects of debilitating disease, reduce stress and eliminate insomnia." He put the brochure down and added, "It's also supposed to cure constipation, make your heart stronger and has so many vitamins it's practically its own food group."

"Do you believe that?" someone called out.

"Well, I'm healthy enough and I drink this all the time. So, maybe." He gave a little laugh and turned to the table in front. "So, these are the implements we use to make it," he said, and pointed to objects on the table. "The *wampa*," and he held up a small wooden cup and passed it around. "The *bombilla*," and he held up a slender silver tube, just larger than a regular soda straw, with a small gold-colored mouthpiece at one end and a strainer that looked like a spoon at the other. The center was decorated with a raised design encircled by a ring and bits of colored glass. "And most importantly, the *mate*," and he held up a small plastic bag which looked to be filled with tea leaves and twigs.

Once the items had circulated the room, he put the *bombilla* in the *wampa* then stuffed it almost to the top with the *mate* before adding boiling water which he had simmering in a kettle on a little hot plate.

"Let it steep for a minute or two, then it is always passed to the right. Everyone shares the same *bombilla*, but don't worry. I think it's too hot to spread germs. And sip carefully," he added, "it's quite hot."

Rachel, a dark-haired Trainee from Texas, took the first tentative sip. She just wrinkled her face in disgust and passed it to me. I took the cup and tried to slowly suck on the scalding hot, metal straw, finally catching a burning trickle. I groaned involuntarily.

"Oh my God, Mark, it tastes like cigarette butts," I blurted out.

He just laughed. Still grimacing, I passed it to Chuck. He looked at the straw tentatively, then bravely put it in his mouth. When the liquid reached his mouth his eyes squeezed shut. He swallowed resolutely and passed it to the right. "You say we can get coffee, right?"

Mark laughed again. Everyone had the same reaction; it was perfectly dreadful. If you emptied an ashtray and poured hot water over it, that was *mate*. Chuck and I had seen Digna sipping on just such a straw as we left the house that morning and I was now especially grateful that she had made us the fake coffee instead.

"Is it addictive?" I asked, thinking that no one would continue to drink the vile stuff if it wasn't. Mark said it wasn't, but I didn't believe him — especially since it stank of tobacco.

4 Basic Training

By the end of the first week, training had settled into a routine of technical training and language classes. Most of the time was dedicated to technical instruction, a mistake I thought, since hours were wasted on the simplest of concepts. Our instructors would present an idea then have us break into focus groups of two or three, develop examples then come back together to share thoughts and ideas.

Our first big assignment was called Mission Impossible. We were put in groups of two and given scraps of paper with names and addresses of two government officials working in Asunción. We were to find their offices, meet with them and be back in Aregua by 1:30 p.m. I was paired with one of the young guys, Greg, and Chuck was paired with the young Texan, Rachel.

Without Spanish, the assignment could have been tricky as it was designed to force you to ask questions and directions in Spanish — a worthy enterprise if your Spanish was limited. Just getting back to Asunción involved a bus change, and there was no telling where to get off once in the city.

For me, however, I was beyond that point with my Spanish, and I thought the easiest way to track down the officials would be to call a cab (very un-Peace Corps-ish), give the driver the addresses and go directly. But I played by the rules, and Greg and I wandered around asking directions, slowly progressing to our destinations. We discovered that Paraguayans all wanted to be helpful and give directions, even if they didn't have a clue as to where you needed to go. If someone said, "Go up two blocks and over one," it was pretty much the same as "I don't know." Greg and I surmised that following the instruction would get us just far enough away from the person to be able to ask someone else without embarrassment.

When we finally found our designated offices, neither official was available. One had gone out for something and would be back, but no one was sure when, and the other was tied up with someone who was obviously more important than we were. We decided our mission was completed enough and headed back to Aregua.

Chuck got off easier since Rachel's host family didn't like the idea of her being alone in the big city, so they sent an older cousin with them who quickly found the right buses and right office locations. The three of them completed their interviews and still beat Greg and me back by an hour.

Digna continued to feed us well and keep us healthy, two of her main concerns. Some days we were able to have lunch with her and she always served some kind of hot stew or soup with salad, which was wonderful. We heard from several other Trainees that they never were served fresh vegetables, so we were lucky. The two vegetarians in the group were discovering that Paraguay was pretty close to being vegetarian hell. Being next to Argentina, land of the cattle ranches, beef played a major role in the diet. Fresh vegetables were hard to transport so many families just lived on variations of *mandioca*, rice, beef, eggs and cheese and gallons of *mate*. The cheese wasn't exactly cheese as we knew it, but rather a softened variety called "fresh cheese" that didn't have any flavor at all. Digna would mix this with chopped up *mandioca* and with every serving I liked it less. It had gone from being bland, to unpleasant and then just about

28

made me gag, but I always choked down a few bites to be polite.

What I wouldn't have given for a fresh bread roll, but they didn't exist. At least not in Pindolo. The few times we had been to small road-side cafes we were asked if we would like bread, since they had learned foreigners preferred it over *mandioca*. They tried to accommodate, bringing out what looked and tasted like very old, stale hot dog buns. Of course, these were uniformly terrible, and the Paraguayans thought so too, so they couldn't really understand why we liked "bread." There seemed to be no concept of fresh bread or bread made with yeast. Their local bread roll, often sold by vendors in the mornings, was called *chipa* and was made from pig fat and *mandioca* which had been ground into *mandioca* flour. Someone in our group dubbed it the instant heart-attack. The closest proximity to any kind of bread at Digna's were the rock-hard bread balls we crunched through every morning with the *dulce leche*. After seeing Digna open a new package of them, I realized they came dried and hard.

We played with the kids a bit in the evenings, but there really wasn't much time. Most days, we didn't get back to Digna's until after dark and it was so cold, we just retired to our room. That, plus the fact that we had homework and assignments coming out of our ears. There were daily language assignments and individual class presentations to prepare, plus we were supposed to work up a community project in Pindolo and plant a garden for Digna. Since classes were six and a half days a week, there wasn't much free time, especially since we wanted to check our email on Sundays which involved a bus trip into Asunción.

At the end of our second week, we went out with Digna and kids one night to the local San Juan Festival, a national celebration held in every town. It was originally a religious festival, but over time had become more of a local fair with a symbolic burning of Judas thrown in for good measure.

Coming from the States where everything is sanitized and designed not to injure anyone, this fair appeared to be a litigation landmine. The first activity we encountered was avoid-the-burning-ball. A flaming ball, about the size of a soccer ball, was kicked helter-skelter through the crowd causing bystanders to jump quickly out of the way if the flaming missile came in their direction. There were all sorts of kids running about, unattended, which worried me, but no one seemed to pay them any mind. Digna, I noticed, wasn't about to let little Victor join them, as she had him firmly by the hand. We watched at what we hoped was a safe distance as the ball careened through the crowd until it finally burnt out.

We then progressed to the center of the square where the locals had erected a tall, greased pole. At midnight there was to be a competition of shinning up the pole without sliding back to the ground and retrieving something that was nailed on the top. It was the safest activity at the festival.

In a tree near the open area of the pole, there was a full-sized, straw-stuffed effigy of Judas hanging by the neck. Digna explained that it was stuffed with firecrackers along with the straw so when they set fire to it, it would really blow. We were peeking from behind a parked truck when they torched it and true to expectations, flaming debris exploded in all directions. The crowd scattered, screaming with terror or delight, I couldn't tell which.

But the *pièce de résistance* was the family-fun activity of walking on burning coals. There was quite a lengthy path of burning embers that hardy souls ran down barefooted. I'm not sure how it worked exactly, but no one seemed to be getting too burned. Maybe if you ran fast enough it didn't hurt, but I wasn't about to try it, nor was Chuck. I turned to Digna and asked her what she thought of all of these activities and she replied, "*peligroso y tonto* [dangerous and stupid]." So I wasn't the only one of that opinion. A couple of our Trainees actually took off their boots and socks and ran down the path. They said afterward their feet felt fine, but I wasn't sure they would admit to just having voluntarily burned the bottom of their feet. They kidded with Chuck and tried to get him to do it, but he passed, telling them it was a "young person's sport." We wandered around a bit more and decided we couldn't stay up long enough to watch the pole-shinny contest. We were tired and despite all the flames and burning activities, we were cold.

M *mmbaee-chee-pa.* That's "how are you" in Guaranie. Our language classes were now divided between Spanish and Guaranie. I tried to make an effort, but Chuck resisted, maintaining that improving our Spanish was a better option. He may have been right, but I couldn't help trying to be the "good student." Like any language though, it would take practice to get anywhere and between classes and speaking Spanish at Digna's, I didn't see where that was going to happen. Worse, it wasn't a Latin based language and sounded oriental, with tonal changes in meaning, like Japanese.

The group was then divided into two sections — Trainees like John, who had city government backgrounds, and Trainees with business backgrounds like Chuck and me. The city government group, now called "Muni" Trainees, would spend afternoons learning how to help local governments, while we business types would be learning about small businesses and reviewing balance sheets of *cooperativas.*

The next week we were all to be sent to out in the *campo* [country], to stay with some of the currently serving Peace Corps Volunteers in their homes, and to observe for ourselves our future Peace Corps life. The instructors said that often Trainees requested to go home after this sojourn.

Chuck and I were assigned to visit another married couple named Tim and Pam Barnes who were our age and had been in Paraguay for a year. She was an Education Volunteer and Tim did something with the municipal water system.

T im and Pam met us in Asunción, and the next morning the four of us rode the bus to their small town about three hours away. The town was even smaller than Pindolo, just a few houses and buildings along one street and everything else was scattered out in the countryside.

When Pam and Tim arrived in the town they had only two options for housing and naturally had taken the best one, but it was far cry from the comfortable digs we had enjoyed in Kabul. It was very small, with just their bedroom, a small living room that doubled as a dining room, and a hallway that had been converted into a kitchen. That was it. The shower was a three-walled affair outside the kitchen and the toilet was an outhouse — also a three-sided — about fifty yards away in a pasture.

They had done a good job fixing up the house with screen doors, windows, an overhead fan — which they said you really needed in the summer, bookcases and cotton rugs; and they had done an amazing job of squeezing a stove, refrigerator and double sink with running water into the narrow hallway. Outside they had a good-sized garden, which Tim had completely enclosed with chicken wire, explaining that if you didn't the chickens or pigs or cows would eat everything.

They made room for us to sleep on the living room floor with an inflatable mattress that was fine for us, but it entailed pushing the dining table to the wall, restricting its use for eating.

Chuck and I both woke up Sunday morning with the first queasiness of bad stomachs. We blamed the lettuce salads we had eaten at a supposedly "clean" restaurant in Asunción the night before. I felt lousy all day and took a long nap along with Chuck in the afternoon, but Chuck felt worse and couldn't rouse himself for dinner.

I awoke in the middle of the night and definitely felt I needed to make a bathroom run. Chuck was sound asleep so I quietly got into my clothes, found the flashlight and made my way down the moonless, dark path. It certainly didn't seem to matter that the front of the outhouse was open to the world, since it was inky black and I could barely see my hand in front of my face.

For some reason, the Barnes had never installed an actual toilet seat so the seat was just the bricks the latrine was made of with a rectangular slot for your use. Pam had told me earlier that I might want to sort of balance over it, supporting myself with my hands on the sides. I put the flashlight on the floor and did just that, wondering again why in the heck they hadn't put some kind of toilet seat on the thing. I had a hard time in the dark trying to make sure my pee stream was going in what I thought was a rather narrow slot. When I felt warm urine splashing on my hands, I readjusted and tried for a better direction. Concentrating on this maneuver, I wasn't aware of any other thing until suddenly I heard something breathing. I froze; it sounded close. I slowly lowered myself onto the wet toilet bricks, picked up the flashlight and shone it outwards, bravely calling, "Who's there?"

Two, big, brown eyes looked back at me.

It took a second and a skipped heartbeat to realize it was a cow — only a cow — maybe three feet away.

"Shoo, shoo," I said but the cow didn't move. I raised my voice, "SHOO," I said again as fiercely as I could, waving the flashlight in front of her. That seemed to work and she ambled away. I quickly pulled my pants back up and hurried to the house.

The next day the three sided shower bothered me a bit more as I swore the children next door were sneaking peeks through the bushes. Had it been my place, there would at least have been a curtain, but it obviously hadn't been a matter of concern for neither Pam nor Tim. Whether the children were my imagination or not, I made Chuck hold up a towel in front of me while I showered — which was done in record time, since the hot water drizzle couldn't compensate for the cold and rainy day.

I felt pretty good that morning, and by the afternoon Chuck was on the mend, too. We tromped through the rain a mile or so to visit Pam's school, where she was teaching small children how to brush their teeth. She sang a song in Guaranie (her own composition) about brushing your teeth, and she distributed a whole box of free toothbrushes that she had managed to get from the States. The kids were delighted. As we had already noted, dental hygiene was a huge problem in rural Paraguay. Almost everyone we met had horrible teeth, and it was rare to find someone like Digna, who had a "Colgate" smile. Even young teenagers would be missing several front teeth. Pam blamed it on the sugar pops and cookies from Brazil that had reached every corner of Paraguay, while toothbrushes and toothpaste had not. I thought Pam's school presentation was outstanding and she seemed to exemplify what a Peace Corps Volunteer should be.

Tim's project on the other hand, seemed to have fallen apart. In his first months in the town he was involved in some type of water system work that he attacked gung-ho, but somehow the whole project seemed to have dissolved. His other occupation had been fixing up their house — but that was losing steam too. The landlord had reneged on his promise to plaster the house so Tim wasn't anxious to add more effort either. Now he tended the garden, took care of shopping and meals — no small matter — while Pam did her work at the school.

We were to leave the next morning, but we awoke to heavy downpours.

"No buses," Tim explained. "Everything in Paraguay comes to a stop when it rains because of these dirt roads."

At noon we finally found a small mini-van headed towards Asunción and were able to catch a ride. We waved good-bye to Pam and Tim through the rain-streaked windows, having enjoyed their hospitality and company immensely, but still without any feeling of how we would adapt to our final site. I wasn't ready to throw in the towel, but wondered if I could be as stoic with the bare amenities as they were, and what we would do if our jobs fell apart.

By the time we finally arrived in Asunción, caught a bus to Pindolo and walked a mile in the mud back to Digna's, we were a sight.

She shook her head sadly over the state of our tennis shoes, which we had mistakenly worn instead of our boots. The red dust of Paraguay, she informed us, will come out only if it doesn't get soaked in. But once wet, you were doomed to stained tennis shoes forever.

I hadn't even thought about washing our tennis shoes. I figured they would just get filthy, which they already were, and that would be that. But Digna took it as a major source of pride that her house was clean and everyone left the house in clean pressed clothes, and she didn't want us leaving HER house with such shoes. So the following morning we wore our boots, while she scoured the daylights out of our Nikes. She was right. They were never white-white again, but were presentable enough in Digna's opinion, to leave the house.

5 Unexpected Reunions

We had been looking forward to the 4th of July. As Peace Corps Trainees we were part of the American community in Paraguay, and we had been invited to the annual Embassy picnic held at the American School grounds in Asunción. Chuck and I remembered the great cookouts the American Embassy had sponsored in Afghanistan so we were salivating at the prospects. To make it even better we had been given Saturday morning free from classes so we could have the whole weekend off.

We had made reservations to spend the night in Asunción at the Gran Hotel del Paraguay, an old restored mansion not far from the picnic grounds. Several Peace Corps staff members had recommended it, and Julie, the Peace Corps nurse, had shown us a brochure about it. It looked to be quite pleasant, set in lush gardens — definitely not a "Peace Corps type" place. It made me feel slightly guilty about considering staying there, but Tim and Pam had told us they treated themselves to a favorite hotel in Asunción every time they went there. They felt that as long as they were living like Volunteers in their village, they could treat themselves as they wished when they were away. I decided this was good reasoning. Unfortunately, most of our fellow Trainees didn't have a Visa card, so when they went to Asunción they stayed at various low-end dives, usually dormitory style with grimy toilets at the end of the hall.

On the Fourth, we caught an early bus out of Pindolo, made the necessary bus change in San Lorenzo, then craned our necks out the window, trying to spot the landmark near the American School where we were supposed to get off. We got off too early, but it didn't matter as the walk felt good in the cold morning air.

When we arrived at the school grounds there didn't seem to be much going on. Some picnic tables were set up and a few Volunteers ambled about, but no signs of any big July 4th barbecue doings. We spotted a table where some embassy women were selling raffle tickets for a concert, brownies, old paperback books, and, we discovered, our lunch tickets — there was nothing free at the party, not even water.

The big 4th of July barbecue turned out to be hamburgers from McDonald's.

About 11:00 a.m., a McDonald's truck pulled up offering the choice of a plain burger or the "fun-pak" which included the burger, fries, a cookie and a Mickey Mouse glove. We went for the fun-pak — it was the Fourth after all, and Digna's children would enjoy the gloves. After a while, someone dressed as Uncle Sam got up and read the raffle numbers. All attending then stood up, sang the "Star Spangled Banner" — and that was it.

The event verged on totally depressing. The only thing that saved the day was that we tracked down Aaron Hohl.

Twenty-eight years before, back in our first Peace Corps days, we had been close friends with a couple named Mike and Elana Hohl. In fact, during our training days in Kabul, the four of us lived together. We had kept in contact, sending Christmas cards every year, but had never managed a visit. We lived in California; they were abroad for many years and then had settled in Ohio. Between careers and their extra work of raising five children, there was never the time or opportunity for get-togethers.

When we mentioned in our last Christmas card that we were

rejoining the Peace Corps, we discovered that their son had joined the Peace Corps — and of all the places in the world he could have gone, he was in Paraguay! Mike and Elana had planned to come to visit him, and now they planned to visit us as well. To meet again in Paraguay after thirty years was miraculous.

I spotted Aaron easily, even though I had never met him, as he looked exactly like Mike had twenty-eight years before. He was easy-going and pleasant and even reminded us of Mike in the way he talked and moved.

We planned a dinner reunion with him and his folks when they arrived in two weeks for their visit. It was also going to be a celebration for me as it was the day before my birthday.

If the embassy 4th of July celebration was a little flat, it was made up for by our night at the Gran Hotel del Paraguay. It lived up to its billing. Set in manicured gardens, it even had a swimming pool in the back. It was too cold for swimming in July, but we both thought how great this place would be for a summer visit in December. Our room had a big, queen-sized bed, with huge white pillows against a dark mahogany headboard. An old French chandelier hung above the bed. There was cable TV and a spotlessly clean white-tiled bathroom, and the only reminder that we were even in Paraguay was the small sign above the toilet advising us to "Plees put all pepers en the baskit."

You would have thought we had been away for years instead of a month, but it had been a stressful month and an evening in a luxurious and warm room was pure heaven.

My fiftieth birthday was one to remember. It started of course, the night before with our reunion with the Hohls. We arrived early at the restaurant that we had chosen in Aregua so we could come over directly after class. It was a small, cozy place, run by a German couple and had a wide front porch where we waited for

Aaron, Mike and Elana.

The day had turned surprisingly warm and by the time they arrived they were sweating profusely from the long walk from the bus stop. Elana was carrying a cake that she had managed to balance horizontally on both the bus and the walk, but it now listed dangerously on its cardboard platter.

"I had to get you a birthday cake," Elana told me. "There was a wonderful bakery in Asunción and I was afraid the restaurant wouldn't have anything nearly as good."

It was terrific to see them and there were great hugs all around. We all declared that we hadn't changed a bit and as old friends do, we picked up conversations and stories as if we had just left them the week before. With Mike and Elana were two of their other teen-agers, plus Aaron of course, so we made a jolly group, laughing and chattering, trying as fast as we could to catch-up in a few short hours.

The four of us had begun our married lives with the Afghan experience, but had taken different paths after our Peace Corps service. We had all done additional overseas work, but Mike and Elana had stayed in the Middle East for years working in education. We had returned to the States and gone into business. They had five children; we had none. But, despite these differences, we were as close as ever. Somehow that initial bonding in Afghanistan was forever. We talked and laughed for hours until we looked around and realized there was no one left in the restaurant and the proprietress was looking at us wearily from a chair in the corner. We left with more hugs and kisses, and I wondered if our next reunion would be in such an unlikely spot. Wherever it was, we definitely needed to have it before another thirty years went by.

Back in Pindolo my birthday morning was more leisurely than normal as we didn't have to rush to catch a bus for class in Aregua because all the Trainees were going to be sent off on field excursions for three days, and would be split off into the muni and business groups. This time Chuck and I would not be together — something we had agreed on, since we thought we could get more out of the trip with two different experiences. That meant my birthday, with the exception of the morning, we would be apart; the first time that had ever happened in our marriage of twenty-eight years.

But the morning celebration started well with our usual rock-rolls dipped in *dulce leche*, and a big manila envelope of birthday goodies sent by my sisters. Digna's children were wide-eyed. Not only did they never get birthday gifts, but were amazed at the idea that this envelope had come in the mail — something they were only vaguely aware of. There was no mail delivery in Paraguay and Digna told me she had never received a letter in her life. The kids hung over my chair as I opened the large sack. First out was a bag of Werther's candies, which I promptly passed around. That pleased everyone.

Next out of the sack was a paperback novel, a *Sunset Book of Gardening* and some gardening gloves. We had been told by our trainers that if we wanted fresh vegetables at our sites we would probably have to plant them ourselves.

Gardening hadn't been an activity for me since I was ten and I had planted a row of peas, but I thought I would be able to find a gardening book in Paraguay. Wrong. There were none in Spanish nor English, and the nearest thing I found were some yellowed, fly-speckled magazines in the back of the Peace Corps library donated by someone about thirty years ago. They contained such useful information as where to call in the States (in 1969) to order special tulip bulbs. So I had emailed my sisters with a plea for help.

The Sunset Book was great — it told what to plant, where to plant, when and how to plant. Now all I needed were seeds, but that would be easier. Our trainer, Mark, had already told us that we would be going to a big farmers' *cooperativa* in a few weeks and could buy seeds there.

A half an hour later, I was waving good-bye to Chuck as the jeep with our group took off to the north. The rest of the morning was spent bouncing along to a small town north of Asunción where a Volunteer named Dawn lived. She had a successful project going — a *yerba mate* factory, and had spent the past month arranging homes for us to stay in, and demonstrations of her project. She had thought Chuck and I were coming together so we had been assigned the richest house around — the only one that could accommodate two people. So I now had a spacious bedroom all to myself and the luxury of an indoor hot shower. I was a little embarrassed about it, especially after learning that some host families only had outdoor cold showers. Shon reported that he tried his shower at noon, the warmest part of the day, but with fifty degree temperatures and a brisk wind, all he washed was his face.

The group met about ten of the farmers in Dawn's cooperative later that afternoon and were introduced while standing in a circle. They were a distressed looking lot, with tattered clothes and thin faces embedded with grime. Few had any teeth. The *yerba mate* was passed around and we all dutifully sipped, resisting the strong urge to wipe off the metal *bombilla* before putting it into our mouths. One trainer announced that it was my birthday and gave me a large, flat Nestle chocolate bar. I opened it, broke it into the little squares and passed it around, following the *yerba mate*. The farmers loved it and they sang "Happy Birthday" to me in Guaranie. It certainly wasn't a regular birthday dinner with Chuck, but one I wasn't to forget either.

The three days went quickly. We visited Dawn's *yerba mate* warehouse where the dried *mate* was stored and of course, were treated to their best blend. She had a women's group, and I learned, if nothing else, how they toiled from sunup to sundown and had little to show for it.

Our afternoons were spent in the cold open office of the cooperative where we attempted budget examinations. This was good for me as my knowledge of accounting was zilch. In college I had majored in drama and any math I had needed as a stockbroker had been done for me on the computer.

We also visited a World Bank project that had been a total screw-up as the people on the end with the money had no idea

41

of what was happening at the end where the money was needed. In this case, a farmer wanted help with starting a small dairy and needed money for a couple of cows and a small barn. After months of paperwork, with each level of Paraguayan bureaucracy trying to get part of the pie, the farmer ended up with an expensive array of stainless steel milking machines, which now sat rusting out in a cowless and barnless field.

When Chuck and I returned to Digna's we met Victor Senior, the never–at–home truck driver. This, it seemed, was about to change.

Apparently his truck had been caught transporting an illegal shipment of CDs instead of the crates of tennis shoes listed on the Bill of Lading. The truck was now impounded. Digna explained that Victor was innocent, but authorities would hold his truck and he had to sit unemployed until it was decided who would pay the fine. Or, more probably, who would pay off whom. Paraguay had the unhappy distinction of being number three in the world on the corrupt county list — Haiti and Somalia taking spots one and two.

Victor Senior seemed unsure of how to deal with us and I wondered if he understood why exactly we were living in his house. He was a bit sullen and I couldn't tell if it was because we were there or that he was currently unemployed. His Spanish was weak and we found him taciturn and hard to understand. After a bit, we gave up and retired to our room.

I was happy to spend the time comparing notes with Chuck about our differing experiences on the field excursions. He had stayed with a Volunteer couple in Encarnación, a city on the eastern border with Brazil, and had a relatively comfortable stay at their place, an apartment in the city. Like me, he had visited various projects and spent time with bookkeeping exercises. Even though most of our experiences were similar I was still pleased we had been able to see different Volunteer situations.

A few days later the household expanded again with the arrival of Digna's sister and infant. There was mention of an errant husband; we didn't get the whole story, but their stay was going to be longer than just a visit. They shared the kids room, which made us feel like we were definitely in the way — and actually we were. We couldn't all fit around the dining table that evening so we ate in shifts.

To make matters worse, in the last rainstorm, the roof had started leaking above the TV in Digna's bedroom and completely ruined it. Despite a trip to the local repair shop, it now had a big black blob in the middle of the screen and did absolutely nothing when turned on. Even more depressing, we discovered they had bought it on time and still had nine months of payments to go. No guarantees of course and no brand you ever heard of. I suspect it was just parts of other TV's, cobbled together.

Somewhere they found a little black and white set and they moved that into the living room. It flickered so badly it hurt your eyes and the sound fizzled and cackled. Despite these drawbacks, the members of the family crowded around in the *sala* after dinner to watch it. Even if Chuck and I had wanted to try and decipher the program, there was nowhere to sit but the floor, so we retired to our cold, dim room and went to bed.

6   Pigs and Chickens and Beyond

Training had taken a new twist as well.

We were given a partner and would be going out to various farms or *campesino* locations to learn the nitty-gritty of raising animals for profit. Chuck was assigned to a pig farm with a young woman named Katie, and I was assigned to a chicken/egg farm with Todd.

I was pleased with my draw of Todd, a funny, easy-going guy. He had been one of the first Trainees to present his report on some aspect of cooperatives. He stood up in front of the class and talked nimbly, while referring to his chart (had to have a chart — Peace Corps loved them) expounding on various facts and figures. When he was finished, Mark asked him where he had gotten his numbers. Todd looked at him with total innocence and said, "I pulled them out of my ass." We exploded with laughter; all the more funny because the assignment was impossible in the first place, and that was probably where the rest of us were going to find our numbers. It was a full five minutes before Mark could restore order and even he was having a hard time with his let's-be-serious rebuke.

We were supposed to spend sufficient time — twice a week for three weeks — at our assigned farms to learn the business, and in six weeks to present a report on how that farmer could improve his business. A somewhat presumptuous task, in my opinion, given that I knew nothing about chickens and our chicken farmer had been doing just fine for ten years, but off we went.

It was a fairly warm, sunny morning when Todd and I set off with directions to our assigned farm. It was just east of Pindolo — within walking distance. We'd been walking quite awhile and hadn't found the place and thought we might have missed our turn-off when we got a whiff of something that smelled like ammonia. The more we walked, the worse it got. By the time we spotted the chicken coops, housing some 6,000 chickens, the odor had become a gagging stench of manure mixed with lethal ammonia.

We didn't see anyone around, just a small shack to the side and a white dog lying lazily in the front. We clapped and called out and presently a small Indian man came around the corner. He had been expecting us and shook our hands heartily. He introduced himself as Pepe and quickly added proudly that he wasn't Paraguayan, but Peruvian. He was about my size, with jet black hair cut in a bowl fashion, black eyes and a small beaked nose. He had a cheerful demeanor and seemed happy to have company.

Pepe led us between the chicken coops, stepping over dead chickens here and there that hadn't survived the night.

"Pecked to death," he told us in rapid Spanish. "If they get a sore or a bloody spot, the other chickens attack. Food for the dogs," he added.

Sure enough, up ahead there was a second white dog chewing on another dead chicken — blood, feathers and chicken innards in a dark pool in the dirt. I felt my stomach turn. It didn't bother Pepe though; it might as well have been a bowl of dog kibble. He walked up to the dog, reached down and patted its head.

"*Esto es Alba. Desayuno bueno, no?* [This is Alba. Good breakfast, no?]"

Alba raised his head, stopped chewing on some indiscernible

piece and closed his eyes. A thousand flies stirred up for a minute then settled back down.

Pepe continued on, lecturing as he went, followed by Todd, with me bringing up the rear, choking on the stirred-up dust and chicken feathers. I could barely understand what Pepe was saying between the squawking, the rapid Spanish and the fact that most of my concentration had broken down in an effort to continue breathing.

Pepe suddenly stopped in front of a ramp leading up to a small wire door.

"*Vamos, vamos* [go, go]," he said, waving towards the ramp.

Todd and I exchanged worried looks, but Pepe was insistent.

"*Muy interesante* [very interesting]," he declared, and motioned to me to go ahead.

I ventured up the ramp, turning once to make sure Todd and Pepe were still behind me, then opened the little door and stepped off into a sea of chickens. If the cackling was loud before, it was now hysterical. The birds fluttered about my legs screeching with panic, flying and scrambling, as though I was murdering them one by one. I tried to step slowly and carefully, thinking that might quiet them down, but every movement made them frantically flap and screech. I finally just stood perfectly still, but that didn't help either. Pepe ignored them and plowed ahead of me, parting them like a white sea.

Hollering over the pandemonium, he pointed to fans, water troughs burlap bags strung together like curtains, nesting boxes and feeding trays and with every description he used the words "*muy importante* [very important]." I gathered that heat was bad for chickens or at least bad for chickens laying eggs.

The only thing that was *muy importante* in my mind was getting out of there. I edged towards the door and after several long minutes, Pepe waded back through the chickens and led us out and down the tiny ramp.

We spent another half an hour outside the door, baking in the sun, while we learned that raising chickens was a very time consuming business.

"They need constant water," Pepe explained. "If they go without water for even a few hours, the egg production will drop in half. And they will die if they get too cold or too hot, and they must have seventeen hours of light a day, *el minimo*!" He pointed to the large fans inside the coops, strung with electric lights. Pepe continued non-stop about how they needed the right food, the right vitamins and constant care.

He finally led us back to the barn, which was a cool, quiet refuge by comparison. There was a big refrigerator which held medicines and vaccines, and the eggs were stacked along the sides in big crates. Near the entrance there was an old and battered roll-top desk with little, school notebooks poking out of all the pigeonholes. Pepe pointed at them.

"*Vacunaciónes, medicinas, y producción* [vaccinations, medicines and production]."

He pulled one out and proudly showed us pages of detailed notes and numbers. Based on his presentation one thing was certain — between buying the chickens, caring for the chickens and gathering and selling eggs, Pepe was doing yeoman's duty. He had an old bicycle that he used to go from the owner's house to the chicken coops, but he confessed that he rarely left the chickens. It didn't matter, he said, he didn't like Paraguayans anyway. He stayed right there night and day and sent a Paraguayan woman out for his supplies.

After a never-ending morning of breathing chicken stench, I felt like I had never left either. Todd and I kept edging toward the barn door and finally choked out polite thank-yous, good-byes and left. I couldn't imagine what more we would learn on subsequent visits.

"So," I asked Todd on the walk back. "How do you improve that business?"

"Bomb it," he replied.

I didn't get any sympathy from Chuck at lunch. "I don't care how bad your chickens smelled," he said, "my pigs were worse."

I couldn't imagine that. "No," I countered. "I'm sure my chickens

47

would stink your pigs under the table."

"Nope, pigs are the worst." He wasn't budging.

I bet him a gin and tonic, hoping that someday we might be in a place where we could actually have one.

July 20th was going to be the big day. That was the day we would be assigned to our future sites and find out just where and what we would be doing. Our Peace Corps training group director had interviewed each of us twice, trying to match our skills with community projects and honor individual requests. Chuck and I had repeatedly said we wished to be close to a big city with Internet cafés. I hated the thought of not having easy Internet access with my family. While in training, I had been able to communicate with my sisters and Mother every week, and it would be very hard to give it up.

Our trainers handed out thick manila envelopes to each of us. We quickly opened ours to read the first line: General Artigas. Where was it? They had put up a big map of Paraguay in the front of the room with flags for each of our locations, and we hurried up to look. There was a cluster of flags around Asunción and then a few scattered East and South. We finally found our flag, a long ways from Asunción, somewhat north of the southern city of Encarnación, on a thin black line which indicated a dirt road. We already knew that there were two kinds of towns in Paraguay: those on the smooth paved road that circled the country, called the *ruta,* and those on dirt roads off the *ruta.* Cities on the *ruta* had fast, modern buses, fresh produce and restaurants. Off the *ruta* meant none of those things. General Artigas was definitely off the *ruta.* Only two members of our training group were further out than we, Todd and Shon, whose flags were near the Brazilian border.

Mark, our trainer, came up beside me. "Don't worry," he said, "you're only a couple of hours from Encarnación and it has Internet."

With that information, I was more optimistic and Chuck and I returned to our chairs and scanned through the rest of the packet. General Artigas was a good-sized town of about 5,000, and several Peace Corps Volunteers had served there before us. We had been assigned there with the first consideration that it was a large enough place to give both of us work. This wouldn't have been possible in many of the other sites where Volunteers were in tiny communities of fifty families. That had been Tim and Pam's situation and when Tim's job evaporated, there was nothing much for him to do.

Our assigned jobs were to develop and improve business with the *cooperativa*.

The more we thought about the assignment and read the description, the better we liked it. Being far from Asunción and the Peace Corps office might be a positive thing: more autonomy and less bureaucracy.

Everyone, though, no matter where they were going, was excited and ready to get started. We would all be going to our sites for three days and then return to Pindolo. In that time we were to meet our contact person, find a house to rent, and wander about getting to know the town. We were to come back with a detailed hand-drawn map of our new community showing all the stores and businesses. Just to make the assignment perfectly clear, we had been required to draw maps of Pindolo the week before. Those were now pinned to the wall, like grade school art work.

7   Welcome to Artigas!

Chuck and I spent the night before our departure back in the Gran Hotel in Asunción so we could get to the bus station for the 7:30 a.m. bus.

Our information packet had said to take the bus called *La Fletcha* [The Arrow] as it went directly to General Artigas. There was another bus, but taking it involved what was described as a lengthy and complicated bus change, so we opted for *La Fletcha*. A few hours down the road, however, we concluded that might have been a mistake. In addition to the bus being run down, having no bathroom, and no heat, it was a classic milk run. As other buses sped out of town, the *La Fletcha* stopped five more times. By the time we had cleared the outskirts of Asunción, all the seats were taken and the aisle was jammed with standing passengers who jostled from side to side as the bus turned corners. School children got on and off, workers of every description would hop on for a few blocks, then hop off. Every few stops, vendors selling juices or *chipa* rolls, would hustle down the aisles. Chuck and I hadn't had breakfast so we shared one of the *chipa* rolls, which we both found to be dry and tasteless.

At noon *La Fletcha* stopped for lunch at a pleasant little café. I began wondering how long the trip would have been in a real bus, even with the bus change.

It was dark by the time the bus left the *ruta* and started down the dirt road to General Artigas. It occurred to me as we bounced along in the now almost empty bus that we didn't know where in Artigas to get off. I worried about it a few more miles, envisioning a long walk in the dark, trying to drag all our bags.

"I'm going to ask the driver if he can let us off in the middle of town," I announced to Chuck and crawled over his legs to the aisle. I practiced the phrase "*Puede dejarnos en el mitad de Arigias?*" under my breath as I made my way forward. As I approached the driver I saw the road in front was bathed in white moon light, and that was all — he was driving with no headlights! I thought briefly about asking him if that was safe, then discarded it as useless and probably irritating, and stuck with my original request. He didn't look at me, but barely nodded, so I assumed it was a registered request.

"And?" Chuck asked as I crawled back into my seat.

"He nodded," I replied, "and he is driving without any headlights." There didn't seem to be a good response to this so we just sat there silently in the dark. I leaned against the window and closed my eyes, and maybe dozed a bit, but I awakened when the bus slowed. I looked out the window and saw a weathered wooden sign with a light over it, illuminating *Bienvenidos a General Artigas* [Welcome to General Artigas]. We passed what looked like the main church, slowed even more over some railroad tracks, went a couple of more blocks, and stopped next to a small outdoor café with a thatched roof, several wooden tables and plastic chairs. This appeared to be the main stop in Artigas, maybe the only one. The other few passengers on the bus got off as we retrieved our bulky backpacks from the overhead bins. The driver followed us down the bus steps and unloaded our yellow duffel containing our sleeping bags and heavier clothes from the compartment under the bus.

"*Gracias,*" I said to the driver, who again only nodded.

There were no other passengers waiting to get on and the few who had gotten off, had already dispersed into the darkness. The bus was off down the road before we could even heft our luggage up onto the high stone sidewalk in front of the café. We looked around. According to the information in the packet, we were to be met by the President of the Cooperative, Ramón Acuña. There wasn't a soul anywhere. It was only 7:30 p.m., but the town was as shut-up and dark as if it were 3 in the morning. A few lights were strung along the thatched roof of the café and I spotted a phone booth to the side.

"I can call," I said, "I've got his number right here," and I pulled out the small scrap of paper with Ramón's phone number from my front jean's pocket. I took a handful of change from Chuck and went over to the phone booth. I looked for the slots for the coins, but only found a thin slit and a *noticia* above saying it only accepted phone cards. I stared at the little slot pondering my options. One thing was certain: getting a phone card in General Artigas on a Saturday night wasn't one of them. Now feeling more discouraged than anxious, I returned to Chuck with the news.

"Well, we can find Ramón tomorrow," he said and looked around. "A bite to eat might be nice and I guess we can find a hotel," he added with surprising cheerfulness, as if we were in a busy, sunny plaza instead of an abandoned, dark café.

Looking up and down the street, straining to make out any specks of light, I commented, "I see zero lights."

"The packet said there was a hotel, so there must be a hotel somewhere. I'll go exploring and you can stay here with the luggage. Where'd we pack the flashlight?" He knelt known and started digging thought the duffel.

"We could always sleep here," I ventured. "We've got our sleeping bags and camping pillows. This is a café after all. Sooner or later it should open."

Chuck still had his head buried in the duffel.

"Found it!" he announced, holding up the flashlight, and he shone the beam out into the empty street.

Just as he stood up, a door suddenly opened from the side of the café. A short Indian-looking woman appeared, wearing a cotton dress and a ragged sweater, her long, black hair pulled back into a braid. She came to the table where I had just seated myself, and without a word handed me one tattered, plastic-covered menu.

"*Gracias, gracias,*" I told her, full of relief, and now, for the first time in hours, optimistic.

The woman merely nodded, then padded back to the open door. Chuck turned the flashlight back on to read the menu and we scanned down the list looking for words we knew like *pollo* [chicken] or *carne* [beef]. There were several combinations, but given the darkness of the house and the total lack of customers we thought the daily special might be the best bet.

"*Dos platos del dia y dos cervezas* [Two daily specials and two beers]," I said when the woman reappeared, and then I added, "*Donde está un hotel?* [Where is a hotel?]" The waitress gave me a quizzical look and fearing she didn't understand, I repeated myself.

"*Aqui* [here]," she said, and leaned forward to look at me more closely, as if trying to figure out what particular impairment I might have.

I wasn't sure how I had missed the notice of an entire hotel, so while we waited for our *platos*, I walked around the building with the flashlight, looking for an entrance. There wasn't one. The only clue was a faded, painted word on the back wall: *hospedaje* [hostel]. I looked again down the dark street and realized this was it. Hotel, cafe, center of town and the only bus stop. The bus driver must have thought I was nuts, asking to be let off in the "middle" of town.

By the time I sat back down the *señora* had brought us two beers and in another twenty minutes our daily specials of rice, some kind of meat in sauce, sliced tomatoes to the side and the customary rock hard, little rolls. We devoured everything. I was even thinking of asking about dessert, but the woman seemed eager to clear the table and be done with us. Chuck asked for the bill, but she just waved her hand in the air and rattled off a rapid line of Spanish of which I caught three words: tomorrow, husband and follow.

We left our luggage, which seemed safe enough given we hadn't seen another person or a car since we had arrived, and followed her to the door which opened not into a kitchen, but a small living room that had a crib in the middle. I peeked in and saw a very new baby. I would have stopped to admire it, but the *señora*, in an amazing burst of energy, was already half way up the stairs on the other side of the room. Upstairs she showed us three identical rooms, each with two cots, a small dressing table between them and an armoire for clothes. The bathroom was down the hall. We took the room closest to the stairs and Chuck went back to the patio twice more to get our bags. The price had never been mentioned, but given the sparseness, it wouldn't have been much and it didn't matter at that point anyway. It wasn't as though we could drag our bags up and down the pitch black street looking for a better deal.

Since there were no other guests we had the communal bathroom all to ourselves. I took first dibs and found the electrical ring, water heater set-up in the shower, just like in training. It seemed old hat now and I achieved a warm little spray with only a minute of fiddling with the water handle. I went back to our room in higher spirits and dug out our p.j.'s while Chuck took his turn. In short order we were tucked into our cots, clean and fed. Everything else could wait.

The town came awake with the sun, first with roosters crowing, then with barking dogs, and finally with the motors of cars and trucks rumbling down the cobblestones on the main street. Chuck and I exchanged sleepy glances as we heard the *señora* down below, banging pots and pans.

"Think we could get a cup of coffee in this joint?" Chuck asked.

We made our way downstairs, back through the living room and out to the café patio. The proprietress was at our table right away — no surprise since we were the only early morning customers — and nodded when we asked for coffee and breakfast. She was back in minutes with two cups of instant coffee, strong and already sweetened to the gagging point, more small, hard rolls and scrambled eggs.

I sniffed the coffee, "Ah, the Nescafé salesman, once again."

Chuck and I had often laughed over the mythical Nescafé salesman who had somehow managed to cover every corner of the earth. No matter where we were, however remote, there was always Nescafé. And sure enough, the guy had been to General Artigas, too. We weren't complaining though. We gulped it down and were ready for more, but this time I thought I'd throw in *sin azucar* [without sugar] first.

I looked up, nudged Chuck and whispered, "Look, an Argentine cowboy."

He had ridden up on horseback, dismounted and was tying his horse to a hitching post in front of the café. Then I noticed there was a post in front of every building up and down the street. He was a picture-perfect Argentine *gaucho*, dressed with knee-high boots, a wool serape and a wide-brimmed hat. He took long, dusty strides to a corner table where the *señora* quickly brought him a *wampa* with the metal *bombilla* protruding out of it. He pulled out a small pouch of tobacco from his vest, rolled it into a long brown cigarette and actually lit it by striking a match on the bottom of his boot. I was transfixed.

I stopped staring at him long enough to notice a yawning man standing in the doorway. The *señora's* husband, I presumed. He stepped out into the sunlight, gave a mighty yawn, and stretched his arms over his head. He looked like he had just crawled out of bed, wearing rumpled khaki shorts, a stained t-shirt pulled tightly over a sizable belly, and, despite the cold morning, only rubber flip-flops for his feet. His hair was a tangle of light brown curls and he scratched them vigorously, then noticed us and came quickly to our table.

"*Hola* [hello]," he said with a big smile, "*Bienvenidos!* [Welcome!]" He stuck out his hand and gave Chuck an enthusiastic hand shake. I held my hand out too, but he just grabbed it, pulled me towards him and gave me a big kiss on each cheek, scratching me with his whiskers. He seemed delighted to have us in his café. "*Soy Cha*

Cho, y ustedes son de Cuerpo de Paz, no?" It took a second for me to recognize that his name was Chacho, and he knew we were *Cuerpo de Paz* [Peace Corps].

"*Si, si*," said Chuck enthusiastically. "*Conoces Ramón Acuña?*"

"Ramón! Ah, *si. El viene pronto.* [He comes soon.]"

With that knowing proclamation he looked down at our empty coffee cups, "Ah *mas café!*" he said arching his eyebrows and before I could stick in my no sugar request he had our cups and was gone. In minutes, he was back, this time with new cups and a thermos. He carefully poured out even darker, thicker Nescafé than before, and asked if we needed anything else and did we speak Guaranie? He pulled up a chair, sat down and proceeded to rattle off in rapid Spanish something about the previous Peace Corps Volunteer who spoke perfect Guaranie. "Teach me English," he said in Spanish, "and I'll teach you Guaranie." He threw back his head with a big laugh, clapped Chuck vigorously on the back, then got up and went over to sit with the Pampas cowboy.

"'Ramón is coming pronto?' I wonder how long pronto is?" I asked, not expecting an answer. For the time being, just sipping the coffee seemed the best course of action.

We watched the town awaken as various old pickups bumped down the main street, dogs trotted along the high sidewalks sniffing for food and a very cute green parrot hopped under tables on the café patio. We hadn't finished the coffee when a small, faded car pulled up next to the curb. The man who got out was neatly dressed in slacks and a checkered shirt with carefully combed black hair. He looked across the patio, saw us, smiled and walked to our table. It was Ramón.

After introductions and profuse apologies about not expecting us until today, he said he had to go, but to meet him at the *cooperativa* that was just down the street, and he would show us the town. After lengthy assurances that we were fine, he left us and we waved at Chacho to pay our bill. Once again we were dismissed with a wave of the hand and a "*mas tarde.*" I decided to make a rough estimate and keep tabs, just in case there was a giant discrepancy at the end.

I wasn't sure what I would do about it if there was, but I jotted my estimates down on a scrap of napkin and stuffed it in my pocket.

As we began our walk we could see that the main street wasn't all that long, but was the only one paved with the stony *empadrada*, a poor version of cobblestones, made from jagged flat rocks instead of rounded, small stones. All the buildings were fronted by curbs two feet higher than the street surface with cement sidewalks topped with large slabs of rocks. Some street corners came with steps, on others we just leaped down, crossed the street and jumped back up on the next one. We passed a leather goods store, a school supply store, a place that looked like a small factory and several all-purpose looking places that reminded me of old-fashioned dry-goods stores. There were already two horses tied up at hitching posts along the way. It looked like a stage set for *Gunsmoke* except that the saddles were different. Instead of a large western saddle, there was a sheepskin over the back of the horse, held in place by a simple leather strap and the stirrups were plain, like the kind they use in English riding.

The main road extended about four blocks in each direction from Chacho's, making me smile to realize that yes, we had been let off in the middle of town. The Catholic Church occupied a big square a couple of blocks away, but the town lacked the Spanish plaza layout I would have expected. Instead, there was a large grassy area with a few pine trees on one corner.

Opposite was the *cooperativa*, by far the grandest building in town. It was two stories high and had been freshly painted with the words "Cooperativa General Artigas" in big letters on one side. The main business of the cooperative was its supermarket, and it actually looked like a supermarket with big panes of glass across the front. We went in and found rows of metal shelving with an amazing variety of goods, everything from sacks of *yerba mate* to refrigerators, but no apparent order to anything. Chuck asked one of the clerks where Ramón was and she took us through the back to a small cramped office where Ramón was sitting at a desk surrounded by stacks of canned goods.

"*Hola!*" he greeted us cheerfully and squeezed around his desk to give me two kisses and shake Chuck's hand, like we were old friends. He proudly showed us around, starting upstairs with a spacious, empty room. It had gorgeous, polished wooden floors and was used for meetings and special occasions. Downstairs, next to the supermarket was a small office and a waiting room where loan transactions took place and next to that, "*el mas antigua edifcio en Artigas* [the oldest building in Artigas]," he told us. With thick mud walls and a heavy wooden door, it looked like, and probably was, the original Spanish mission.

Ramón led us down the street to the Mayor's office where Mayor "Pete" was equally pleased to meet us and offered to help us with anything. When I told him about our assignment of drawing a map of the city, he just laughed and handed us a perfect map of the town with the names of all the streets. Technically, all the buildings and houses had numbers, but few knew them and nobody posted them. Shops were known by location and what they sold and houses were known by who lived in them, for example, "Edna's pink house," or for some historically or distinct feature like "the old mansion." The map Pete handed us had the names of the major buildings: the Church , the Cooperative and his office and I could add the names of others. In Spanish he told us a little of the town's history and explained how he wanted to get a town identity. Apparently there was a sign on the edge of town which we didn't see the night before, that proclaimed Artigas as the Garlic Capital of Paraguay. Mayor Pete wasn't sure that was true, but he did want to be on the map for something. Thirty years before, Artigas had been a railway stop on the way to Encarnación, and with the flow of people and goods, it had been a growing community. But the government had let the railroad system collapse. Trains hadn't been running for fifteen years and now the only way to Artigas was the twenty-five mile dirt road from the *ruta* that we had traveled the night before. He suggested we might want to walk to the end of town and see the old depot. We thanked him for his time and he reaffirmed our welcome.

8   Handshakes and Kisses

Next on our agenda was to find a house to rent.

We told Ramón that we wanted to rent one with a phone line in order to use the Internet for email. He didn't exactly say it wasn't possible, but cupped his chin in his hand and looked thoughtful before brightening and suggesting we try the previous Volunteer's house, the old Spanish mansion, which had a line. Phone lines, he explained, were expensive and it took years of waiting to get one, meaning either find a house with a line or forget it. We walked first to the caretaker's house to get the keys, then headed west a couple of blocks. The house was surrounded by a high stucco wall and along one side was a small door — very cute and very little, like a door to fairy house. Even I had to duck to enter and Chuck practically crawled.

I was charmed until I got through the door and looked up. The place looked abandoned. Not just vacant for five months since the previous Volunteer had left, but more like abandoned for fifty years. The area around the house was a wreck — weeds, overgrown brambles, discarded piles of lumber and rusted metal parts. The house was arranged in a Spanish square around an interior patio (hence the "Spanish mansion"), and we entered into the salon, often just called the *sala*, or living room. It reeked of mold and the ceiling bowed down suspiciously as if it were full of water. Several windows were broken and the paint was peeling off the walls in big strips. The floor was so dirty I couldn't even tell what it was made of, and as we picked our way across the room Ramón pointed out the telephone. It was on the floor in the corner and had an old, ragged, fiber-covered cord that disappeared into a large hole in the wall. Ramón bent over, picked up the receiver and upon hearing a dial tone, smiled at us hopefully, sensing our dismay. We proceeded to the next room which was similar to the living room, but with even filthier walls. Ramón had to tell us that it was a kitchen since the only clue was a lone, brown-stained sink in one corner. The small bathroom was unspeakable with a toilet and shower that even the strongest cleaning agent anywhere couldn't remedy. The bedroom the Volunteer had used was another disaster with holes in the wall, a dripping ceiling, broken windows and a rusted bed spring against one wall. I was staggered that anyone, much less an American Volunteer, could have lived in such conditions. If it had just been a matter of cleaning or painting I wouldn't have minded, but this place was beyond "fixing up." It needed major construction or tearing down all together. Chuck and I exchanged horrified glances behind Ramón's back then as politely as possible I told him I didn't think it would do.

He had guessed as much and took us to the only other house with a phone line. This house was spic and span compared to the "mansion," but its drawback was that it came furnished with dilapidated furniture, stained and broken, taking up almost all available floor space. Plus the owner's mother lived in a small house so close it was almost attached. We nixed that one, too.

Ramón had another idea, "Why don't you look at Kitty's house? It doesn't have a phone line, but you might like it anyway. Besides, she's my cousin."

We walked to the south end of town — happy at this point the town was small — to meet Kitty, who owned and ran the town's hardware store. She led the way down the street to a small yellow house with a red tile roof, surrounded by a trimmed, large yard. On one side was a huge flowering, purple bougainvillea bush and on the other, a small tree with yellow flowers There was a barbed wire fence around the perimeter, essential for keeping out the free range livestock, and in front of the house there was a cute gate with a little stone pathway leading to the front porch. It had what a realtor might call "curb appeal." Chuck had to duck to get through the gate as there was a wire, at about the 5'7" mark, stretched across the top poles of the gate for support. High enough for Paraguayans, but it caught Chuck at the neck.

Kitty watched him duck, and said "*Lo arreglaremos* [we will fix it]."

We followed her to the front porch, which was covered with red tile instead of plain cement, and watched as she opened the wooden door with the customary skeleton key. We stepped inside to a small square front room, with the same red tiles covering the floor. The room was bright with windows facing the porch and the side yard. To the left were two small bedrooms, each with windows and the far end of the living room opened to a kitchen with a small bathroom off to the side. We took turns peeking into the tiny bathroom featuring a flush toilet with its tank mounted head-high on the wall, a single sink, and a mirrored medicine cabinet. The shower was about one yard square with the standard electrocution-heating ring. I stepped in to look at the coil more closely.

Kitty quickly assured me that it was in good working order, "*Si no, lo arreglaremos.* [If not, we will fix it.]"

The kitchen was a good sized room — three times bigger than my galley kitchen in San Diego. At one end was a window, with cupboards to each side, and below them a sink with a tiled counter top. I could envision doing dishes there and looking out the window. There was a wooden door to the back yard which had a large 4 by 4 beam that fit across in a wooden holder, instead of a key. Amazingly secure in comparison to the modern front door and its skeleton key. To the side of the back door was a small hallway with a utility sink and more cupboards. I liked everything I saw.

"Look Chuck," I said," pointing to the ceiling, "an open-beamed ceiling!"

Here, of course, it was because they just didn't add a ceiling. From the inside we looked up at the wooden poles supporting the roof and the underside of the tiles. I thought it added a rustic cabin feeling.

Ramón lifted off the cross beam securing the back door and we went outside to look at the yard. It was huge. There was a grape arbor right outside the back door, but it was now a broken down with a twisted mass of rebar supports. Kitty explained that the previous spring a tornado had come through and wrecked everything. Since then there hadn't been any renters so there had been no reason to repair it. But as she continued to assure us, "*lo arreglaremos.*" The grape vines looked dead too, but Kitty said no, they were fine, it was just winter. They would have leaves in a few months. Beyond the grape arbor was a line of five massive mango trees and scattered among them were orange trees, banana trees and others I couldn't identify. Kitty pointed to one with pride and told us it was an "*arbole de limon!*" We had already learned that the fruit the Paraguayans called a lemon was actually sort of an orange-lemon cross. Not like a lemon, but a rather a tangy orange. None-the-less, we were pleased to see it.

The place did need some work, mostly outside, as the yard was overgrown with grasses and weeds. The inside could get by with cleaning and new paint. Kitty promised us that it would be repainted and everything would be *perfecto* by the time we came back in three weeks. Chuck and I exchanged a glance on that statement, but it didn't matter. If it wasn't "*perfecto*" we could fix it up ourselves. We stepped to the side and instantly agreed that this house was the one. We would just have to come up with another solution for the phone line.

The Paraguayan rental contract was not too official looking, but did include the rental price of 200,000 Guaranies a month (about $60.00) and our occupancy date, the third week of August. For a single Volunteer this would have been too expensive, but with two

Peace Corps salaries, this fit within the budget. Kitty repeated that she would *arreglaremos* everything, and we said we would be back in three weeks. A handshake took the place of a deposit.

We were both delighted. Ramón, looking visibly pleased about the rental, left us and we walked around our new neighborhood, chatting excitedly about the house. It had an instantaneous good feeling about it, same as our old house in Afghanistan. A good sign, we thought, making our future life in Artigas seem promising.

There was a lot to buy and we walked back to Chacho's to do some list-making. The Peace Corps recognizes that most houses come completely unfurnished — no lights, appliances, drapes or floor coverings (which was the same as it was in Afghanistan), so they provide each Volunteer with what is called a "living allowance" that is actually an extra month's salary for getting basics for a house, or in the case of some really rural Volunteers, building a house.

We immediately started our search to determine what we could purchase in Artigas and what we would need to buy in Asunsción. Much to Ramón's delight, we found we could get a simple stove and a small refrigerator at the *cooperativa*. The refrigerator was beyond our Peace Corps budget, but we decided we would just buy it with our own money. We hadn't had one in Afghanistan and had managed OK, but there we had Dad Ali, our part-time servant, who bought everything fresh every day, plus a cold winter season. Here, in the sub-tropics, it would be another story. We decided we could treat ourselves, and it made two big sales for the *cooperativa*. Not only was that good for the *cooperativa*, but every dollar we spent in town would circle around and benefit the entire community.

Ramón told us that the neighbors to our right, the Barbosas, not only ran a *chipa* business, but did carpentry on the side.

"*Ellos hacen camas, mesas, sillas, todos. Puedes visitar esta tarde.* [They make beds, tables, chairs, everything. You should visit this afternoon.]," he told us, adding that in the mornings they did their *chipa* rounds, but should be home all afternoon.

Earlier we had already learned that there were no doorbells in Paraguay. Given that most houses were surrounded by a fence, and inside that fence was a snarling dog, no one would ever make it to a front doorbell anyway. The custom was to stand outside the gate and clap your hands. In the States it might seem inconceivable to hear anyone clapping out in the street, but it worked amazing well in Paraguay. Partly, I was to discover later, because the windows and doors were full of cracks and gaps and were usually open anyway so it was easy for the occupants to hear.

After lunch we headed over to meet our new neighbors, stopping at the gate and clapping loudly. Instantly, three snarling and barking dogs rounded the corner of the house and charged the fence, and Chuck and I both took a startled step backwards. Across the yard, the front door opened and a small girl stepped out.

"*Tu padre alli?* [Is your father there?]" I called out, but as I said it a short, stocky man joined her in the doorway, then came out to greet us. He was a small man, not even meeting my 5'2," with a shock of straight black hair and dark eyes. Like Chacho, he wore flip-flops, but had on old khaki pants instead of shorts and a thin shirt. He shouted something at the dogs that sent them trotting away, then he looked at us curiously and opened the gate. We introduced ourselves as his new neighbors to be and he was instantly delighted.

"*Soy Rudy,* [I am Rudy]," he said and shook our hands heartily, pumping them up and down while repeating "*Bienvenidos, bein-venidos* [welcome]."

He turned and shouted something in Guaranie to the children, who then ran back into the house and returned seconds later, each dragging two plastic chairs. Rudy motioned for us to sit down while his wife and more children appeared. I counted eight: three little girls that hid behind their mother, four other children who stood about shyly and one boy who seemed the oldest, stood by his father. Rudy introduced his wife, Delma, who was about his height, but stockier, with a square body, no waistline and stout, rounded forearms. Like Rudy, she wore flip-flops, and she had on a cotton skirt and a thin blouse. The children were introduced from the oldest to the youngest: Jorge, Miguel, Jose, Claudia (pronounced Clouw-dia), Fatima, Maria, Samuel and Martina. There were actually two more children, but they were grown and had gone off to Argentina for work. No jobs here, Rudy explained.

He was very pleased that we would be moving in, saying, "*Es mejor tener vecinos.* [It's better to have neighbors.]"

We made simple Spanish conversation under the big tree while the *mate* was passed around. We graciously took sips on each passing. Chuck mentioned that he played the guitar which brought forth a request for lessons from the oldest boy, Jorge.

"*Si, si,* " Chuck told him, and Jorge gave him a big smile and a handshake. He was a handsome kid, with dark eyes, and a shock of dark hair that fell over one side of his face, giving him a rakish rock-star look. I also noticed that he had a beautiful smile with perfect teeth — the first I'd seen in Artigas. With that arranged, Chuck came to the point of our visit.

"Do you do carpentry? he asked. "We need a table, a bed, all sorts of things."

If Rudy had been a *Norte Americano*, he would have said, "Do I do carpentry? Is the Pope Catholic?" But instead he simply replied "*Por supuesto* [of course]," and with great enthusiasm, jumped up and led us over to one of the two front doors to the house. He opened it and instead of a living area there was a workshop.

There we saw two completed wooden bed frames — a double and a single. Chuck pointed at the larger one and asked how much.

"*Setenta mil Guaranies* [roughly $20.00]," Rudy replied.

Chuck replied "*Dicho y hecho*" ["said and done"], an expression that cements a deal.

We also agreed to purchase a table and six chairs. Rudy was ecstatic; we were ecstatic. In one day we were well on our way to setting up our house. Later Ramón told us that he could bring over an old free-standing kitchen cupboard called an *alacena* if we didn't mind fixing it up a little.

Ramón had invited us to dinner at his house that evening and had carefully showed us on the map where his house was located.

"*Vengan a la siete*, [come at seven]," he told us, and then repeated it. He laughed and told us that he knew *Norte Americanos* were "*puntual* [punctual]," a habit he thought was *muy bueno*.

When evening came Ramón's house was easy to find as it was on a corner, and we could see his car parked in front. On our limited walks, we hadn't seen any garages, but only a few people had cars.

The house resembled our new rental from the outside, with a simple stucco exterior and a small, fenced yard. We clapped at the gate, and the obligatory dog came rushing out, barking, but Ramón was right behind him calling him off. He ushered us through his front door and motioned for us to sit on the velveteen-covered sofa in the *sala*. It looked new and I suspected that, like Digna's, most of the time it was probably covered with a sheet.

Ramón brought out a plate of olives for the hors d' oeuvres, which we knew from training, were not customary for Paraguayans, but rather a special treat for us. He introduced us to his wife, Anjelica and his son, Fernando, who was sixteen. Anjelica was pretty woman, maybe in her forties. She taught school in the mornings and ran a small school supply store in the afternoons as teachers and students in Paraguay only had classes half-days. Fernando had a sturdy build, a round face like his fathers and a pleasing smile. If he had lived in the States, he might have played football or been on the wrestling team. Unlike teenagers in the States, he didn't seem put out by his mandatory appearance. He appeared to be perfectly content to chat with us and showed no sign of wanting to leave to do something else.

For dinner Anjelica had prepared a tasty meal of roasted meats and a salad. It was clear they were trying to serve what they felt *Norte Americanos* would like. *Mandioca* wasn't in sight. The evening was pleasant as we chatted in Spanish on various topics. I especially liked Anjelica — she was intelligent, down-to-earth and interested in learning all she could about us and our customs.

We didn't stay long after dinner. I wasn't sure what the Paraguayan custom might have been, but we were both weary from a busy day and I was finding my ability to concentrate in Spanish faltering. We graciously thanked them and walked back to our room at Chacho's.

The next morning we headed back to the meeting room above the *cooperativa* where Ramón had arranged for us to meet with the numerous directors of the organization. We sat in a circle of chairs and were introduced to each director, and then were asked to introduce ourselves.

We both spoke, telling a bit of our past and our mission. After we finished, there was a long silence. Chuck and I exchanged a nervous glance thinking that maybe we hadn't said enough or hadn't explained our purpose, so we ran through our Peace Corps agenda, telling them that we were Business Volunteers and wanted to help with business projects. Again nothing but stoney silence. Now we were stumped. We just sat there; they just sat there. It was so unlike an American meeting where everyone is clamoring to talk and you have to interrupt someone to get your turn to speak. A long, empty minute ticked by before Ramón finally said they were all pleased to have us.

"*Hay mucho trabajo aqui* [There is much work here]," Ramón said, but he didn't specify anything.

Finally, one woman spoke of needing better education and more modern methods of teaching. Ramón expounded on that, explaining the sorry state of Paraguayan education where it was based on rote memory. They had started a new kindergarten, he went on, to try to develop a more modern system from the ground up. "Could I teach English to the kindergartners?" he asked. I blanched at the thought. Not only did I not want to do it, it seemed totally impractical and far from the Co-op business training we had received. Everyone in the circle looked at me. I sighed internally but said yes, I was sure I could help some with that. There didn't seem to be any other answer.

As I discussed with Chuck later, and he agreed, I couldn't very well say NO, I'm not going to help with that, especially since it was our first meeting and their only request. I imagined that a couple of lessons a week wouldn't kill me, but I was a little concerned with the fact that I didn't know anything about teaching little kids. My only previous exposure had been decades before when I was working as a high school substitute teacher, but was asked to take an elementary class — just to help out. It had been a disaster and had stuck in my memory as one of my worst days ever.

9   The Final Stretch

On our third evening in Artigas, we asked Chacho if we could settle our bill and he shrugged and said we could, although he seemed perfectly happy to wait until we came back. The hotel was about $8.00 a night and the food bill equally cheap, just a few dollars per meal. I had stopped keeping track since there was one price for breakfast, one for lunch and one for supper. A little more if you had a beer at night or the wonderful Nescafé in the mornings.

Chacho —who was also the bus station manager — told us to be out front by 6:30 a.m. to catch the bus to Asunción. He also gave us careful instructions on how to transfer to the "fast" bus from Bogado to Asunción.

We made the change without problems and were back at Digna's by supper.

All in our training group were excited and optimistic in class the next day, chattering about how we liked our sites.

With the knowledge of our locations and a better idea of our jobs, we were allowed now to pick and choose what training classes we wanted to take during our final three weeks. Chuck immediately opted out of the rest of his Guaranie lessons. The citizens of Artigas, being close to the Argentine border, were good Spanish speakers and although they did speak Guaranie, it didn't seem like it was necessary. I stayed with the classes though, thinking a little would be useful and diplomatic, although in truth, I didn't have the courage to tell my Guaranie teacher I would be dropping out too, knowing how disappointed she would be.

Because there was plenty of water in Artigas, we attended a lecture on fish farming and left enthusiastic — but realistic. One lecture was hardly enough to plunge us into aquaculture projects, but there were, supposedly, other Volunteers who could come and help us should the need arise.

I thought the bee-keeping class might be useful too, but to attend, one had to first get stung. Understandably, they didn't want someone in the class who was allergic to bee stings since the first class involved traipsing out through the underbrush to break apart a bee hive and capture the queen. Chuck said I could go, but he didn't want any part of it. He reasoned that he had been stung enough on his own without signing up for more. He did have a point. I decided instead to get the names of some actual bee-keeping Volunteers.

Meanwhile, Todd and I trotted out to the chicken farm Pepe managed although there was little more we could learn, and really nothing we could help him with. The original idea of sending us out there had been to learn about chicken farming, but also to assist the chicken farmer with our supposed better business acumen and turn his supposedly lackluster operation around. It was a complete joke. I didn't know enough about accounting or chicken farming to give Pepe the slightest advice and besides, he didn't need any. Although he wasn't computerized, the records he kept were perfect and in fact, everything was perfect except that to be really profitable, they needed to add more chickens and another employee. Could we give them money from the U.S.? That was the only help he wanted.

As Chuck was preparing his final pig report, Tony, the pig owner (who also needed zero help from Volunteers) invited our entire group out to see the birth of a new batch of piglets. His computerized system (and practiced eye) predicted the birth day with precision and he had told us to be there at noon on Wednesday. We arrived promptly at noon and Tony greeted us warmly announcing that the piglets were just about ready to come, but in the meantime he would show us around the ranch.

It didn't take me long to realize I had lost the bet with Chuck for the gin and tonic. The pig smell was worse than chickens. It was bad enough strolling around the outside pens, but worst yet was the shed were they concocted their own pig feed, a nauseous combination of dead chickens and something that smelled like rotten grain. It absolutely knocked me back. Two of Tony's sons were stirring and slopping around in the wretched stuff, proudly getting the mix "just right." What must have made the smell palatable to them, was the money rolling in.

Unlike my chicken farm, Tony was making real money. He led us to his office where he had a computer with all the data on every pig, from conception to sale, with detailed entries of everything from exact times of conception to birth weights and growth charts. There were so few quality pigs being bred in the country that Tony just had to announce that the pigs were ready to be sold and the buyers came to him, ready to load them in their trucks. Even counting food, medicine and all that went into the pig raising process, Tony almost tripled his money on every single pig. In less than five years he had developed a thriving business.

We circled back to the barn where the first piglet was about to arrive. Ten minutes passed and still no piglet. Tony looked concerned and instructed one of his sons to get the veterinarian.

He looked at us and said, "*no está en posicion correcto.*" Then, to illustrate his point, he made a fist with his hand, then turned it sideways.

Since the vet was just down the road it wasn't but a few minutes when he walked into the barn, looking very much the veterinarian, wearing tall rubber boots to his knees, a checked shirt and carrying an old-fashioned doctor's bag. He spoke in Guaranie for a minute with Tony, then knelt in the straw and massaged the sow's huge belly. He took off his shirt, revealing a thin T-shirt. He rolled the small sleeve of the t-shirt over his shoulder, then scrubbed his right arm thoroughly and bathed it in an antiseptic before rolling on a long, latex glove.

I was surprised by the thorough sanitizing. I would have thought the glove would have been sufficient, but obviously not.

Now sterilized, he bent over the sow and talked to her, patting and stroking her head with his left hand while inserting his right hand slowly up the birth canal. When he was up to his forearm he started making "hm-hmmm" sounds, then finally, "*bueno*" and he extracted his arm with a tiny piglet, the size of a mouse, in his hand. It was white, wrinkled and very still. Even to my unpracticed eye, it looked dead.

The vet still massaged it for a minute before announcing that it was "*muerto*." But, he added, all of the piglets should come now. And sure enough, in about ten minutes the sow showed more activity and a new piglet was deposited in the hay. This one was pink and was already wobbling its head around as the vet picked it up. He handed it over to one of Tony's sons, who was clipping the umbilical cords and applying some sort of antiseptic.

The clipping part made me feel faint and I had to walk outside. By the time I returned, the vet had left and Tony's sons had taken over, carefully putting each little piggy next to one of the sow's teats. Tony explained that the number of piglets had to be the same or fewer than the number of teats as they didn't share. If a pig had thirteen babies and only had twelve teats, one would starve. We left after the arrival of the seventh piglet, but later learned there were a total of eleven healthy piglets. The sow had twelve teats so all had a place on the chow line.

There were two closing ceremonies for our training. One with our host families, and one at the Embassy. The host family ceremony was held on the last day of class and turned out to be a nostalgic affair. Digna had been chosen to give a talk on behalf of the families and coincidentally, I had been chosen to speak for the Volunteers. She started crying during hers and continued crying during mine. This set me off and I practically sobbed through my whole speech, which fortunately was short. It was hard to believe I was such a crybaby when I was anxious to leave and ready to start our new life in Artigas.

The following day the official ceremony to swear us in as Peace Corps Volunteers — PCVs — was held at the Embassy where we gave an oath of allegiance and ate cake with red, white and blue frosting. We all dressed up for the occasion. I actually had on nylons and pumps and Chuck wore a jacket and tie. It was the first time in three months that we didn't look like scruffy backpackers.

10   Back to the Future

We were more confident on our second trip to Artigas and took the fast bus, now that we were familiar with the switch we would have to make in Bogado. All of our luggage plus extra supplies were stuffed into three big duffels stowed under the bus. Since the only coffee we had noticed in the *cooperativa* were tiny packets of Nescafé, we had gone to one of the big stores in Asunción and stocked up with several big sacks of coffee, plus a coffee pot, four bottles of wine and several cans of Campbell's soup, just for nostalgia.

We were assigned a Peace Corps adviser who would come to Artigas in a couple of weeks, ostensibly to bring us bicycles (now provided whereas in Afghanistan we had to buy them), but more likely to check on us and see how we were doing. At this point we were feeling very good as we were way ahead of the other Volunteers in our group. We were the only ones who had already rented a house, not to mention lined up furniture.

This time we rolled into Artigas in mid-afternoon and were greeted with big waves from Chacho. He called Ramón for us and by the time we had finished some Nescafé, Ramón had pulled up in a pickup and was waving the skeleton key to the front door.

Being a bit cynical Chuck and I had made a bet on the bus that probably none of the things that Kitty had promised to be "*arregla-remos*" would be done, but I didn't really care. I could roll up my sleeves and scrub, paint or do whatever, and live in our unfinished new home at the same time. But we were pleasantly surprised. Upon approaching the house, the first thing we noticed was the house was now green, not yellow. The entire outside had been repainted and that wasn't even an task that had been mentioned. When we came to the gate we laughed. The wire that previously was holding the posts together — at neck high for Chuck — had been replaced by a heavier one that was shaped in a large arc about seven feet high. Ramón smiled at us, pleased.

"*Bueno, no?*" he chuckled.

The inside was also clean and ready to go. The bathroom and kitchen cupboards still needed some work for my standards, but I was expecting that to be the case. Overall, we were delighted and praised Ramón for all his efforts. He shrugged modestly and claimed it was all of Kitty's doings.

We heaved our bags in the corner and looked around, not sure where to start.

"*Quieran escoger una refrigeradora?* [Do you want to choose a refrigerator?]" Ramón asked.

Why not, we thought and went back with him to the *cooperativa*. We picked out a small basic model, with an itty-bitty freezer compartment; definitely NOT frost free. I wondered if you could even buy a non-frost-free fridge in the States. The stove was equally basic, four small gas burners and a small oven. It had a lid that covered the burners when down, but when open, acted as a back-splash.

Chuck pulled out his big wad of Guaranie bills and paid for the stove in full. We had agreed to pay for the refrigerator over the next four months since we didn't have that much cash with us and had not wanted to carry that much money from Asunción. Ramón was most pleased about our purchases and assured us they would be delivered the next morning.

That task completed, we walked back to our new home, stopping first at the home of Rudy Barbosa, our new neighbor and furniture builder. Rudy was also delighted to see us and said he could bring over the bed and the table and the four chairs, *pronto*. He and Jorge were at our door in minutes each carrying one end of the table. In a second and third trip, they brought over the bed and chairs. We paid them with our dwindling cash bundle, thanked them again and closed the door with a feeling of accomplishment.

Then we took a second look at the bed frame. In Rudy's workshop it had looked large, but now in our new bedroom, we realized it was a very small bed — a double perhaps, but more like a fat single. It would never work.

"So now what?" I asked "We can't very well take it back." We both looked at the tiny bed for a few minutes remembering how comfortable we had been in our big king-sized bed in San Diego. "Let's make it the guest bed," I suggested, and Chuck and I each grabbed an end, turned it sideways through the door, and positioned it in the second, smaller bedroom. It fit nicely.

"We needed furniture in here anyway," I said, offering an optimistic note. "And the size is perfect." I doubted if we would have more than one visitor at a time, if we had any at all

"I'll just buy a bigger bed for us," Chuck added confidently, not letting this slight disappointment spoil our day.

We returned to the living room, sat down at our new table and discovered another sizing problem. Rudy had made the table tall, thinking, perhaps of how tall Chuck was, then made the chairs the regular height. When I sat in one of the chairs, the table came up to my chest. This problem was easy to fix; we could just have Rudy come over and saw a few inches off the table legs.

After a simple dinner at Chacho's, we returned home, opened a bottle of wine and, with two small glasses I had brought from Asunción, raised a toast to the first night in our new home. Finally! We had made it through all of the trauma of leaving the States and then the summer of training and living with another family. We congratulated ourselves until the bottle was empty then blew up our air mattresses, unrolled our sleeping bags and curled up happily on the floor of our bedroom, in our own house.

For once we could take our time getting up. There were no classes, no buses to catch, no time to be out the door. We awakened as the sunlight brightened our amber colored windows and I lay there quietly for a while, listening to roosters and dogs, and suddenly, the sound of someone clapping at our gate.

"Who could that be?" Chuck mumbled, as we both jumped out of bed pulling on jeans and sweatshirts. I followed Chuck out to the porch to see a boy on a bicycle in front of our gate.

"*Soy Samuel*," he told us, "*Y tengo el periódico* [I have the newspaper]," which was apparent as he had a canvas bag full of newspapers slung over his shoulder. He could bring one by every morning if we liked.

"*Si, si*," Chuck told him enthusiastically.

Ramón had told us there was no need to start any projects right away and to spend the next couple of weeks getting settled. A couple of weeks seemed too long, but I didn't argue.

We sat down to make major lists. It was easy: I needed everything. The only thing in the entire house was a small roll of toilet paper and the obligatory waste basket that Kitty had been thoughtful enough to supply. That was it. With the exception of the two small glasses, I had no dishes, no cutlery, no pots nor pans. Every room lacked something. Other than the dining table and chairs, the living room was totally bare. The kitchen needed a working table and a storage cabinet. The bedroom needed a bed! And without closets, an armoire of some kind was necessary, and night stands too. And that was level one.

The level two list included finishing touches like pillows, blankets, throw rugs, towels, linens, and curtains since all windows were bare. All the windows also needed screens and we needed two screen doors.

I decided to shop initially for cleaning supplies and dishes. No point in loading up on food without a dish in the house. It was going to take a number of trips regardless, since I'd have to carry it all back in my plastic shopping bags and backpack.

Chuck's plan was to wait for the new stove and refrigerator to be delivered while I shopped, then scout around to see if there was anything resembling a furniture store.

By nightfall we had a humming refrigerator with cold milk, a working stove and oven, clean cabinets holding a few dishes, two plastic chairs with seat cushions, and best of all, a real queen sized bed and mattress.

Chuck had discovered a sort of combo saddle shop and furniture store that had a *grande* bed that they were more than happy to sell. Delirious to sell, actually. Chuck said that given the dust on it, it had probably been sitting in there for years. They were so excited, they loaded it on a truck and delivered it instantly, afraid Chuck would change his mind.

After the bed was placed in the bedroom, I carefully cut the plastic wrap from the mattress, deciding I could cut the plastic into a perfect shower curtain, since there wasn't one and water splashed over everything, including the toilet paper.

We decided to celebrate with a simple dinner at home, buying one of Chacho's chickens and heating up one of my Campbell's soups.

I had not been able to find a can opener for the soup in the *cooperativa* so I quickly went next door to ask the Barbosas if I could borrow theirs. They didn't have one. The house across the street was my next option. It had a satellite dish in the yard so I thought possession of a can opener might be possible. I clapped at their gate and repeated my request, holding up my soup can. The man looked at me, nodded and took my can. After what seemed to be quite a while, he finally returned, smiled and handed me the open can. The top had been opened all right — by pounding a nail around the edge some fifty or sixty times. I thanked him profusely. Just like with directions, Paraguayans always tried to help.

Meanwhile, Rudy had come over with his saw and reduced our dining table to normal height standards. He also advised us to go to Encarnación, the *cuidad grande* [big town], to buy our household items as their markets had everything and were cheap. This we would do the next day, plus we could check out the Internet café for email.

Chuck asked Rudy what time the bus came that would go to Encarnación and received an ambiguous shrug of the shoulders and an explanation that it was sometimes just before 6 a.m. or sometimes just after unless it rained, then it was usually 6:30. But if it rained *mucho*, then it wouldn't come at all.

The alarm clock was set for 5:15. We thought that after a quick cup of coffee, we could stroll up to Chacho's and get there before 6:00.

I awoke in pitch blackness with roosters crowing. I looked at my watch — only 4 a.m. I tried to get back to sleep, but various dogs chimed in, then more roosters and then it was 5:00. "I thought roosters just crowed at dawn," I mumbled to Chuck, pulling on my jeans.

He just eyed me sleepily and shrugged. "Stock brokers from San Diego. What do we know?"

The sun began to rise just as we made our way to the main road. Sure enough, at about five minutes to six, here came the old *Fletcha*, rumbling towards us. In less than an hour, we changed buses in Bogado and caught the super bus to Encarnación.

It was a pleasant ride with farming country most of the way and as we neared the city, it didn't seem as grey or depressing as Asunción had so many weeks before. I couldn't decide if it was due to the sunny day or the fact that I had gotten used to shabby buildings and roadside shacks and now they didn't bother me. Or maybe I was just excited about getting things for the house.

Before we'd even gotten off the bus we spied the Internet café, so we back-tracked to it as our first stop of the day. I had received three letters from my family that we printed to reread, and I was able to send one. It had been almost two weeks without any news from the States and I was elated to hear from my sisters.

Next we caught a taxi to what was a huge open market at the

end of town. Sidewalks were jammed with vendors selling every product imaginable, and each one was competing with the stores behind them that were filled with the same products.

We split up with Chuck going in search of hardware items while I would purchase items for the interior of the house. My plan was to do comparison shopping for the linens as I would have done in the States, but when I stopped to look twice at an item, the merchants were on me, bargaining furiously, so I finally just settled on shopping at one store for the lot — sheets, blankets, towels, pillows, tablecloths, material for curtains and several throw rugs. I discovered the best thing about buying everything from one store, was now the owner was my very best friend and he would happily watch my pile of merchandise until I was ready to take a taxi.

In the meantime Chuck had returned with an enormous roll of green, plastic screening for our windows and doors, plus an assortment of tools. There was more we needed and special foods we wanted, but we realized we had to stop shopping as our carry-home pile was getting too unwieldy.

As it was, we looked like Ma and Pa Kettle getting on the bus. The driver had to load the screen and rugs in the luggage space below, and I managed to stuff my large plastic bags of linens in the overhead compartments.

The transfer in Bogado wasn't too cumbersome, but by the time the *Fletcha* had made countless stops on its way to Artigas, the bus was jammed full. To get off we had to force ourselves through a full aisle of standing passengers with our big sacks knocking into everyone. "*Perdón, perdón,*" we apologized with every step.

It was late by the time we dragged ourselves and our bundles from Chacho's to our little green house, making two trips to carry it all. I made the bed, which looked quite smart with pillows and the most colorful blanket on top. We got out the mosquito netting that the Peace Corps had provided and strung it up on the beams over the bed. It fell nicely around the bed and looked very tropical. It was designed long so you could tuck it securely around your mattress once you were in bed. We planned to do just that. Chuck declared it would be the final perimeter for all things that flew or crawled . . . or slithered.

The next morning I made my way to the *cooperativa* as soon as it opened. From old habit, I had made a list, but I didn't really need one since I needed everything and planned to go up and down the aisles buying anything that looked useful or edible. The store had two check-out counters, two carts and one customer — me. No clerks were at the counters, but I could hear noises in the back so I guessed that there must be an employee around somewhere. I pulled out the first cart; the front wheel didn't turn so I pulled out the second cart, which tilted to the right, but did roll.

The store was large, but there were no signs indicating what was in each aisle, so I slowly started down the first one. In the first section I found rat poison, fly-paper, men's shaving lotion, disposable diapers, shampoo, rope, plastic bowls and wrapping paper — all covered with a layer of dust. I took some shampoo.

The other aisles were equally chaotic and I slowly rolled along, discovering huge sections of cookies and candy, canned goods and enormous sacks of *yerba mate*. No bread except for the omnipresent hard little rolls we had been crunching since our arrival in country. No spices at all, I thought, until I discovered them in little sacks hanging from a fly-specked poster board at the end of an aisle. Most of the common ones, like oregano, sage and thyme were there. Someone back in the States had told me that chili powder didn't exist anywhere south of Mexico so I had brought two large bottles of that with us. I looked for at least ten minutes for something like mustard or mayonnaise, and finally found a box with tiny little packets, the kind you get at fast food restaurants, and I took handfuls.

The most astounding section was the canned peas aisle. I was stunned! There must have been 1,000 cans of canned peas — almost rivaling the cookie section. I wondered why Paraguayans loved canned peas so much until I came across the produce department. It consisted of three boxes on a bench in the back of the store. One contained some tomatoes that looked decent, the second, some onions that also passed muster, but the third held two rotten pineapples, with flies buzzing over them and two bunches of brown-spotted, squishy bananas. Below the bench were rotten potatoes in a disgusting box with thick black mold growing in fuzzy abundance, and a large bin of something I couldn't identify — roots or beets or God-knows-what, covered with dirt. I made a mental note that starting a garden was a project that was going to be moved to the top of my to-do list.

I was heartened to find that there was a large variety of yogurts in one of the two refrigerated cases, made by the Paraguayan Mennonites. They obviously hadn't progressed to aged cheese though as the only choice was the "fresh" cheese that Digna used. Near the refrigerated cases was a freezer jammed full of frozen bags, each covered with thick frost. I scraped my fingernail over one trying to determine what was inside and it appeared to be chicken, but most of the lettering came off with the frost so I couldn't determine if they were bags of thighs or breasts or what. I passed — we could always buy our chicken freshly roasted by Chacho. I stocked up on basics like sugar and flour and did find some dried soup mixes.

When I got to the check-out counter I found a pleasant young man and I asked about meat.

"*Carne?*" he questioned back, then explained in rapid Spanish that I had to go to a *carcinero* [butcher shop], and proceeded to give me directions that I didn't exactly catch, but heard enough to decide it was close. Of course this was Artigas, everything was close.

I took my two big shopping sacks home then returned to look for the butcher's shop. It was tucked away on the main street. It had a small doorway with no sign and inside, a single counter and a large, shiny, white refrigerator. A very short, stocky, bald man stood behind the counter,with his sleeves rolled up and a big smile displaying front teeth capped prominently in gold. He looked as if he had been waiting for me.

"*Beinvenidos, señora, soy Alejandro.*" He came around the counter, took my hand and kissed me on both cheeks. Even acknowledging the cheek-kissing custom, I was startled to get such an enthusiastic welcome and couldn't decide if he really liked me, really wanted my business or maybe this was how one greeted one's only customer of the day.

"*Soy Eloisa*," I replied, stepping back just a little and explained I wanted ham, beef and bacon. He smiled at me some more, nodded and went back around his counter. He opened his refrigerator and pointed proudly to a large of hindquarter of beef and explained in careful Spanish that he was the beef butcher and for pork there was different butcher and bacon? He wasn't sure what bacon was. He turned and pulled the whole beef hindquarter out of the refrigerator, hefted it onto the counter and asked how many kilos I wanted. I started at it dumbly, trying to calculate kilos and the stew I had in mind.

He watched me patiently and finally asked, "*Señora, como va a prepararlo* [Madam, how are you going to cook it]?"

I said for a *cocido*, which was the word I had learned for stew, but that didn't seem to register. I added *sopa,* which meant soup, and he flashed me his golden smile, turned the big end of the hindquarter to the saw and in a flash, buzzed off a huge chunk. He then picked up an enormous cleaver and with a great whack cut that section in two.

"*Bueno?*" he asked, and held up a hefty piece.

I was still hypnotized by the saw blade that was a wicked looking vertical blade with no guard or shield of any kind. I realized I had been holding my breath and now exhaled, since it appeared he still had all of his fingers and nodded yes. He weighed it and wrapped it and charged a few Guaranies. I'm sure if his hands had still been clean, he would have repeated his warm handshake and kisses, but I quickly thanked him, waved good-bye and backed out of the door.

Chuck was waiting for me when I got back, anxious to have something in the way of a stateside soup-and-sandwich lunch.

"Any bread?" he asked.

"Nope."

"Cold cuts?"

"Don't exist."

"Cheese?"

"Just like Digna's."

"Tuna?"

"Nope."

"Peanut butter?"

"In your dreams."

"So, what is for lunch?"

"Well, I think some soup, hard crunchie bread things and some yogurts. But, I did manage some beef from the butcher's so we can have a big stew tonight although it won't have potatoes — those were rotten. And I think the butcher is in love with me. I got two cheek kisses just for coming in the front door."

Chuck raised his eyebrows, "Just for coming in the front door? There's a marketing strategy."

And we both laughed at the prospect of American merchants kissing all of their customers.

11 Home Sweet Home

It seemed like the best thing to do after lunch in Artigas was to take a nap. All stores were closed for two or three hours and no one stirred.

We decided that the small bed in the front bedroom would be our napping spot. I liked it because from that position I could peek out of the window and see what was happening in the street. We laid down with the idea of resting for ten minutes, then were out like lights, waking forty-five minutes later wondering what planet we were on. I then rose up on my elbows and watched as the town slowly came back to life, first with a motorcycle zooming by, then a truck, then a cow ambling along, then dogs, more trucks — activity was picking up.

I saw that the two dogs belonging to the neighbors on our left, were in our yard doing their business. The fences on both sides of the backyard were in poor condition and the only thing that they kept out were cows. Earlier I had tried to introduce myself to these neighbors, but it was obvious that they didn't speak any Spanish, and the wife seemed reticent to even approach me or smile. Our landlord, Kitty, came by and I asked her about them and only got a wrinkled up nose in response and the words *malo* [bad] and *bajo* [low]. She didn't expound on the matter, so I let it drop. I had noticed that Paraguayans were decidedly prejudiced against people with darker skin and these neighbors were quite dark and obviously quite poor as their house was just a shack. It was ironic that as much as the Paraguayans disliked the Spanish conquistadors, they did seem to like Spanish blood in their veins.

Fences, we noticed, surrounded most yards or anything green since all animals were free range. There were three little trees planted in front of the *cooperativa* that Ramón had proudly pointed out, along with the tall barricading fences around them. If not so protected, the cows would eat them down to stumps. He had told us that a law had been passed forbidding free-ranging animals, but it obviously wasn't enforced. It was a problem if someone had only a cow but no pasture. It was much easier just to let it roam. The house just up the street on the corner had one such cow. It grazed all over the place and then ambled home and actually laid down at the feet of the owner, who sat in a plastic chair in front of his house watching the world go by.

But free range chickens were the worst. I observed that these highly touted non-caged chickens, the pinnacle of healthy eating according to Stateside information, ate a diet of dog excrement, cow excrement, pig excrement, rotten food, bugs, anything green and anything in front of their voracious little beaks. So far the only item I had seen them not eat, was a lemon peel.

At any rate, Chuck said he would fix the holes in the fence to keep the neighbor's dogs on their side.

We were beat after a meager dinner that night.
I was amazed at how long it took to do everything by hand and without a car. The two trips to the *cooperativa* had taken all morning. Dishes — even the few we had — took time to wash because I had to first boil water on the stove. At least I had realized that I needed to set the kettle on the stove while we ate so that the water was ready for clean-up.

We decided that we'd celebrate our progress with one of our

bottles of wine when we heard clapping at the gate. Looking out we saw young Jorge from next door with a guitar in one hand. He was a bit sheepish and just stood there when we went out, but Chuck invited him in and graciously said that this was a good time to start lessons. And it probably was the only time for Jorge, between school and helping his parents with the *chipa* business.

His guitar was a hand-me-down from some uncle and had two strings. Luckily Chuck had brought a couple of extra packages of strings from the States, so the main part of the first lesson was spent in restringing and tuning, while Jorge looked on. Chuck wrapped up the lesson by teaching him the basic C, G, and A7 chords. Jorge was ready to come back the next evening, but Chuck told him that once a week should do it, as it was important to for him practice. Jorge promised to practice *mucho* and sure enough, the next morning I awoke to roosters crowing, dogs barking and distinct repetitions of the chords, C, G and A7.

M orning deliveries weren't limited to the newspaper. After coffee and our paper we heard clapping at our gate, and exchanged the quizzical looks of "Now what?" Both of us went out to discover a man on a bicycle with big boxes of vegetables tied to the front and back.

"*Soy Crispin*" he announced with a big smile filled with gold capped teeth. "*Vendo vegetales* [I sell vegetables]."

I couldn't believe my eyes. There in his boxes were fresh tomatoes, cabbages, limes, carrots, green onions, cauliflower and green peppers. I wanted to buy it all, but decided I couldn't possibly use that much and besides, Crispin informed us, he would be by about every three days, weather depending. I was ecstatic and had him fill my arms with produce. Back in the kitchen, I sorted it lovingly into the refrigerator.

"I love this place," I told Chuck. "You just wait a little, and what you need just comes to your front door."

The truth of what I'd said was further reinforced in the afternoon when a woman came by asking if she could do our laundry. Her Spanish was very weak and it took me a while to get it arranged, but it was finally decided she would come every Wednesday, weather permitting and bring everything back on Friday, weather permitting. Clothes had to dry outside, so any time it rained, there would be a delay. Plus, dry or not, the custom was to iron everything, underwear included. Digna had done the same thing, saying that it kept the bugs out of the clothes. Or it at least fried them.

I had seen two more home delivery services. One was a fellow on horseback who had two long metal canisters tied to each side of his saddle. This was fresh milk. Since we had a ready supply of low-fat boxed milk at the *cooperativa*, which didn't even need refrigeration, I decided to pass on the non-pasteurized variety, especially since I had no idea of the condition of the farm or cows it came from.

The second delivery service came rolling down the street in an old wooden cart, pulled by a big draft horse that looked exactly like it was lifted from an old European painting. It was piled high with mandioca roots. They were incredibly cheap, so I bought one to see if I could somehow make them tasty. I peeled it and boiled it, just like Digna had, and then spiced the devil out of it, but we both still pushed it around on our plates. Chuck asked me if the cold cuts and cheese man had appeared yet.

I had purchased yards of pretty, yellow-flowered fabric in Encarnación to use as curtain material. I had even gotten plain muslin for a lining. I wasn't a good enough seamstress to do any fancy curtain making, but even I could hem the two fabrics together and make a fold at the top to slide onto a pole. Chuck had found some long bamboo poles in the house and wall brackets were already in place. Back in our Afghan days, I had made our curtains and had made the mistake of buying just enough material to cover the window size. When I pulled them closed, they looked skimpy. This time, I bought double the width so they would look full, but double the width was taking double the time to hem. Make that quadruple. In

Afghanistan, another Volunteer had loaned me her very cute hand-crank sewing machine. Here I just had my self-operating fingers.

While I was hemming, Chuck had been making friends with Oscar, the owner of the local radio station, which was located in a small annex of the church about two blocks away. The radio station filled a big need in the community for entertainment and information because few locals took the newspaper, and all printed matter — books or magazines — was too expensive. The broadcasts were in Guaranie as many *campesinos* [farmers] living in outlaying areas didn't speak Spanish.

As we were new residents and foreigners, Oscar wanted to interview us on the radio so we went down to the station that afternoon. Oscar asked us questions in Spanish, then translated into Guaranie for his radio listeners. It was pretty standard stuff — the facts that we were American Peace Corps Volunteers, we would work with Ramón and the *cooperativa,* and so far we liked everything about General Artigas. Now, Oscar assured us, everyone would know who we were.

He was especially keen to know if we had brought any music with us as he was eager to add new music to his selections. Later we brought over our three cassettes for him to copy, but the only one he wanted was the country music one.

"*Weelie Neelson, muy popular,*" he exclaimed.

We promised we would try to get some tapes for him.

12   Compost R Us

While I was happy to have time to get the house in order I was also anxious to find out more about what we would be doing. What was our Peace Corps job going to be?

We pestered Ramón to organize another meeting for us with the board at the *cooperativa*. He complied and in a few days we were once again sitting in the uncomfortable circle with the *cooperativa* board.

Chuck and I rattled off all the projects we might help them with and added brightly we could bring help for bee keeping or fish farming. Once again quiet, passive faces looked back at us. Chuck and I had made a pact that this time when we were done with our spiel, we wouldn't utter another word. So we sat and stared back at them.

Finally, Ramón picked up the slack and talked again of the need for better education. Then one woman spoke up and said they were going to have a cooking class using soy products, maybe I could help there. The town nurse wanted to do a better job on garbage pick-up and recycling. Someone else spoke of the need for exercise classes. Oscar's mother said he needed help in the radio station.

When Chuck tried to steer suggestions back towards business or helping develop business projects Ramón said we could do whatever we wanted to do. There was a special Education Committee we should meet, someone suggested, and Ramón reminded me again about the kindergarten. They all looked hopeful and confused.

We thanked everyone and walked back home. "I think they want us here, but have no idea of what to do with us," I told Chuck.

"I wonder whose idea it was for Business Volunteers?" he asked. "Theirs or Peace Corps'?"

"Maybe it doesn't matter. We can fill in doing whatever. And we were Education Volunteers before."

Chuck just shrugged. "I'll start with Oscar tomorrow."

"I'll see what I can do with the kindergarten."

It was a sharp contrast with our Peace Corps experience of thirty years before. Then, we were assigned to be English teachers at a specific place and at a specific time. We just had to show up and start teaching. Paraguay's business program wasn't as solid.

I left for my kindergarten class the next day with major trepidation. I knew I had to be entertaining and keep their little minds engaged, but that was it.

I followed the directions to the location of the class and easily found an old house that had been converted into a school. It had a big, shady back yard with a large area of sand, encircled by logs. Inside there were cupboards with school supplies, little tables and chairs and a portable blackboard. The children's art had been hung along one wall. A woman who had been at the *cooperativa* meeting welcomed me and introduced me to her sister, the principal teacher who seemed lukewarm at best about having me there, said I could have fifteen minutes as the children didn't have a capacity to sit longer than that.

Fifteen minutes was fine with me.

She introduced me to the eight children in the class, some of whom were only three and four years old. They all stared at me, much the same as they would have stared at an alien from space. I had decided that I would start with "hello" and "good-bye" and if that went well, maybe the numbers one, two and three. I pantomimed, moved around, tried to engage each child, and in the end maybe one or two actually said, "Hello." It was like pulling teeth.

The teacher gave me a perfunctory *gracias* and said I could come back in two days, my schedule being twice a week.

I walked home, discouraged. I didn't feel I was any good at teaching preschoolers, and I had the distinct impression that the teacher didn't think so either.

Chuck wasn't much more enthusiastic about his experience at the radio station. Oscar had him running the show, but it was just a matter of sitting there for two hours making sure the music tapes ran smoothly. We were both glum, but after discussing the situation for a we while decided that with these projects we were getting known in the community and other possibilities would open up.

Our best success had been in making our house cozy and livable. My curtains were finally finished and we hung them in the living room, and the walls went instantly from bare to warm, plus now we had privacy from the street at night when we had lights on. A brick and board bookcase placed against one wall, a map of the world — that my sister Linda had sent — hung behind the table, and two bright throw rugs on the red tile floor nearly completed the room. I just needed one more trip to Encarnación for some odds and ends, notably some chair pillows for our plastic chairs.

Chuck commissioned a fellow to make screens for the windows and screen doors so we could let a breeze blow through the house as the temperatures got warmer — then we started thinking about the outside of the house.

With Crispin bringing fresh vegetables to the door, the immediate need for a garden seemed less important. But I had been getting ahead of myself anyway as it had been pounded into us in training that the first step to a good garden was good compost. And to make that we needed to have a compost heap.

The next Saturday Chuck suggested we start, so I dug out —
no pun intended — my notes from training. "Ingredients," I
read cheerfully. "Carbon from dry leaves, dried grass or sawdust.
Check! Nitrogen from fresh grass, manure, vegetable scraps and
coffee grounds. Check."

We had everything, but first we needed to decide on a spot, and
then gather the materials. Where to put it was easy. A compost
heap should be located in a partly sunny/partly shady area — and
there was a perfect spot just under the edge of the first mango tree.
Unfortunately, there was already something in the perfect spot —
an enormous stack of old bricks and lumber that must have been
used when the house was built. They appeared to have been there
forever. We decided they could easily be stacked against the fence,
and in fact, we might kill two birds with one stone by stacking them
next to a section of the fence that was falling down. We started
carrying as much as we could in our arms and stacking it along the
fence line. I was arranging the stack when I heard Chuck give a yell
and saw him grab the shovel and start pounding it into the dirt.

"What it is?" I shouted, but Chuck was so absorbed in his
whacking he didn't even look up. "Chuck," I yelled again, "what's
the matter?"

Chuck stopped, put the shovel to the side and looked down in
the grass. "It *was* a snake."

I went over and bent down to try to see. It had been small to
start with, but now it was in tiny pieces, scattered in the dirt.

"I wonder if that was a 'one-second-and-you're-dead-snake'?"

"Whatever it was, it is now a 'one-second-and IT'S-dead snake,'"
Chuck said, still breathing hard.

I poked at one of the pieces with a small stick; it was definitely
not alive. I picked up a little piece and put it to the side on a rock.

"Did we get any snake pictures in our Peace Corps books?"

"Don't think so. Maybe you can take it over to the Barbosa's
and see if they know what kind it is."

I was ready to call it a day, and go find out about the snake, but
Chuck wanted to at least finish clearing the spot. We proceeded,

but at a much slower pace since Chuck had to poke each brick first to see if another snake would slither out. By dinner we had a clear spot and had even gathered a few items for our compost pile, but it was going to take longer to assemble than we thought.

By the time I returned to my rock for the little snake piece it was covered with ants and had no remaining color or markings. I went over to the Barbosa's anyway and clapped at the fence. Delma came out, shooed the dogs away and came to the gate. I explained our finding the snake and showed her my little piece. "Could it be a good snake?" I asked.

"A good snake!" Delma practically choked. "There are no good snakes."

We decided to gather more compost ingredients during the week and try to put our pile together the following weekend. We had a big yard of grass — the easiest source of the nitrogen, and it was in need of cutting, but we pondered how to cut it. I had been wanting more exercise and thought that a push mower might be the solution.

On our next trip to the *cooperativa* we asked Ramón where we might buy one and he said there was an old one out back we could use. We went around and found an extremely decrepit mower with rusted blades. It didn't push very well, but we rolled it home and tried it out. Chuck couldn't even push it a foot. The blades barely moved and they cut nothing. We rolled it back to the *cooperativa*, thanked Ramón anyway and discussed the possibilities of buying a new one in Encarnación.

That evening a bedraggled man clapped at our gate. He looked homeless and hungry and wore a threadbare shirt with only a couple of buttons. I wondered if he was looking for charity.

"*Soy Cabana,*" he told us. "*Puedo cortar su cesped.* [I can cut your grass.]"

He had heard from Kitty who had heard from Ramón, that we were in the market. His price was almost nothing, so we instantly

94

agreed and he said he would be there the next morning. Sure enough, he was clapping at our gate at 7:00 a.m., standing there with a young son.

"*Donde está su máquina?*" I asked, expecting him to bring some type of lawnmower.

"*Aqui,*" he said proudly, and held out his machete for me to admire.

Cut the lawn with a machete? I couldn't believe what a back-breaking chore that would be. Even worse, both of them only wore flip-flops, leaving toes exposed to not only the machete but stinging ants. I had already discovered the lawn was full of the nasty *colorados* and despite being careful, I was recovering from a cluster of bites on one ankle. These ants were tiny and would swarm up your leg in an instant. By the time you realized they were on you and tried to fling them off, they would bite in unison — every bite formed an itching, angry pustule that took a week to heal. I looked at their feet, and saw that they were already covered with open sores and scabs.

I pointed at their feet and protested, "*Pero los colorados.*"

Cabana glanced at his feet and shrugged, "*No importa,*" then entered the yard and started swinging the long blade through the grass, barely missing his toes. His son trailed behind, gathering the grass in piles.

It was painful to watch. I went inside and returned with water and cookies for snacks. It took them all morning, and while I was happy to give them employment the working conditions depressed me. They did leave us, however, lots of green grass that we could add to our compost pile.

We scavenged around the rest of the week, trying to gather up the other ingredients. Chuck got sawdust from a local carpenter's shop and piles of ash from our fire pit out back. I set out with a bag and picked up dry cow patties in a nearby field to use for the "dry ingredient" pile, plus I figured they must have other good compostable stuff in there as well. Wet cow patties probably would have been a better source of nitrogen, but scooping them up seemed way too gooey. As it was, I wore my heavy gardening gloves and picked up the dry ones gingerly on the edge only after kicking them first to make sure nothing too creepy was living underneath.

After breakfast on Sunday we went out to our cleared spot and carefully layered our ingredients according to the manual. We sprinkled it with water, covered it with the other half of our plastic mattress cover and stuck a big, long stick down through the center.

From our training we had learned that if the compost was "cooking" the stick should be hot to the touch in a day. We anxiously waited two days and then went out to the pile for the big test-of-the-stick.

"Drumroll," I cried, and Chuck pulled it out. Stone cold.

"Maybe it's too early," I suggested, so we stuck it back in and waited another day. Again, the same result.

Chuck went into the house discouraged. When I joined him I found him digging through a stack of old Peace Corps newsletters we had been given in training.

"There was something about compost in one of these," he said, then brightened when he found it and pulled it out. "What to Do if Your Stick Is Cold," he read triumphantly. He scanned through it. "Probably needs more nitrogen," he concluded, "and guess what it says is the best solution?" I looked at him blankly. "Pee!" he declared.

So for the next two weeks, Chuck tripped out and merrily relieved himself on the pile. Not to be outdone, I peed into an old can, but it was a killer on my thighs, trying to squat over the toilet and hold the can at the same time. None the less, I sprinkled on my contribution too. Plus I added more kitchen scraps and coffee grounds, also listed as boosters of nitrogen.

In two weeks we tried again and met with success. We were "cooking"!

13 Guests

We finally met with the Education Committee and discovered they wanted to expand the arts. They were keen on adding drama, music or dance to the community, but weren't sure where to start.

Having a drama background, I offered to direct a community play and they all thought this would be grand. After some consultation and several trips to the local school, I was given the suggestion to put on a play called *Sombrero Ka'a*, a well known and popular Paraguayan farce about a cuckolded husband. The play could be performed in the local outdoor auditorium, they told me, and they would be happy to help with whatever.

I spent the next week checking out the auditorium, selecting parts of the play to read for try-outs, making signs for the try-outs, asking Oscar to advertise the try-outs on the radio station, and setting up in a corner of the *cooperativa* for the reading. I had set the time from 5:00 to 7:00 p.m. — after work and before dinner. There were signs out on the sidewalk announcing the play and try-outs, and I thought I had covered all my bases.

I had, except for one. No one in the entire town wanted to actually be IN the play. I sat there for three hours without a soul coming in or even stopping. I suspected they read the signs from afar, then walked on the other side of the street just to make sure they were not going to be yanked in. At eight o'clock I gathered up my signs, locked the door and went home.

"So much for that idea," I told Chuck gloomily.

He tried to offer encouraging words, but didn't have much to suggest. His own enterprises weren't exactly house afire. He was getting bored to death at the radio station, and the only other thing he had going were his porch guitar lessons. Now he had a second student, Alfred, who was also coming about twice a week, so at least that was something.

We went back to Ramón who suggested yet another meeting with the committee. This time they had more suggestions, the main one being a children's Christmas play, but not in Artigas. There was a town a few miles away called San Pedro, where the *cooperativa* had a second branch, and some women members there were organizing a Christmas show, but needed help. Chuck reminded Ramón that we didn't have a car and our bicycles hadn't arrived from Peace Corps yet.

The bus goes all the time, he told us — "*no problemo.*"

They also suggested that I could help Ida with her new class on Saturdays teaching cooking with soy — which was being grown locally, or I could help the town nurse, Margarita, who was interested in improving health and hygiene. And Chuck could teach more guitar.

I left the meeting feeling a little dubious about working in another town, but that's what they wanted and Ramón offered to take us there the next time he went.

We went the following week and met the two women who were running the show. They were very pleased to have us on board and said they would do all the costumes and make sure the children were there if I could run the rehearsals and Chuck could play the guitar for the singing parts. It was basically the standard nativity play with a Mary, a Joseph, the three Kings and a host of shepherds. It was still only October, so we had plenty of time.

With that project on the boards, I set off to the soy cooking class. Soy had recently been introduced to the farmers as an alternative crop and was also a good source of protein for many families who couldn't afford meat.

The class was in the same school house as the kindergarten. Hilda, the teacher, had set up a cooking area with two hot plates and all the necessary bowls and ingredients on a large table. I offered to help but she told me she had it all under control.

Quite a few girls were there, and the lesson for the day was making soy milk. Hilda took them through the steps; they got to observe and do a little themselves and I sat and watched. She spoke only in Guaranie, so I was taking notes from observation until she got to the sugar adding part. After I saw the cups of sugar that were poured in to make it palatable, I lost interest.

Everyone was quite nice to me though and welcomed me back anytime I wanted to come. Hilda had an entire cookbook of soy recipes she was going to go through —the next week it was going to be soy burgers or something. I thought I'd show up just to learn some soy recipes, but I didn't see where my presence was going to add anything other than the fact that if I, the *Norte Americano,* thought it was useful it might draw others.

I also made a couple of trips out to visit with the town nurse, Margarita. The first time I went to see her she wasn't there — gone to a funeral, I was told. I was beginning to discover that without telephones, missing connections was a common occurrence. Since the town was small, people just went to someone's house. Usually, the person was home. If not, so what? Come back another time.

When I finally met with her she spoke of many improvements the town needed, like reinforcement of the animal free-grazing laws, new municipal garbage cans, and the importance of screening windows and doors. Her house was the first one I had seen besides ours, with screens. Every summer, she told me, there were outbreaks of dengue fever throughout the country that she felt could be eliminated with screens. Fortunately, there had only been a few isolated cases in Artigas, and those were from people who had been visiting in Asunción.

Margarita spent much of her time at the town's clinic and at various other clinics around the Itapua region and she nursed her mother.

"Would you like to meet her?" she asked me.

"*Por supusto* [Of course]," I answered.

She led me out of the house and around back to a small shed. The room was dim and it took me a second to see a small figure curled up in the bed — I couldn't tell at first if it was even human. The person was drawn up in a fetal ball, with a face so sunken that it was just a skull. Her closed eyes were just dark sockets and small skeletal hands were drawn up under her chin.

Margarita leaned down and I guess heard her breathing and told me she was asleep now, so I would have to meet her later. Asleep! I had never seen someone who looked so close to death. I was already tiptoeing backwards, anxious to leave, but Margarita seemed to find nothing out of the ordinary. She mentioned that her mother was old and not too well. Still shocked, I couldn't think of a thing to say as I followed her back to the house.

We picked up our conversation on town projects where we had left off. She assured me she would help me with whatever project I wanted to work on and I could come and visit the clinic if I wished.

I definitely didn't wish to do that. I felt I had strayed far enough from my business development directive and more importantly, I would be zero help around anything medical.

Towards the middle of October I felt organized enough to entertain dinner guests.

I had told Ramón that he and Anjelica would be our first guests as I was eager to pay back his hospitality and help, so they received our first dinner invitation. I decided to serve spaghetti as I could get almost everything I needed in town, and on our trip to Encarnación I had even purchased a small can of mushrooms. The only thing missing was the Parmesan cheese, but I decided they wouldn't know it was missing and the dish was good enough without it. I planned to have nuts for an hor d'oeuvre; instead of a lettuce salad, a cabbage coleslaw, and for dessert, Mennonite ice cream. I had only four plates and four bowls, so while I simmered the spaghetti sauce and re-mopped the floor, Chuck went down and bought four small plates for the salad.

I had invited them to come at 6:30 and Ramón, conscious of American punctuality, was clapping outside precisely at 6:30. He came up the steps followed by Anjelica and to my surprise, their son Fernando. I tried not to look surprised and welcomed them all into the house, mentally scrambling on what I was going to use for a fifth place setting. The food wouldn't be a problem —I could always make servings for four serve five, I just had to put it in something. As they sat in the chairs at the opposite end of the living room from the table, I left for the kitchen, ostensibly to get the nuts, but as I passed the table I quickly picked up a couple of plates and silverware so they wouldn't notice the table was set for four. Chuck was close on my heels.

"We didn't invite the son, did we?" he whispered.

"I didn't think so." I whispered back, "But it's OK." I took down one of the tin bowls and an extra spoon. "This is what you'll use," I said quietly and we both returned to the *sala*. Chairs weren't a problem since we would just pull over one of the little plastic chairs.

Meanwhile, they were enjoying looking at all the things we had done for the simple room, like the rugs and a brick and board bookcase, which Ramón thought was especially clever. I had recently completed my coffee table too, using a square of plywood. I had painted a geometric looking sunburst on it, then applied three coats of varnish to give it a polished and water resistant top.

For the legs I had covered two apple crates with a bright cotton print, then just laid the plywood piece across the top. It was a bit wobbly, but it looked good, if I did say so myself.

The dinner went well. They were effusive with compliments on my "American" spaghetti, a dish new to them. I served the ice cream in my little glass coffee cups since I had six of them and it looked rather cute. They didn't stay long after the ice cream, but we did enjoy their visit and I felt especially proud of handling my surprise guest. I don't think they had a clue that I was not expecting all three of them.

Later, I realized the mistake I'd made. In Paraguay, families stayed together, went places together and the idea of leaving someone behind was just unthinkable. Of course in the States, we always assume when you invite a "couple" they will get a sitter for small children and wouldn't even think of bringing a teen-ager. And what teenager would want to come?

When we first moved in we had intended to buy an electric water heater like Digna's, but we were slowly growing accustomed to the electric, water-ring gizmo in the shower and the idea of the water heater had faded. The water-ring was hardest for the first person in to adjust the exact amount of water, and hence, the exact amount of heat, but once that was done it was easy for us both to take showers, one after another. Chuck usually went first, then called me as he was stepping out. It was much easier than our old routine in Afghanistan, where we had to build a fire in the water boiler tank, wait a half an hour for it to heat the water, then run in quickly one after another before the hot water ran out and reverted back to freezing.

One evening, not long after our dinner party with Ramón's family, Chuck had just gone into the bathroom to get showered and I was dealing a hand of solitaire while waiting my turn. Suddenly I heard a gargling cry. Chuck came rushing out, totally nude, his mouth foaming with toothpaste.

"What on earth?" I jumped up, frightened.

"Something's in the sink!" Chuck shouted, looking around for some kind of weapon. He grabbed one of his muddy boots next to the back door and cautiously tiptoed back towards the bathroom holding his boot up menacingly.

I followed silently behind.

He looked at the sink from the doorway and I peeked out from behind his back. Nothing.

"Well, there certainly was something! It came through the overflow vent."

"Let's turn out the lights and wait a minute," I suggested. "Maybe it will come out again."

Chuck turned off the bathroom light and we stepped back outside the small doorway.

"Look," I whispered, "here it comes." A black head appeared cautiously out of the rectangular vent in the sink; little arms appeared next, then a long body of about six inches, and finally legs and a tail. It was a long, black lizard. Chuck raised his boot and stepped towards the sink. It disappeared back down the hole.

I couldn't help it; I started laughing.

"Well, it wouldn't be so funny if you had your face down there rinsing your mouth when it came out," Chuck said defensively.

I tried to stop laughing, but Chuck standing there nude, his mouth covered in foam, holding his boot over his head, was just too funny. I finally composed myself and went in and ran the water full force down the drain.

"Bye lizard," I called. "Hope you can swim."

As extra insurance Chuck taped the vent closed with duct tape and returned to his shower.

As funny as it was watching Chuck, I really didn't want that thing running around while I was in the shower so I carefully scanned the walls and corners of the bathroom as I entered. It wasn't that I was afraid of lizards, I reasoned, I just didn't want to be surprised by lizards.

The next morning Chuck decided it was time to get a plumber.

In addition to the bathroom episode, the leak under the kitchen sink was getting harder to ignore.

At first I had just washed the dishes in a small plastic pail, but even so, water was coming through the cabinet doors below. It hadn't taken a plumbing genius to discern the problem. The pipe from the bottom of the sink didn't go into the floor or to another pipe. It didn't go anywhere. Coming up from the floor, ostensibly to connect with it, was another pipe. But it was too short — there was a nice gap of several inches between the two pipes. If there wasn't much water or just a trickle, the water from the first pipe would actually fall into the second pipe, but any amount of water and it was like holding a ketchup bottle under a waterfall. Sure, some went in the pipe, but most went on the tiles below and out to my feet.

During our first week Chuck had made a make-shift connection sealed with some dubious Chinese putty, but it still leaked like crazy and the putty was now falling off in obscene grey piles.

We needed a real plumber and Kitty told us she would send one over. The next morning, promptly at 7:00 a.m. there was Cabana, the machete-welding lawn cutter, clapping at our gate.

"*Soy el plumero mejor*, [I am the best plumber,]" he told us brightly "*Puedo arreglar todos.* [I can fix everything.]"

Chuck explained the problems, Cabana nodded sagely, and in a half an hour he was back with a large hammer, wrenches, pipes, sacks of fittings, shovels and an old railroad spike. The bathroom sink was fixed in a jiffy, just a matter of putting a screen in the pipe.

In the kitchen, he crawled under the sink and using the spike and the hammer, took out the floor tiles around the pipe then began digging. He dug furiously, like a dog digging for a bone, making a small earth mountain in the middle of the kitchen. Finally he eased himself out from under the sink, wiping his forehead with his sleeve.

"*No es bueno* [It's not good]," he told me. "*Mira* [look]."

I took my flashlight, and on hands and knees peered down into the hole. The bottom pipe, which of course didn't reach the top pipe, didn't connect to the opening in the horizontal pipe in the ground below either. It only rested on top of the pipe about an inch away from the connection. Good thing, I thought, that I hadn't poured much water down the drain, the whole house would have floated away. But Cabana seemed undeterred and in a couple of hours had a sink pipe that actually went from the sink to the leave-the-house-pipe. Supposedly it went out to a cesspool, but I had serious doubts about that.

It had started to rain by the time Cabana had finished and rather than let him walk home and get soaked I insisted he wait a while until it let up. He stood awkwardly in the living room, turning his baseball cap over and over in his hands, refusing my admonitions to have a seat, saying that he was "*demasiado sucio* [too dirty]." He finally agreed to sit in one of the plastic chairs we had out on the porch.

To pass the time I brought out my USA wall calendar to show him pictures of the United States. I carefully explained each picture and knew he could understand my Spanish, having told me he had lived in Argentina for years.

He finally looked up at me and asked "What is it?" when I had stopped on a picture of the Oregon coast.

"*Es la mar* [It's the ocean]," I replied, adding that it was on the western coast of the United States.

"Yes, but what is it?" he had asked again.

"You understand what the ocean is?"

"Yes, yes, of course, but what is this?" He grabbed the calendar in frustration and shook it.

I suddenly realized he had never seen a calendar before. He didn't understand all the squares and numbers. It dawned on me that the only calendars I had ever seen in Paraguay were the miniature ones, where the entire year is printed on a small card. Cabana had never seen a large calendar with a page for each month and squares for every day. I carefully explained what it was and saw a light go on in his eyes.

"Aaah" he had said, now understanding. "*Que maravilloso.*"

14   The Great TV Caper

O ur evenings were getting wearisome.

In Afghanistan we had read every night and listened to the BBC. But we each had comfy cushions to sprawl on and there was a good ceiling light. Our living room in Artigas was dark. We remedied the lighting situation by hanging a bulb from the ceiling between our two plastic chairs. I inverted a wicker basket over it as a shade so it looked rather cozy and worked fine, but the hard plastic chairs challenged the concept of "curling up" with a good book. And our small radio didn't pick up anything but Oscar's station, which mostly played accordion polkas. We played gin rummy on the dining room table and there was a solitaire game on the laptop computer so it wasn't as though we had nothing to do. Just almost nothing. Chuck decided we needed a television.

"A TV?" I questioned. Chacho had a TV set up at the café and the few programs we had glimpsed were pretty dreadful — either soccer or soap operas.

Chuck said we should also get a VCR and then rent movies that we had seen stacked along the back wall of the hardware store. I thought that it didn't seem very Peace Corps-ish, but Chuck reminded me that as far as living "like the people" we were about the only ones in town who didn't have at least a small TV. Even the shack to our left had an antenna sticking up.

Televisions, of course, could not be purchased in Artigas so it meant another trip to Encarnación. And, while we were at it, Chuck wanted to see what we could do about an Internet connection. This was of big interest to me. I was missing my weekly calls to my Mother and frequent emails with my sisters. It had now been four weeks since I'd been able to communicate and I was feeling anxious.

Chuck headed over to our hardware store first to see about antennas. No use buying one in Encarnación and trying to get it on the bus if we could get one here. In fact, I had been wondering how we were going to get a big box containing a TV on the bus, but Kitty solved our problem. Her neighbor, who was also her brother-in-law, was going to Encarnación in three days and he would be happy to take us in his truck.

And so we met Roberto. He had moved to Paraguay from Argentina, having met and married Kitty's sister when she was down in Buenos Aires for some reason or other. They had come to Artigas so she could be near her family, and Roberto had opened a small auto-parts store across the street from Kitty's hardware store. We liked him instantly. He was Chuck's height and build with dark hair and eyes and a cheerful smile of perfect teeth. While he said he spoke a little Guaranie, he preferred to speak Spanish, his native tongue, and would love to come and chat with us.

"*Cualquier tiempo* [any time]," we both gushed, happy to have a new friend. Any time turned out to be that evening after supper when he strode up to our gate and clapped, holding up a small bottle of *caña*, as his contribution to the evening.

Caña was advertised as "almost whiskey" and I supposed it almost was. It was also almost undrinkable — a sticky-sweet, high-alcohol concoction that we could barely choke down. Soon after our arrival in Artigas we had tried it thinking that maybe it might be an after dinner aperitif that could replace wine. Straight-up definitely didn't work, nor did any combination with fruit juices or colas.

"What is it with the beverages in this country?" Chuck had asked.

We welcomed Roberto to the front porch and brought out an extra chair. The evenings now were warm and it was more pleasant sitting outside than in the house. For the sake of good manners, we mixed the *caña* with some coke and added ice and lemon to ours. Roberto wanted to know all about us and where we were from, with each answer opening more conversation.

"*Área cincuenta uno, sabes de esto*? [Area fifty-one, do you know of this?]" he asked us with wide eyes.

Chuck replied that yes, we had heard of it and Roberto launched enthusiastically into stories of flying saucers, aliens and all sorts of strange doings that governments (ours in particular) didn't want us to know about.

We just laughed and said "*Puede ser* [perhaps]," and for Roberto that was the same as saying we were ardent believers. We, at least, knew what he was talking about, which was probably more than most Artigas residents.

Discussion of area fifty-one was followed by that of the Bermuda Triangle and its numerous maritime disasters, then we were off on the subject of Russian submarines. As the *caña* dwindled, so did my Spanish ability until I felt I couldn't say anything and decided to call it a night.

The trip to Encarnación was arranged for Saturday, but because Roberto was taking another friend, there was only room in the truck for Chuck. It was fine by me. Chuck knew what he wanted and Roberto assured him he could get the very best deal.

Chuck left early that Saturday after a quick breakfast of coffee and the ubiquitous little crunch rolls dipped in *dulce leche*.

It seemed way to early for me to launch into any house cleaning projects, so I poured another cup of coffee and dawdled over the paper. I managed to read an entire article on *gobierno corrompido* [government corruption], specifically dealing with the fact that the Paraguayan president was driving around in a Mercedes, which would have been bad enough given his salary for the year couldn't buy a used pickup, but rumor had it that this particular Mercedes was supposedly "hot" merchandise, stolen from God-knows-where and brought over from Cuidad del Este in eastern Paraguay, a rather notorious city located on the border of Brazil, and apparently was the clearing house for stolen goods coming into Paraguay. And worse, the U.S. State Department said it was a known location of terrorist training since it was lawless and any weapon could be purchased there. I scanned forward to the end of the article and sure enough, the car had been "bought" in the lawless city.

I did have to hand it to the Paraguayans though for a free press. The two main newspapers continually attacked one side or the other of the political scene, unearthing an endless stream of scandalous behavior. In the States, one day's paper would have kept platoons of lawyers happy with libel and slander suits.

I finally got to the end of the article and decided that was enough Spanish reading for the morning. My brain seemed to un-do after about forty-five minutes of Spanish reading and I would find myself comprehending less and less. I was at that point — it was time to quit.

I folded the paper in case Chuck wanted to read it later and took my empty coffee cup back in the kitchen noticing the layer of dust on the floor tiles as I went.

Dust was always with us. It blew in around every loose window pane, under the door and sifted down from the crumbling red tiles on the roof. If I mopped in the morning, by late afternoon, I could wipe my finger across the floor tiles and leave a mark. After two days I could write my name across the front of the refrigerator. I mopped the floors with my new Paraguayan method, copied from Digna, who used a long handled squeegee with a wet towel wrapped around the head. It must have been the accepted mopping method as I saw these squeegees in many of the small markets, but never saw anything that approximated a mop. Of course after two or three swipes the towel came undone, which meant a stop and a re-wrap. A few swipes after that and the towel was too dirty to continue. That meant unwrapping it, rinsing it out, squeezing it, and re-wrapping it around the squeegee again.

The front porch was easier to clean. There I could just pour a bucket of water over it and then squeegee it all over the side. It was a far cry from the Swiffer mops in the States with their disposable heads, but I did feel some satisfaction knowing that it was much more ecologically friendly, and easier for us, since there was no garbage pick up.

There actually was a dump on a road leading from town, and garbage was collected from various barrels around town on some sort of regular basis. So, if you really had something to be thrown away, like a glass bottle or tin can, you could take it to one of the barrels and it would be carted to the malodorous hill. The barrels themselves were a problem though as they were hung between two posts and swung back and forth. Ostensibly they were designed to swing so it would make it easy for the collector to just tip the barrel over to empty it. Unfortunately, it was also easy for the dogs. When we first arrived, we made the mistake of throwing a huge sack of garbage containing meat scraps in one of the barrels and discovered all of it strewn up and down the street the next day.

Now, like everyone else, we burned our own garbage (and toilet paper) in a burn pile way in the back section of the property, past the five mango trees. It was surprising how little garbage we had, since we bought no packaged food and very few things in containers. Chuck, who had taken on the job of fire-man, only had to do a burn once or twice a week.

The afternoon began to seem very long and I felt strangely anxious with Chuck gone. With the exception of the one training weekend, we hadn't been apart. I recalled our Peace Corps time in Afghanistan where in two years, I was only apart from Chuck once — for a baby shower for an embassy woman. Back then we were all young married couples and the forced closeness either solidified the marriages of the Volunteer couples or broke them apart. Many couples were divorced after the Corps, or in some cases, the marriages fell apart during their stay. The two couples we had stayed in contact with, the Jacksons and the Hohls had had long, durable marriages, like ours.

I was also feeling a bit melancholy and sat staring out the

window, sorely missing my Mom. I missed my sisters too, but they were busier, had more going on in their lives and I didn't have to worry about them. Or maybe it was that I didn't have to feel guilty about having left them. While in Afghanistan, I never thought about any of them, so it seemed to me now. At the time, my oldest sister Rita, was in Guam with her Navy husband and Linda, my second sister, was up in the Oregon woods somewhere with her forestry husband. We all wrote when we could and didn't worry much about it. It felt different now. I thought for the first time how selfish it was of me to be seeking another "adventure" when I probably didn't have that much time left with my Mom.

I brooded on that for awhile and realizing there wasn't much I could do about it, I decided to start one of the needlepoint kits I had brought. I dug the easiest looking one out of the bottom of the duffel. By coincidence it had bright yellow flowers, similar to those on my new curtains. By the time I had the yarns sorted out, found masking tape to secure the edges, stopped to make a pot of tea and actually worked a few rows, I heard Roberto's truck.

Chuck climbed out looking hot and dusty, but also enthusiastic about his purchases. He and Roberto unloaded a big box that held a TV and a smaller one that appeared to be a VCR, and carried them into the living room.

"And, we're good to go on the email, too," Chuck announced proudly, pulling a business card from his pocket. "Now we just take the laptop to the phone store, dial this number," he said waving the card, "and we're in business. Plus, look at the letters I brought," he said, waving a packet of printed emails. "And to celebrate, some real bottles of wine!" He pulled one triumphantly out of a sack — it was Concho y Toro from Chile, a wine we used to buy in San Diego.

Roberto had his own supplies to get home so we waved good-bye from the porch and returned to look at the big boxes in the living room. But the first order of business was to sit in our little plastic chairs and read the emails. I read them, Chuck read them and then I read them again. I loved hearing about all the little details of my family's lives and I felt better having news from my Mom. My sister Rita wrote that a publisher was interested in reading the entire manuscript of my book, *The First Big Ride,* and so she had sent it off. That was interesting. I had forgotten all about it. It reminded me that I wanted to start working on a new draft, something that I should have been doing instead of needlepoint.

The next day, being Sunday, was a perfect time to start the TV project. Chuck suggested we make the second bedroom our entertainment room, so he would set the TV and VCR up in there. To watch, we could sit on the small bed and lean against the wall.

I cautiously asked if he wanted to wait until Roberto could lend a hand, but Chuck was adamant.

"Easy deezy!" he exclaimed, full of confidence. "Up and running in no time."

I had learned years before that on such put-together projects it was best to back off, go do something else and try to ignore the occasional cursing when something didn't fit, something broke or a finger was smashed. I stood around long enough to see the TV out of the box. It wasn't a state-of-the-art television. It looked pretty much like it came from the nineteen fifties — small, no remote control of course, and a little rabbit-ears antenna. There were Chinese characters stamped all over the box as well as an instructional booklet in Chinese.

I returned to the kitchen to put away Crispin's vegetables and waited to hear sounds of victory from the small bedroom. It was nearly 11:00 before I heard Chuck exclaim, "All-Right!" I returned and stood in the doorway. Chuck had positioned the TV on the top shelf of another of our so-called "bookcases" built of planks and cement blocks. The VCR was on the wooden plank directly below.

"Ok," he informed me, "We've got power." He turned the front knob and the screen flicked then came in as a gray-snow static. He changed the channels. Roberto had told us we would only get three channels, no matter how good our reception was, so Chuck clicked around and tried the other two. On one channel we could see shadows and hear a garbled noise. The other two were solid gray blizzards.

"I'll move the ears," I offered, "while you try the different channels." I moved them from side to side and back and forth with no discernible results. I remembered that people used to cover the ends of the ears with tinfoil for better reception, so I ran off to the kitchen for some foil. I came back and covered the ends with big crinkly masses. Chuck clicked again, nothing. He was visibly disappointed.

"I had it all planned that we would watch a show and have a glass of wine tonight." He sat back glumly on his heels and flipped aimlessly through the Chinese instruction book.

"Well, we'll just have to get an outside antenna," I said encouragingly. "Didn't Kitty tell you that she had everything you need for them in her store?"

"Right." Chuck's face brightened. He took off down the street, still confident that he could have his TV humming and wine in hand by nightfall.

He was back in twenty minutes, this time with Cabana, who was helping carry the antenna paraphernalia as well as two long bamboo poles and a homemade ladder.

"Cabana knows all about setting up antennas," Chuck declared, as they deposited all of their items in the front yard. Hearing his name, Cabana smiled and nodded.

"*Que bueno* [great]," I said, trying to muster enthusiasm, as Chuck and Cabana dragged the whole lot to the front right corner of the house where Cabana commenced to wire the antenna and loops of cable to the top of one of the bamboo poles. Chuck leaned the rickety ladder against the house and held it while Cabana clambered up and down, securing the pole to the side of the house by pounding nails into brackets, each blow raining chunks of green-painted plaster. It was a bit distressing to watch the new paint being pounded off, leaving big brown splotches, so I returned to the kitchen to make lunch.

I called out to Chuck to see if I could treat Cabana and him to something, but he hollered back, "Not now. Later." I shrugged, and made myself a sandwich. In a while I heard Chuck calling. He and Cabana had managed to keep the pole upright and had fed the cable through the quarter inch crack at the top of one of the window panes in the bedroom, across the inside sill and over to the back of the TV set.

"Can you turn it on now?"

I turned it on to channel fuzz.

"Nothing," I yelled back.

"Try the other channels."

I clicked to the other two. One had a glimpse of images and some sound, the other was non-existent.

"Well, the second one's a little better," I called through the window, "but still pretty bad."

Chuck turned the angle of the antenna, "Now try it."

"Nope, nothing."

I heard him swear and come down the ladder. He and Cabana were now discussing the problem. In a few minutes I saw them dragging their entire contraption to the northeast corner of the house. Now the cable to the TV was too short, so Chuck headed back to the hardware store for more wire. He came back in a half an hour, re-threaded the cable to the TV while Cabana stood on the ladder rotating the flimsy pole.

Chuck then came in, went to the TV, clicked the channel dial and proceeded to yell to me in the kitchen to yell to Cabana, who was in back of the house, perched on top of the ladder.

"Turn it," Chuck hollered to me.

"*Puede muevealo.*" I relayed the message out the back door.

"*Si, señora,*" Cabana called from the roof.

"Damn it. Doesn't work at all." I heard from the bedroom. I hesitated as I didn't know the Spanish for "damn it."

"*No funciona,*" I finally called to Cabana.

"*Ahora, tratalo.*" Cabana shouted down to me.

"Now try it," I yelled to Chuck. I heard the clicking of the dial

114

and a big sigh.

Chuck came in the kitchen shaking his head. "It's just got to be higher."

"Can you tie two bamboo poles together?" I asked.

"Look outside. We've got two bamboo poles together. It's too flimsy anyway, we're going to need some kind of metal support."

He went out to the yard, conferred with Cabana, then the two of them went off in search of a long metal pole and a better antenna. It was nearing supper time when Chuck returned, dragging two seriously long metal poles.

"We'll have to finish this tomorrow, not enough light now, but I did get a video for tonight."

He smiled and produced a dusty, torn plastic video box from behind his back.

"Mind you, this may not be the best movie you've ever seen, but look here," he said proudly, reading the back of the box, "action, adventure, thrills." He scanned down the rest of the review. "Doesn't say anything about academy awards, but says *Pancho's Escape* is, and I quote, 'gut-wrenching drama.'"

After dinner Chuck carefully poured two glasses of our Concho y Toro into our all-purpose water glasses and beckoned me to our new entertainment room. He put the video in the new VCR and we sat back on the single bed, leaning against pillows.

"Now this is the life, no?" Chuck asked. He got up, turned it on and returned to settle back against the cushions.

The video started and was rolling through the credits when great sections of static filled the screen. Chuck jumped up, hit the fast-forward button and it started smoothly again. It lasted almost ten minutes, then more static. Chuck got up again, and after a few seconds whirring on fast forward, the movie was once again rolling. Chuck sat back on the bed and I handed him his wine. We got a full fifteen minutes that time, then back to the drill of fast-forwarding.

"This isn't the VCR, it's the damn video."

Chuck was up and down a half a dozen times before he threw

in the towel.

"I heard they copy the videos illegally here. That's why it's such a poor quality. Some guy was probably running a video camera under his shirt."

"Well, it's not too good anyway." I said. "Not nearly gut-wrenching enough. How about just nice wine by candlelight?" I roused myself from the bed-sofa, got a candle from our candle supply, returned and set it up in a saucer next to the TV. I returned to my spot next to Chuck, gave him a kiss and we toasted to our new, not-quite-functioning entertainment center with the glow of the moon coming through our window.

The serious antenna-raising resumed the next morning. Cabana secured the poles together with bolts and nuts and wired the new antenna with coils of cable to the top, while Chuck dug a deep hole next to the house. The cable was fed back down through the bedroom window and attached to the TV. Chuck clicked the channel selector around.

"Victory!" he shouted. "One channel is working."

"*Si, es bueno,*" Canaba chimed in, "*pero necesitas otro antennae for los otros caneles.*" Chuck frowned while Cabana explained that we got the one channel because our antenna was pointed to the northeast, towards Asunsción, where the station was. To get the other two, whose stations were located in Argentina, we needed to point it to the south or just mount a second antenna permanently pointed south. Chuck asked him about buying a motor to turn the antenna. Cabana looked at him blankly, then burst out laughing.

"*Motor? No hay motor. Necesitas otro antennae.*" He chuckled again shaking his head, obviously thinking how crazy we *Norte Americanos* were.

It was already noon and this time they accepted a lunch break and a cool pitcher of *ted-er-ray*, a cooling Paraguayan drink of herbs and water I had learned to concoct, before they returned to the "easy-deezy" television reception challenge. Chuck and Cabana

116

returned to the yard, and erected a new pole towered on the opposite corner from the first antenna, making the cute, red tile roof look like some kind of giant alien bug. This time we did get a picture, not a great picture, but a picture. Now a second wire from the second antenna came in with the first line, squeezed through the quarter inch gap at the top of the bedroom window pane.

"And how does this work, exactly?" I asked, looking at the second wire lying on the floor.

"Well, when we want to change the channel, we have to take the wire off the back of the TV from the metal pole antenna, then hook in the wire from the bamboo antenna."

I nodded. I could see this meant the end of channel switching as I knew it. We did sit down with more wine that night to enjoy the television. The program on the clear channel seemed pretty insipid so Chuck squeezed behind the bookcase and on his hands and knees unwired antenna number one and wired on antenna number two. After he was comfortably settled back on the bed we decided that shows on the two other channels were even worse and not as clear as the first. Chuck crawled behind the bookcase again, undid the second antenna wire and put the first one back on. He dusted off his knees and got back on the bed with me.

"That's it," he said flatly. Entertaining or not, that was our program; further channel surfing was not an option.

The electronic challenges with the Internet were more merciful. All we had to do was take our laptop and a long extension cord to the telephone office in town. Once we got our turn in the little phone booth, we undid the phone jack to the phone, plugged it into the computer, then ran the extension line for electricity out the door and across the waiting room to the back of the office where the telephone clerk plugged it into the wall. Then we dialed our connection and we were in. Or sort of in.

While we waited for the slow, dial-up connection, the Paraguayans waiting for the phone were most curious as to what was going on.

"*Computadora*," the telephone clerk explained to them with great seriousness. "*In-ter-net*," he added with a nonchalant air as if hundreds of people came in every day and hooked up their laptops. The waiting Paraguayans peeked into the cubicle and watched us typing and reading the small laptop screen. I kept my back to the door so as not to be distracted, but I could hear their excited whispers.

15   Seeking Employment

Chuck was keeping busier than I was with his multiple guitar lessons and daily stints at the radio station. My twice weekly ordeal at the kindergarten and once a week sitting in the back at the soy cooking class, was hardly inspiring. I was busy enough because the housekeeping and grocery-getting was almost a full time job, given that everything was done by hand and we went everywhere on foot.

The Peace Corps had delivered the rest of our supplies and brought us mountain bikes from Asunción, but the bikes weren't much help for errands as the roads were so rutted and so deep with dust that the smallest excursion left you filthy, and the few roads that had the stone *empadrada* were so rough that you were rattled to your bones in short order. So around town it was easier to walk, but we did take the bikes out for longer exercise excursions although that was equally challenging.

I decided that I would try to get more involved with the *cooperativa* and somehow help with sales. Ramón seemed receptive to my ideas of helping and said again I could do anything I wanted. He wanted us to be happy and was trying to be accommodating, but I knew he had nothing in particular for us to do. I wandered around the *cooperativa* and took stock. There were never any items on sale or specials, everything was covered with dust, there was no advertising, there was no organization to the product placement, and the produce was a disaster.

The manager of the store was a little woman named Alicia and she was enthusiastic about any improvements I could bring, and she arranged for all five employees to meet with me in the upstairs conference room. After introductions, I told them I was there to help with sales and opened the floor to their ideas. There were none. I kept quiet, but after a minute I mentioned a few of the ideas I had been thinking of. And what did they think? This brought some nods and agreements; these were good things, but after some prodding I discovered the real issue for them was that each one felt he or she had no time to do any extra work. And it was true. For example, the checker, when she wasn't checking, had to be stocking the shelves, or cleaning or bringing in supplies from the back, and the man who unloaded the produce from trucks, also had to drive to Encarnación to get more and stock shelves and keep the generators running. I said I would help with cleaning and organizing and would make signs for the sales. Everybody liked this idea. I wasn't sure if signing on as a volunteer employee was the right direction, but at least it was some direction.

For the next ten days I cleaned shelves. With the doors opening all day long and dust blowing in from the street my wiping down shelves made scant progress. By the fourth day my clean shelves from the first day looked pretty much like I had never been there. The only noticeable improvements were neater stacks of goods. Disheartened, I kept it up anyway, working my way across the store to finish the job.

I talked to Alicia about arranging products together in similar groupings and while she never said no directly, there was always a reason it couldn't be done: all the little things had to be in front or people would steal them; the heavy things had to be in back because she couldn't move them; the paper diapers were with the plows because no one ever bought them anyway. To be fair, many things were in groupings already, such as all the sweets, candy, toys and gifts, canned vegetables and all the grains. The produce was all together in the back which was a good thing because it was uniformly awful and buzzing with flies. I brought up the idea that as the items got older, maybe they should be sold for a cheaper price. I carefully used the words *mas viejo* [older] instead of the true description, which was *podrido* [rotten]. Alicia agreed that this made sense so she gave me paper and markers to make some signs. I brought this home and with some enthusiasm, created large announcements in Spanish proclaiming the newer prices and sales. She put them up and if nothing else, it did brighten the store a little. No one seemed to buy more though. They knew rotten stuff was rotten and that was that.

B ack in our old Peace Corps days, there was little going on in the way of Volunteer meetings, get-togethers or job assessments. Once you had your assignment, off you went and that was pretty much it. I guess if you hated your job or had some problem, you could complain to the country director, but if things were going along OK, you were left alone, except for your monthly shot notices.

In the new Peace Corps the staff kept tabs on us more. We had already had one visit from our project director and now we were headed back to Asunción for a big weekend conference with all the Volunteers in country. Once again, we were back at the "retreat" center, which didn't seem as shocking this time around although I did a careful inspection of my bed for ants. The meeting's theme was safety issues that weren't of much concern to us in Artigas; more interesting was learning how our compatriots were faring. Over half of them didn't have housing yet and most were — like us — still fumbling around trying to figure out what they were doing. John, our lawyer friend, had secured his housing, but was not making any progress working with his town's city hall. He couldn't even get into a meeting. We were all advised to just keep at it, get to know the community and have patience.

At the conference we met our closest Peace Corps neighbor, Mandy Baily. She had arrived the year before and was about five miles from us as the crow flies. Her project was farming development, and she was to try and persuade farmers to try new crop methods or new crops. She was young and bubbly, about my size, with blue eyes, a wide smile and dark blond hair pulled back in a ponytail. When I asked her about her success with her project, she just smiled and shrugged. "I keep trying this and that," she said. "I work a lot with the women." She promised to visit us after the conference and sure enough, the day after we returned home she came by on her bicycle, a large pack on her back.

"Mandy," I cried, coming out on the porch. "So good to see you!" I wasn't kidding. It was wonderful to have a fellow Corpsman coming by, someone who could relate to your existence and someone who spoke English. "Come in, come in, make yourself at home! Leave your bike by the porch. I just made some banana bread. Would you like some? Can I get you something to drink?" I stopped suddenly, fearing I was babbling.

She graciously said yes to the banana bread offer and followed me into the kitchen.

"Wow," she said looking around. "Some kitchen, about the size of my whole house! I love my house though," she quickly added. "It's only one room, but it's all I need. You'll have to come out and visit." She went on to explain how she had her simple house built. It had taken months, not in the construction, but just in getting the necessary paper work and permissions. In the meantime she had lived with a family. "And the consequence of that," she said, "is that my Guaranie is pretty good, but my Spanish is awful."

She had decided to spend more time with the women as her influence in talking to the men was limited. This seemed the practical approach as I couldn't envision these old farmers paying any young girl much attention. In fact, I couldn't even envision why the Peace Corps would send a single woman out to rural Paraguay to tell farmers how to plant crops. It wasn't as though she wasn't competent, but Paraguay, like much of South America, was extremely *machismo*. She could have been the best farmer on the planet and would have had an uphill battle gaining credibility.

We chatted the rest of the afternoon and we invited her to spend the night. She protested, but then decided that our shower and guest room with a TV was too tempting. She warned me that she was a vegetarian, but not to worry, she would eat just the rice and salad. It worked for me, we had a giant bag of rice and a refrigerator full of Crispin's vegetables.

Mandy invited us to visit her, but getting to her house took a little planning. We could take the old *Fletcha* and hop off at the curve in the road and then walk the mile in to her place, or we could skip the bus and go by bicycle.

The bicycles did seem the quicker option and Mandy had given us a map, so the following Friday off we pedaled. Even though is was a short distance it took almost forty-five minutes, with the difficult, rutted roads, and then we had to walk the bikes when the roads gave out. We finally spied her house across a field of tall grasses. It was made of red bricks; small and square with an over-hanging roof on one side that gave shade to a little cement porch.

Mandy was waiting for us and eagerly invited us inside. She was right; it was just larger than our kitchen. Her bed was against one wall, built high so it was even with a window and had space below for storage. Another corner housed a miniature kitchen with a sink and shelving, another spot for the table and chair and a corner for a shower. It was like a tree house — something out of Swiss Family Robinson. Mandy had a garden outside and had cleverly planted a tall hedge against her western windows, which she said would shade her house completely from the intense afternoon sun of summer. She shared an outhouse with her neighbors, about two hundred yards away and since I had to use it, I could testify that it was spotlessly clean.

"The thing I love the most," she told us, "is at night it is totally quiet here. No humming from lights or buzzing from appliances, no traffic, no nothing — just frogs and birds and crickets. You think you know what quiet is until you are here. Unless," she laughed, "they're having a dance in Artigas. Sometimes, if the wind is right, I can hear that, even here."

Living in town, we had first-hand knowledge of these dances. They were open air affairs, on a cement plaza about a block from the *cooperativa*. They started around midnight and lasted until 4 a.m. The volume of the music was deafening and even with our windows closed and our earplugs in it was hard to sleep. Happily for us, they were expensive and weren't held often.

We drank some *tederay*, then Mandy led us through several fields to meet the family she had lived with. It was a pretty poor abode, making our old place with Digna seem the height of luxury. The mother had many children and one at her breast as we visited. She seemed to be very fond of Mandy, and they chatted happily in Guaranie. It was good to know that she did have friends and wasn't totally isolated in her little house. After some chit-chat in Spanish, which the mother did speak, we headed for home.

In a way, I envied Mandy, living the brochure-like Peace Corps existence that I had always envisioned, but on the other hand, I did like my electricity and running water. And I know Chuck did too.

16 November Spring

It was getting warmer and hard to reconcile the weather with the calendar. November was spring! The only reminder that Christmas was coming was our first rehearsal for the Christmas play in San Marcos.

Even though we could take the bus, we decided it was really only twice as far as Mandy's place, so it shouldn't be that hard to get there by bike. That would beat standing out in the sun waiting for the bus on its erratic schedule. Or so we thought. We soon discovered that Mandy's turn off wasn't even close to the half way mark to San Marcos, and after an hour, we still weren't there. At the hour and fifteen minutes mark we could see the town and cranked up our speed, arriving only ten minutes late. We were covered with dust and sweat ran down our faces. Julia, the organizer, looked askance, asking if we were OK and did we need to sit down and could she bring water? Women didn't exercise much in Paraguay and the idea of riding a bicycle from Artigas astonished her.

After she thought we were rested enough, she shouted at the children who seemed to range from preschoolers to about age twelve. They were shrieking and chasing each other in and out of the house, totally out of control. After some hand clapping and repeated commands of "*Siéntense* [sit down]," she had them seated in a circle. I had the older children read parts of the script, deciding the casting as I went. The only speaking parts were Mary — the biggest role, the three Kings, Joseph and the Archangel. Most of the little children could just be angles and shepherds. With parts assigned we planned to meet weekly with the idea of first just reading through the play and blocking out the scenes.

Chuck looked over the Christmas music he was to play — Spanish carols, all unknown to him. Julia added that an English Christmas Carol, translated to Spanish would be nice too, so he had his challenges.

It was a long pedal back, with Chuck cursing the Paraguayan roads and me lamenting our decision to ride our bikes. It was almost dark by the time we got home and we were too weary to even think about cooking dinner. Chuck walked down to Chacho's to buy one of his roasted chickens, while I sliced some tomatoes. We were fast asleep by 8 o'clock.

The rest of our Peace Corps work just sputtered along. Chuck had more guitar students than he could handle and I continued with my sales enhancing work at the *cooperativa*. Mostly, I decided, I was just a janitor, but went down every day anyway, trying to feel useful. I was getting a little better with my bi-weekly kindergarten class activities as I now led them around the playground saying, "Stop," then stopping, and "Go," then going, and trying for other action verbs like "Jump" and "Run." The children seemed to like it well enough and I reasoned they might not be learning any English, but were getting exercise. The teacher still eyed me suspiciously every time I came though, wondering, I was sure, what craziness I would introduce.

Roberto was becoming our best friend. He came by a couple of evenings a week, loving our evening conversations and box wine on the porch. One evening he asked us if it was true, what he had heard about Americans. "*Son todos obesos?* [All are obese?]" We assured him that no, not all were obese, but a great number were and that it was a big problem. He went on to explain how important exercise was and we complained of our lack of it. "*No problemo,*" he told us happily. "*Vengan y corran conmigo.* [Come and run with me.]" He said that there were several soccer fields around town and one in particular had a track around it that he ran on every afternoon about 5 o'clock.

The next day we were there. "Track" might not have been the word, but it did have a well beaten path that was more or less cleared of *colorado* nests. It felt wonderful to run and get my heart beating. We jogged a good thirty minutes and decided that this was going to be a daily routine.

Boys in Paraguay didn't worry about exercise —they had soccer and it was huge. The national team was followed with zealous fervor and any time there was a televised game, you could be sure nothing else was getting done in Artigas; everyone would be gathered around a TV. There weren't any other sports to speak of and for girls, there was nothing.

Artigas had its own soccer competitions, with four teams that played each other and teams from around the province. Since many of the teams were named after important dates in Paraguay and many of the streets were named after important dates in Paraguay, it wasn't uncommon for May 12th to be playing September 3rd at November 11th on September 30th. It was easier to get the needed information from Roberto.

Roberto told us that the next Sunday's game would be in the field where we ran, so when Sunday rolled around we walked down to the field, paid our small admission and approached the field. We discovered too late that we should have carried our plastic chairs from home since admission was only to watch, no seating of any kind, and the *colorados* eliminated the possibility of simply sitting on the grass. Some *campesinos* came on horseback and then sat on their horses, a few pickups were there with families sitting on the hoods and other people from town had carried their chairs. We didn't feel like walking back for ours so we decided to stand

and watch for awhile. I guess it was a thrilling game, but it bored both of us almost to death. It wasn't anything against the Artigas players, it was soccer in general: all the running and kicking and no scores. Chuck tried to like it, but in his opinion it just didn't compare to American football, his favorite spectator sport. I wasn't keen on watching any sport but soccer was way down on my list. I had never played it as a girl and barely knew the rules. We lasted to half-time, greeted many acquaintances from the *cooperativa*, then went home.

The next week Roberto invited us to come to his family's big Sunday meal, called an *asado*. The word *asado* means roasted, and referred to the large piece of meat (beef or pig) that would be roasted, usually in an outdoor oven or pit. I asked Roberto what we could bring and he answered immediately, "*Vino.*" The only kind of wine available to buy in Artigas was cheap box wine, but it was still too expensive for most budgets. We were happy to bring it. It was an easy contribution and it beat the heck out of *caña*.

The Sunday dinner was held at Kitty's house, but Roberto was in charge of the roasting and he had been at it for hours. When we arrived he greeted us with a big smile, wearing a large apron and waving a meat fork. "*Vengan, vengan y miran,* [Come, come and look,]" he called to us and we followed him around to the back of the house where there was a large, clay, outdoor oven. He opened the metal door with a heavy pot-holder and we could see the roast sizzling and the aroma made my mouth water. The entire scene reminded me of a holiday dinner with a big turkey roasting, children running everywhere, and women hustling in the kitchen. I stepped into the kitchen offering my services, but was shooed away so I went back outside and had some wine with Chuck and Roberto.

I would like to say that it was the best meal I had ever had, but it wasn't. I can say that the meat was delicious, the hospitality was wonderful, and we loved being there. The meal, though, was, well, Paraguayan. Since greens were hard to come by, there wasn't any type of green salad and instead there was potato salad, which normally would have been fine. But this potato salad recipe seemed to have the ingredients backwards. Instead of potatoes tossed with mayonnaise, it was a bowl of mayonnaise tossed with a few potatoes. It was understandable, given the deplorable condition of the potatoes in the *cooperativa*, so to make up for that, they had added several cans of canned peas — they obviously had a can-opener. I was beginning to understand why there were so many cans of them in the *cooperativa*. The starch, naturally, was boiled mandioca. Chuck and I helped ourselves to portions of each and tried not to look too obvious adding salt and pepper. I left feeling like I had filled my stomach with lead and we went straight home for a nap.

Paraguay had one food item, though, that undoubtedly was the best in the world — strawberries! We had seen them for sale in Aregua, where we had our training sessions, but living with Digna and taking the bus home, we hadn't bought any. Now, one of the *cooperativa* farmers had fields of ripe berries that he was bringing to town every morning. These berries weren't big and hard and produced for shipping. They were small and dark and juicy, picked ripe at sunrise, put in little baggies and brought to market. The first day I spied them I just bought two little bags, tentatively, to try them out. I had been discouraged for years in the States, buying big, delicious looking strawberries only to find they were either totally tasteless or sour. Chuck and I tasted our Artigas berries after lunch with milk and sugar and just about fell out of our chairs. They were incredibly sweet and delicious — the best berries I could ever remember tasting.

I started buying two or three baggies every day. We put them on cereal, served them with milk, mixed them with yogurt and of course, just ate them with our fingers right out of the sacks. I could have cooked with them, but that seemed a waste and I wouldn't have had the discipline to leave them alone long enough to add them to a batter. As a tribute, Chuck even started strumming and singing "Strawberry Fields Forever."

Despite the fact that we were gorging on strawberries and were able to buy good vegetables from Crispin, we were anxious to start a garden before it got too hot. Mandy told me we needed to plant by early November or it would be so hot the little plants would just fry. We had already purchased supplies in a farming *cooperativa* in Asunción, so we had seeds for cucumbers, green peppers, lettuce and tomatoes, and planned to plant potato eyes for potatoes. I had even gotten some marigold seeds to plant around the garden perimeter, having heard they would ward off bugs. Adding to my birthday gardening book and gloves, Chuck had bought two shovels, two kinds of rakes and a hoe. We were ready.

The next Saturday, dressed in our long-sleeved shirts, long pants, gloves, boots and hats, looking more like we were off to a hazardous materials site than a garden, which considering the *coloradoes* and mosquitoes, we probably were, we marched out to survey our yard. Kitty, our landlady, had already given us permission to make the garden, saying with a shrug we could do as we wished.

There was an obvious sunny spot, so Chuck staked it off and started digging up the grass in large clumps. Clearing the grass was only a beginning as gardens in Paraguay needed to have high flat ridges for the plants with deep canals between them for the water to run off during the heavy rains. If a garden was flat, we had been warned, the whole thing would float off in the first rain. It took us all morning to remove the grass. After a brief lunch and no nap — too dirty to even contemplate it — we went at it again. We knew our compost wasn't quite ready, but decided we could mix some in any way; it had to be better than regular dirt. Chuck went over to the pile, took off the plastic cover, dug in his shovel and started back across the yard, his shovel heaped high. He suddenly shouted and dropped the shovel.

"Snake?" I yelled, instantly panicked.

"No. Ants! Goddamn *colorados*. Look! It's crawling with them!"

I ran over. Sure enough the entire shovel-full of compost was a mass of hundreds of them, now covering the shovel handle as well. Thankfully, due to his gloves and long shirt, he had no bites. We walked cautiously back to the compost pile and took a closer look.

"It's an ant hotel," I said glumly.

"Not for long." Chuck marched to the house for his lethal ant powder and sprinkled it around the base.

"I was tired of doing this today anyway," I agreed, and we stopped for the day.

In two days the ants were gone and we were back to the task, both of us carrying shovels of compost to the garden and working it in the soil. After that came the drainage ditches.

"Why was it we wanted a garden?" Chuck asked me.

"Potatoes." I reminded him. He had been obsessing about scalloped potatoes. "And lettuce and tomatoes." All things that Crispin didn't carry.

After another long afternoon we had a garden plot arranged with neat rows, deep canals and even a trough leading from the lowest end to the edge of the street. Finally, I had seeds in the soil for cucumbers, green peppers, tomatoes and lettuce and had even put the seed packets on little sticks in front of each row. Encircling the whole perimeter were my crop-protecting marigold seeds. I couldn't stop admiring it.

A week later we woke to a strangely quiet morning that was still dark at 7 a.m. By mid-morning the sky was enveloped with low, black clouds and large heavy drops had begun to fall. I hurried out to the back yard to re-secure the plastic over our compost and retrieved my underwear from the small clothesline we had rigged between the grape arbor and a small peach tree.

I had been hand-washing my own underwear because they had told us in training that it wasn't really acceptable for a woman to send out her "private" clothes. I wondered where that idea had come from — certainly not the Guaranie Indians; something probably imported from the aristocratic Spanish. It didn't matter in any case; it was easy to wash my own lingerie and hang them out. Plus, this way, they were still intact. The rest of our clothes were slowly acquiring an array of small holes on the edges, from being hung, Paraguayan style, on barbed wire fences. It didn't bother me much with our t-shirts and shorts and was a small concession for laundry that was returned spotless, ironed and folded.

Chuck came back from a session at the radio, shaking his wet jacket on the porch.

"Oscar says we're in for a good one, whatever that means."

By the time I had served a bowl of soup, it had begun to pour. Chuck picked up his spoon then sat back and stared, transfixed, as a large drop landed in his soup and sent ripples to the edges of the bowl. We both looked up.

"I'm thinking we should move a little," I said as I slid our plates and bowls to the left. I put a glass under the drip and we finished our soup. I picked the bowls and returned to the kitchen, only to discover water dripping off the top of the refrigerator, a big puddle on the kitchen cutting table and two growing ponds on the floor.

"Chuck," I called. "Look, we have leaks everywhere!"

Chuck quickly went to check on the computer that sat on a shelf in the entertainment room and the TV itself, remembering Digna's disaster. They were dry, but he covered them with plastic in case a new leak appeared, which seemed likely. There turned out to be only one leak in our bedroom, at the foot of the bed, two more in the living room and only one in the entertainment room. The floor was now an obstacle course of bowls and cups.

I had to see how the garden was holding up even though there wasn't much we could do about it now. We both threw on our yellow slickers and ran out to take a look. It was holding perfectly. The raised beds were still intact and the troughs in between were filled with water rushing down our canal to the street. We gave each other a high five and ran back to the cover of the porch. The road was a different matter, almost a small river.

"Do you think I can make it to my kindergarten class?" I asked.

"You might," Chuck mused, "but I think you'd be the only one in attendance."

The rain lasted all day and all night, closing everything for two days. It amazed me to see the effects of no paved roads. No school, no stores open, no paper, no Crispin, no laundry. Zip. Old *Fletcha* was out of service for three days. By the fourth day the roads had dried enough for most vehicles, and commerce was slowly coming back to life.

17   A New Beginning

The roads were totally functional by the end of the week when we were due back in Asunción for another training session plus dental checkups. These sessions were being held in a new town, to the south of Asunción where the entire training facility had now been relocated. It was too bad as we all missed the ambiance of the old training house in Aregua.

We were housed with families and although our family was as friendly and nice as could be imagined, we realized our desire for a family stay was approaching zero. Making this stay more challenging was the fact we weren't actually in the house, but in an attached room that looked like a vacant store. It was a big, mostly empty square space with a bed placed in the back, a table, two fluorescent tubes on the walls for lights and a bathroom that was off to the side. The family was pleased that they could offer us the private room, but had neglected to consider the large, curtain-less storefront window facing the busy street. Unless we wanted to provide a peep show we had to shower and slip into bed without lights. This caused banged shins, stubbed toes and no a small amount of cursing. Making matters worse, there were no screens and no fans. Between the heat and the mosquitoes that buzzed continually around my ears, we both awoke the first morning tired and sullen.

We were the first ones in line for the Paraguayan dentist, who Julie, the nurse, told us was the best in town. He checked our teeth, which were fine, then supposedly cleaned them. It didn't compare with the intensity of the cleanings I got back in the States. There, it was something of an ordeal — scraping and scraping while I cringed and waited for contact against a nerve. Here, it was mostly just a floss and a brush. Painless, but I didn't feel assured the job had been done.

It was odd how we felt with our fellow Volunteers compared to the way we had felt thirty years ago. Before, we were a tight band of best buddies. Now, there were only a few that we were close to and we didn't feel part of the group at all. Partly, I knew, it was due to the age and marital differences and the fact we didn't spend outside time with them. Some of the younger members of our group seemed immature, and I wondered if they really were or was I just getting old and stodgy? We noted that Pam and Tim, the couple our age with whom we had stayed, had many close relationships with their younger compatriots. Was our group different from theirs or were we too snobbish or weren't we trying hard enough?

Despite this, we did have a fun at the Halloween party thrown at the P. C. compound on Saturday night. It was a huge bash, with almost every Volunteer in the country attending. Chuck was dressed as a serial killer which involved wearing a cereal box around his neck that had a knife stuck in it. I was a piece of gum. That costume was just a tennis shoe tied to the top of my head. Neither costume was original, but we thought they would be new for this group and we had great fun explaining ourselves all night.

We made one extra stop before we left for Artigas and that was to Pindolo to visit Digna and her family. We called ahead from the Peace Corps office to her cell phone and she was delighted to hear from us, although when we got there she gave us a scolding for not having called her more.

"I have been so worried about you. How are you doing? How is your house? How is Artigas, like Pindola?" She pummeled us with questions as she served us a terrific lunch of stew and a salad, which was a treat. On that particular afternoon Victor Senior was gone and so was her sister and her baby, so it was just Digna and her two children, which made it seem like old times. Little Victor was beside himself to have Chuck to play with and was practically crying when we left for the bus. I hadn't realized how much we had meant to them and felt guilty being remiss in calling Digna. Worse, I hadn't even thought about calling. I now promised to do better.

We made it back to the Peace Corps office by late afternoon, time enough for another discussion with our supervisor on what else we could do in Artigas. He suggested talking more with another member of the *cooperativa* — one who had more time than Ramón.

As usual, we brought back as many bottles of "real" wine as we could carry in our backpacks plus a bottle of gin and one of tonic. Roberto had been telling us that he really liked gin or *geen* as he called it, but, of course, he could never get any. He came by the evening we got home and although we were beat from the trip, we couldn't deny him his long awaited *geen en tonic*. We poured generous drinks all around, topped off with thin slices of our backyard lemon/oranges. We had another conversation about fat Americans and Roberto told us he had read that if he wrapped his stomach in plastic wrap before he exercised he would lose more weight. We argued that it might just be water loss, but he was sure it would do something positive.

"*Estaba escrito por un Norte Americano* [it was written by a North American]," Roberto added, making it irrefutable in his mind. He was going to try it this next week anyway. My "geen en tonic" was rapidly sending my Spanish skills into the toilet, so I offered my excuses and bid Chuck and Roberto a good night. Chuck followed in ten minutes.

Within the week we scheduled a meeting with Ramón Jara,

136

another committee member from the *cooperativa* who was in charge of the savings and loan section. We didn't know him well. I had seen him a few times, as he was often acting as the cashier at the store, but I had never conversed with him.

The three of us sat down and we explained our frustrations of not having enough to do. He said he'd look into it. Chuck and I both thought that it was going to be another dead end, but to our surprise, he spotted me in the *cooperativa* the following day and said to come back and meet with Ramón, he had good news. Chuck and I hurried to the meeting at the appointed time and sat anxiously with Ramón in his little cramped office. He was beaming.

"*Tenemos tres computadoras* [We have three computers], he told us. "*Puedes enseñar computadors a los estudiantes?*" [Can you teach computers to students?]

Chuck and I exchanged a glance, not sure exactly what he had or what he was thinking. We had enough trouble trying to get an email sent home every week, much less having to file students into a phone booth, one at a time. Ramón was reading our minds.

"I know, there is no Internet," he explained in Spanish, "but you could teach the basics?" He looked at us hopefully. I looked at Chuck.

"Well, sure," he said.

"We could teach them how to how to type and use the word processor for starters," I added, and looked over at Chuck, who nodded in agreement.

"Come," he told us, I'll show you."

He took us upstairs where there were three large boxes with the familiar Intel logo on the sides. He opened one box and we could see a modern, brand new computer inside. He pulled out the keyboard, still in its plastic sheath and let us admire it. I noted it was the Spanish keyboard with all the proper punctuation marks and accents, which was essential as it wouldn't do to teach the kids on an English keyboard.

I had discovered, much to my frustration at the Internet cafés, that Spanish keyboards had totally different locations for their punctuation marks. Every time I had tried to use an apostrophe, I got a semi-colon. Periods were commas, commas were brackets and I never did find the question mark. My first letters home had looked like a monkey at work. And, of course, English keyboards had no accent marks or the little squiggly "n-yea" mark, which could be an important distinction. Without the precious ñ, for example *Feliz Año Nuevo*, Happy New Year, becomes, *Feliz Ano Nuevo*, Happy New Ass Hole.

"You could teach in the annex," Ramón continued happily, and led us downstairs to the small adobe building that sat at one side of the *cooperativa*. "This is the oldest building here," Ramón said. "The first fortress of General Artigas." It was a squat building with thick adobe walls, totally out of place next to the two-story cement *cooperativa* with its glass windows. He opened its heavy wooden door with a long skeleton key, and we entered into a cool, dark room that smelled of dirt. The door was set a foot inside the front wall and there were twenty inches of wall beyond that, creating an amazing thickness that had obviously withstood time. Ramón lifted a crossbar from a small shuttered window and pushed it open. There was no glass or screen and a breeze blew through the room.

"This looks like the Alamo," I whispered to Chuck and couldn't help thinking of how incongruous it would be teach a computer class in an ancient, adobe fort.

"You'll want the window and door open for light and a breeze," Ramón told us, "but if it rains we have electric lights." He pointed across the room where two of the walls had the typical fluorescent tubes mounted near the ceiling. He promised to have the place swept, tables and chairs moved in, and, most importantly, the three computers plugged in and running by Monday. He would give us a list of students and we could start immediately.

Chuck and I both felt that learning to type was an important prerequisite for the students. Otherwise, when they finally got to a place that used computers or they had the opportunity to send a letter, they would have to slowly peck out words. Not practical when they would be charged by the minute. We decided we could combine the typing with how to open programs, cut and paste and whatever else we could incorporate without an actual Internet connection.

That afternoon I got out our laptop, put my fingers on the keyboard and tried to recall how I had learned to type back in the eighth grade. All I remembered was that I wasn't very good. At Christmas the typing teacher had set up a Christmas tree and the fastest and most accurate typists got to hang gold baubles on the tree. The second best group got to hang silver bells and the rest of the class (which included me) were relegated to hanging paper stars. I stared at the small keyboard and frowned. Start with the middle row, do practices of that, then extend fingers to the top and bottom rows? Yes!

I got out a piece of paper and started making simple three letter combos of middle row letters. And practice? I thought of piano players that practiced on cardboard keyboards. I could draw the Spanish keyboard with all of its keys and give each student a copy of the keyboard page. Ramón had told us that we could use the copy machine and paper supplies from the *cooperativa*. And, I could practice myself to discover where exactly all the punctuation was.

Chuck had gone down to the radio station and I couldn't wait for him to get home so I could show him my ideas. We decided we could start about thirty students, each of us working half days with three students at a time for an hour each. After more consideration, I thought we could get them through all the basics in about six weeks, then could graduate those and start a new bunch.

"I wonder how many students will show up?" I asked Chuck. "Hopefully, it won't be like my play audition."

It wasn't. Word had gone out over the radio and when we arrived at 9:00 a.m., there were already a half a dozen kids sitting on the high stone sidewalk. By the time we closed for lunch, we had a list of forty students, the last ten we put on a waiting list for the next course. Alicia, the store manager, had sent her son. She told me later that he hadn't slept all night and had gone down to sit and wait for us at 6 a.m. in the morning. It was touching to see how eager and enthusiastic they were. No one wanted to miss the opportunity.

When I started the next day my first assigned students were there waiting for me. Chuck took over in the afternoon and, like me, found kids waiting patiently by the front door.

18   LA (La Artigas) Fitness

The classes were a huge success. I had worried that students might find typing exercises a bit pedantic, but they were enthralled to be doing anything that got their hands on a computer. And the typing was going to be useful. After mastering the middle row of letters, I made exercises with the fingers reaching for the letters above and below and we started adding skills like moving icons and changing the type size. It was fun to watch their initial intimidation disappear as they became more comfortable.

With the classes going smoothly, the garden growing and the house more or less in place, we were beginning to feel quite settled. We continued to run laps with Roberto in the evenings and true to his word, he wrapped his torso in plastic wrap for about a week, until he finally gave that up. It was just too hot and uncomfortable and he didn't think it was working all that well. We were glad he had abandoned it as his face had been getting alarmingly red by his second lap around the field.

Our next session with him on the porch led to further discussion of exercise or lack of it in Artigas. He told us that there once had been a sort of gym, but it had closed for lack of business.

"And we had basketball," he added.

"Basketball?" Chuck asked.

"Oh yes. You have seen the basketball court?"

We both shook our heads no and he said we could walk by it on our way to the running field. So the next day we followed him and realized that we had passed it several times without noticing it. Tall grasses grew along the edges of the cement court hiding it, and weeds grew in multiple cracks on the surface. At either end, there was a rusty hoop with no netting. If the weeds were scraped off, the court looked like it might be serviceable enough. In addition there were post holes at the sides for a tennis net. Obviously, someone at some time — maybe a long-ago Volunteer — had tried to make it a full-service community court. Roberto said that play had stopped for lack of a basketball.

Chuck and I decided right there that buying a basketball would be a must for our next trip to Asunción, which was only a couple of weeks away. It seemed like we had just been there, but Peace Corps was having another training session. We weren't delighted to have to go all the way back there again so soon, but now at least, we could buy the basketball.

In addition to the meeting, all the Volunteers were invited to stay at the "resort" on the lake in Aregua where we had trained, and have Thanksgiving dinner there. If I hadn't known better, I would have been thrilled by the prospect, but I knew the lake was polluted, so no swimming or even wading was advised, the shores were covered with litter and the accommodations would be four to a room. There were other hotels of course, but we had also heard that the resort had run out of food the year before. We opted out of both.

I knew that this kind of thinking was the very reason we weren't close to the younger members of our group, and staying apart wouldn't help us get any closer, but I just didn't care. John wasn't staying there either or attending the dinner. On our last trip to Asunción we had been told there was a terrific Italian restaurant near the Hotel Paraguay we might like and we had decided we would have our Thanksgiving dinner there.

By the time two weeks had rolled around, I was more amicable to the trip and as it turned out, the training was more useful than I had imagined since it was a special language session, either in Guaranie or Spanish, whichever you were using at your site. Naturally, we attended the Spanish sessions and enjoyed the opportunity to ask grammatical questions and practice slower conversation. I noted it also helped to be speaking without any wine or *geen*.

The Italian restaurant turned out to serve our best Thanksgiving dinner ever. It was decidedly upscale and we had brought clean slacks and polo shirts for the occasion. The tennis shoes still made me feel scruffy, but there was no helping that. We didn't have room in our backpacks to carry extra shoes, especially for one evening, and there was no way we could walk the distances on the dirt roads with anything else. However, once we were seated, with our feet tucked under the table, we looked as presentable as the other patrons. We both had chicken pastas, which were at least close to a Thanksgiving turkey, plus hor d'oeuvres, REAL bread, salads and wine. It was easily the best meal we had eaten in country. The whole feast cost 60,000 Guaranies, a shocking extravagance for Peace Corps Volunteers, but in the real world it was only about $19.00. Thank God for the Visa Card.

We returned to Artigas, packed to the gills as usual with grocery goodies and wine, plus a basketball! When Jorge's next guitar lesson came around, Chuck greeted him, bouncing the new basketball on the front porch. Jorge's eyes lit up and he would have dashed off to the court right then, but it was dark and, as Chuck pointed out, the court needed some weed cleaning first.

Jorge and his brother, Miguel met us the following afternoon with machetes and two hand-made hoes. The four of us hacked away at the most offending weeds, Jorge and his brother whacking the big ones with machetes, while Chuck and I scraped smaller weeds flat or pulled them out. The boys were wearing flip flops that impeded any serious basketball play, but they assured us they would be back with friends.

The following afternoon I rejoined Roberto jogging around the field and left Chuck to the basketball court. He came home tired and said that despite his height, the boys had given him a good run for his money.

I wished I could get the girls in town interested in some sport, or even an outdoor activity, but I wasn't sure what that was going to be. Basketball for the short girls wasn't going to be an option. The only sport I knew anything about and could teach, was golf, not too likely a candidate. I had never played soccer and didn't know the first thing about it, and baseball was a total unknown for Paraguayans. Very few kids had bicycles and most of the women I spoke to told me they had never learned to ride, nor did they want to. I asked one of my new typing students what she did for exercise and she told me nothing, but she could swim. I was even more surprised when she told me she had learned to swim in Artigas.

"*Aqui* [Here]? " I had questioned.

"*Si, En el camino a San Marcos tenemos un balneario.* [Yes, on the road to San Marcos we have a balneario.]" I didn't know what a *balneario* was, and asked her again. This time she just made swimming motions with her arms. How could I have gone down that road and missed a swimming pool or a lake or whatever it was?

Chuck and I were rather excited; what a treat it would be to have a place to swim! The next Sunday we packed our swimming suits and small camp towels in a backpack and pedaled out of town on our bikes. We followed the directions the students had given us and sure enough, in about three miles there was an unmarked turn-off. Up a little ways on this path we came to a small weathered kiosk, attended by an old woman charging five Guaranies to enter and go swimming. We asked if we could take a look first and she nodded agreeably. We went around her stand and approached a small embankment. There in all its glory was the *balneario*. It was a mud hole and not even a big one. Babies and small children

144

played happily on the muddy banks, oozing mud between their fingers and teen-aged girls sat on towels while they watched teen-aged boys splashing and showing–off in the water. It didn't look deep enough or big enough for swimming and brought to mind all the horrid parasites that supposedly live in Amazonian waters. We didn't so much as want to put our toes in, much less pay five Guaranies for the privilege. We kindly thanked the old woman for letting us look around, then pedaled home and put our swimsuits back into the duffel bag.

The word *balneario* puzzled me as I had learned the word *piscina* for pool, so I looked it up.

"Here it is," I told Chuck. "Spa or health resort."

"So what's the word for bog?"

I flipped back through the dictionary. "*Pantano*," I said. "Truth in advertising, but probably lousy revenue."

19   Christmas Preparations

Mandy pedaled up to the fence in a swirl of dust and waved at me through the window. I came out on the porch as she bounded through the gate.

"Guess what?" she called. "My parents are coming for Christmas!" She pulled a wrinkled copy of her email from her backpack and read me the news.

"That's terrific," I agreed, "and you all must come here for Christmas dinner. And spend the night." I paused, thinking of her small quarters. "Will they stay with you in your house?"

"Oh yes, for a few nights anyway. They won't mind, they're used to camping."

I thought to myself they had better be, visualizing my mother — then I remembered that her parents were younger than I was! And I had the distinct impression their lives were rural and basic, like farmers I knew when I was growing up, so I guessed they would be fine. There was no doubt though, that Christmas dinner at the Hanner Hilton would be just the ticket.

Over tea and cookies Mandy suggested they could bring some of my Christmas presents as well as hers. I liked the idea as I wasn't too optimistic about boxes arriving intact by the local mail. Back in Afghanistan all boxes were routinely opened, rifled through and items were always taken. I wasn't sure Paraguay's postal system was as bad as that; but to be safe, on my next email home I told my sisters they could send small flat packages to Mandy's parents. Linda, as it turned out, had already mailed hers, but Rita thought she would take up the offer.

Roberto had said we were welcome at his family's Christmas dinner, but when we told him that now we would have guests, he was pleased for us, but wondered what we would cook. He couldn't imagine a Christmas feast without a big *asado* roasting on a big spit outdoors. I told him we'd cook a roast in the oven and then said it was too bad there wasn't any pork in town, as a pork roast would be good.

"*No cerdo*?!" Robert had exclaimed. "We have pork, the best pork in Paraguay!"

Artigas had pork? How had I missed this?

"It's on the other side of the soccer field," he told us. "The owner raises his own and it's very clean and very good."

With that recommendation and Roberto's directions, I set off the next morning and found the small *tienda* he had described. The door was open, but no one was inside. I tentatively approached, clapped loudly and called, "*Hola*," several times but no one appeared. I was about to give up when a tiny, stooped, man limped through the back door. He was almost bald, with only a few tufts of white hair over his ears and perched on the bridge of his nose were the thickest glasses I had ever seen. They were, in fact, the only glasses I had ever seen in Artigas. He gave me a black, toothless smile, wiped his hands across his blood-stained apron and peered at me with large, magnified eyes.

Looking down at him I noted that the counter top was also filthy and blood stained. Roberto had said the pigs were clean and I guessed that meant the pigs didn't have diseases, which certainly was good, but obviously cleanliness didn't extend to the shop or shop-owner. The butcher kept looking at me, not saying anything and I finally muttered that I needed a *cerdo asado* [pork roast]. He nodded, crept back through the door and returned in a minute hunched down even lower carrying a huge pig leg on his shoulder. He toppled it to the counter with a thud, then reached over and flicked the ON switch of his saw blade. It was then that saw that he was missing three fingers from his right hand — the thumb, forefinger and middle finger, the three that would have been closest to the whirring saw. He pushed the leg over with his left hand and with his nose about an inch from the spinning blade, sawed off a sizable chunk. He turned off the saw, which made me breathe easier, then reached for an enormous cleaver hanging behind the counter. With unexpected energy, he brought the cleaver down with a blow, severing the piece in half. I flinched. He placed a piece on an old-fashioned and blood-stained scale that used rocks as the counter weights.

"*Es bueno?*" he asked squinting at me.

"*Si, si*" I replied, not caring if it was enough or too much. I didn't want to see him doing any more sawing or whacking.

He pulled out a surprisingly clean piece of butcher paper, wrapped the meat and handed it to me. I thanked him, paid him and left, happy no more fingers had gone missing.

Every day the heat intensified. It was hard to imagine Christmas was coming. With Kitty's permission we had two fans installed in the house — one in the living room and one over our bed. It helped tremendously, but we were still sweating all the time. Nights were the worst. Chuck was getting up about 1 a.m. to take a quick cold shower and after one night I followed suit, since I was awake anyway and it seemed to help. It kept us cool enough to fall back to sleep. I complained to Alicia at the *cooperativa* and she just laughed.

"*Hagalo que hacemos* [Do what we do]," she advised and went on to describe how they filled a small kiddy wading pool with water and ice and sat around it with their feet immersed and ate watermelon. I recalled how wonderful the cold water had felt on our feet during the Big Ride bicycle journey the previous year, and decided to give it a try.

While Chuck was taking his turn with the typing students, I bought a little rubber pool at the *cooperativa* and put it in the back yard under a mango tree. It was pretty apparent that our two small ice cube trays were not going to cool the water so I made a second trip to the *cooperativa* and bought the largest block of ice they had, which was about the size of a shoe box. I got that home, added water, pulled up our two plastic chairs and waited for Chuck. He arrived shortly, sweat dripping from his face.

"Come and get cooled off," I announced and his expression brightened some as he followed me through the house to the back yard.

"Wow," he exclaimed and quickly took off his shoes and socks for the refreshing foot plunge. I had even bought a watermelon, which were now plentiful and sweet, so we could do just as the locals. We sat there spitting the watermelon seeds into the grass and I tried to recall what I had been doing a year earlier.

Schools were now closed until February for "summer" break and we had noticed a decrease in attendance at our typing classes. Ramón told us not to worry, it would all pick up normally after January 6th, the Day of Kings, and the last of the holiday celebrations. This time of year, he explained, families all go to visit other relatives.

This, we discovered, was also playing a part in our children's Christmas play. We held another rehearsal and to my concern, Mary and two of the three Kings weren't there. Julia just shrugged it off. They'll be back, she told me. I had other children read the parts and tried to start some basic stage movements, like when to come on the stage and when to leave. When I told them to wait offstage, they all wandered off.

Chuck did his best to get them all singing. Julia said they knew the Guaranie carols very well but Chuck couldn't get them to sing those either. Even playing the music on the recorder didn't help. I sympathized with them as I couldn't even discern the tune. As far as our "Silent Night" went, even translated into Spanish, it was hopeless. The kids didn't get the song or the melody. A couple of them mumbled a bit but most just sat and looked at Chuck with big eyes. They did like the guitar though and Chuck entertained them, letting them strum as he played chords.

"Scratch 'Silent Night,'" he said on the bus ride back. "I'd like to scratch the whole thing," I told him. "Have I mentioned lately that I hate little kids?"

Walking home from the bus stop I realized I was limping due to a rock in my tennis shoe. When we got home, I took off my shoe, shook it vigorously, and put it back on. I took a few steps; it was still there. I repeated the exercise and had the same results. I took it off for a third time and felt around the sole with my fingers. It was smooth. Then, a light bulb went on in my head; I felt the bottom of my foot. A small hard bump was directly under the heel.

"Chuck," I called. "Can you come and look? What is this on my foot?" I grabbed my toes and held the bottom of my foot up for inspection.

Chuck peered at it, poked it once, and said, "Hmmm." My anxiety level rose instantly.

"Hmmm?! What does hmmm, mean?"

"Well, it kinda looks like that thing they described in the health lecture — the bug that lays eggs and has to be dug out?" He stared at my foot again. "I'll go get the medical notes."

My stomach did a flip-flop with the words, "dug out." He came back flipping through the notebook.

"Well, it doesn't have a black circle around it. That's the kind that you can smother with salve." He picked up my foot and took another look. "It does have a black spot in the middle . . .." He looked back at the notes. "The pique bug, it says."

We looked at each other. "I'm not digging it out," he declared.

That was fine by me — detailed work was not his forte. I didn't want him anywhere close to my foot with a sharp instrument. And he knew by experience what a fainter I was so he didn't want any part of it either.

"Well, it's a long way to Asunción just for this," I said. "People get them all the time. It's really common." I was trying to convince myself that it was no big deal, but to me it WAS a big deal. "I know," I said suddenly, "Delma! Delma can do it! She told me she took them out all the time for her kids." I put my shoe back on, limped over to her house and clapped at the gate. As usual their snarling dogs charged the fence and Delma appeared in her doorway.

"*Necesito tu ayuda* [I need your help]," I called.

She came quickly to the fence, looking worried. I told her, somewhat frantically, that I thought I had a pique bite. Delma threw back her head and laughed.

"*Norte Americanos!*" She continued chuckling, thinking how funny we were to think that growing larvae inside your skin was anything to concern yourself about. "*Es facil removarlo, soy un experto* [It's easy to remove it, I'm an expert]," she smiled. "*Un momento.*"

She returned to her house and came back holding a small plastic bag. "*Agujas, hoja de afeitar, pinza* [needles, razor blade, tweezers]," she rattled off, holding the bag in front of my face. "*Tiene peroxido de hidrogeno?* [Do you have hydrogen peroxide?]"

I nodded, feeling clammy just looking at her baggie of instruments.

"*Vamos a tu casa,*" she declared and charged ahead of me, heading to our house.

Chuck was waiting for us on the porch. I told Chuck to find the hydrogen peroxide and I sat down and showed my foot to Delma.

"*Si, es un pique,*" she confirmed and opened her plastic bag. She pulled out a white handkerchief and spread it open on the other plastic chair, then carefully laid out her instruments. She turned and asked me for a small dish.

"*No aqui* [Not here]," I feebly protested and motioned inside the house where I limped to the spare bed, laid down, and tried to mentally prepare myself for foot amputation. I covered my head with a pillow and hoped for the best.

I felt a couple of sharp pricks, and as I braced myself for more, I heard her say "*Bueno, es finito*." I peeked out from over the pillow. "*Mira* [just look]," she said, and held out the dish Chuck had brought her. I propped myself up on my elbows and stared into the dish. She took her needle and prodded what looked like tiny white eggs. They wiggled.

"Oh my God," I groaned and lay back down. "*Matenlos* [Kill them]." I told her. She laughed and poured a bit of hydrogen peroxide on them which turned them into a fizzing bubble. She then poured an equal amount on the new hole in my foot. When the fizz subsided, she covered it with a bandage.

I thanked her profusely and she just said, "*Es nada. Somos vecinos, somos famila.* [It's nothing. We are neighbors, we are family]."

I offered her ice cream, but she said no, she needed to get back. Chuck saw her to the door and I called out that I thought the patient needed ice cream. I hopped to the table as he dished up two big bowls.

20   Iguazú — Water Wonderworld

Life seemed to grind into slow motion. As the thermometer outside the door rose, our corresponding energy to do anything dropped. Not that there was anything to do. Attendance had become so spotty at the computer classes that together we only had two mornings of students. Both the kindergarten and the soy classes had been canceled until February and even Chuck's guitar classes had dropped to his two faithful students, Jorge and little Al.

When we complained of the heat to Roberto, he suggested we go to Iguazú Falls for the weekend. I had heard of the place from other Volunteers — a magnificent waterfalls, I had been told, in the corner of Paraguay where it joins Argentina and Brazil. And it was only a half-day trip from Artigas.

The only slight problem was we would have to sneak away and not tell the Peace Corps. Even though there wouldn't be a thing for us to do over the weekend and barely anything to do the next six weeks, we were supposed to remain "on site." Any time Volunteers left their sites it was considered "vacation," and that was supposed to be requested and approved in advance. I knew the reasons. In the past — and maybe it still happened — some Volunteers just took off and were away from their sites for weeks.

It was probably because they had nothing to do and were bored out of their skulls — but that's another story. And there was the "how-would-they-find-us in-an-emergency" rational. In addition, a complaint had been filed somewhere in the offices in Washington D.C. about the Peace Corps being a grand junket, so the hammer came down. Volunteers were allowed only two days of approved vacation per month.

Just the same, that night while we lay awake, sweating on top of the sheets, we discussed the pros and cons of going without permission. It would take two days to go to Asunción and back for a pass that allowed us to be gone for only three days. We decided to just go. If we were found out, it would definitely be easier to beg forgiveness than waste the two days asking for permission. As a slight precaution, we would let Ramón know where we were going.

The next day I saw Delma and asked her about the Falls. She went into raptures and quickly ran back to her house and returned with an old tattered postcard of the Falls. It did look lovely with a wide expanse of waterfalls against a green jungle.

"*Que maravilloso!*" she exclaimed. "*Deben ir* [You should go]," she told me emphatically and added that the sprays from the Falls would keep us cool.

On Friday we walked to the main road with the sun barely lighting the sky. We caught the old *Fletcha* to Bogado and then sped on the asphalt highway to Encarnación. After a brief layover and a *chipa* roll (to hell with cholesterol — it was vacation time) and Nescafé, we settled into one of the deluxe, long-distance buses to Ciudad del Este. These buses didn't travel the dirt roads. They were big, slick and most importantly, air-conditioned. Our seats actually reclined and I put mine all the way back, feeling relaxed and luxurious. Out of the tinted window I watched the plains of Paraguay roll into hills and already loved the vacation. I turned to tell Chuck how wonderful it was, but he was fast asleep.

By late afternoon we were at the downtown bus depot in Cuidad del Este where we transferred to a local bus to cross the border to Brazil. We were expecting a long delay at the border, but instead a guard just waved the bus through.

"That's curious," I told Chuck. "What happens now if they check the passport for a stamp when we come back?"

Chuck leaned across the aisle and asked another passenger. The fellow just waved it off, saying it wasn't important, didn't matter. I looked outside the bus window and nudged Chuck. Streams of people were walking across the border carrying or pulling huge bundles of goods and no one was stopping them either.

"Guess border-control isn't much of an issue here," Chuck commented. "I'm not going to worry about it," and he put our passports back into the bottom of his backpack.

We got off the bus on the Brazilian side of the border, hailed a taxi and Chuck told the driver, "Hotel Tropical *en el parque* [in the park]."

We had heard this was a magnificent old hotel and worth staying at, no matter what the price, although one Volunteer had mentioned he thought it cost about the same as stateside hotels. There had been no way to call for reservations so we thought we'd go and just try our luck. The backup plan, if there were no rooms, was to have lunch at the restaurant and a return to Cuidad del Este to find a hotel somewhere there.

In minutes we had passed through the business district along the border and were speeding along on a well maintained road with undisturbed jungle on either side. It could have been the entrance to any US national park except that there was little traffic — only one car in front of us when we arrived at the park gate. We bought our passes and continued another couple of miles until the taxi pulled into a covered driveway of what looked like a colonial mansion, but pink instead of white. Smartly dressed bellboys held open car doors and in front of us, an elegant woman, dressed in a sophisticated linen suit, was being helped from a black Mercedes Benz. I was feeling woefully lower class in jeans and tennis shoes, but we received the same service none-the-less. I crossed my fingers as we made our way over to the reservation desk.

"Yes sir," the clerk informed Chuck in perfect English, "we do have a matrimonial suite. How many nights do you wish to stay?"

Chuck hesitated. Despite the fact that it was worth staying in no- matter-what-the-price, Chuck checked the price anyway. "What is the rate?" he questioned.

"Two hundred and seventy *reais* per night, including breakfast buffet," the clerk told him then reached for a calculator. "In dollars that would be one hundred and twenty-five dollars per night. Do you have a credit card?"

Chuck smiled at me, handed over our card, signed the registration, and before we could protest that we could carry our own backpacks, they had been loaded onto a carrying cart and a bellboy was handed the key. We followed him down thick carpeted halls and he opened the door to a spacious, bright room, featuring a huge, king-sized bed, gleaming wooden dressers, a large bathroom with two sinks, mirrors to the ceiling and an enormous tub with jets in the sides. And no sign about putting the toilet paper in the basket. There wasn't even a basket.

Chuck and I were awestruck, like we had never been in a hotel before. We listened politely as the bellboy pointed out the cable TV and mini-fridge, then tipped him two dollars. The second he left, we whooped with delight and fell across the bed. I already loved Iguazú, even before seeing the waterfalls.

That evening we decided to take a short hike down the trail from the hotel. We crossed the street to the trail head, but instead of starting down the path we stopped dead in our tracks. In front of us was a waterfall that filled the horizon. The setting sun was casting a golden spell across it, turning miles of falling water into falling liquid gold. We both just stood there, transfixed, in awe of the spectacle.

"And there's more?" I finally asked, looking over at Chuck. It seemed to me that would have been view enough, but as I was soon to discover, that vista was nothing in comparison to what lay ahead. We followed the narrow asphalt trail into the jungle and at almost every corner was another dramatic scene — walls of water crashing down. They went on forever, one series of falls cascading into the next. It was getting dark before we were even a quarter of the way down the trail, so we hurried back to the hotel with a vow to spend the entire next day going end to end.

The next two days we were truly in a water wonderland. Not only were the falls something to behold, but the flora and fauna did their part too. Fluorescent blue butterflies flitted by constantly; wild parrots flew across our path and we could hear the screeching of distant monkeys. We even saw a new animal for us, the mandicoti, a raccoon-looking animal, that, like its northern cousin, sniffed eagerly for handouts even though signs were posted that said they should not be fed.

The second day we took a taxi to the Argentine side (still no passport checks) where we boarded a small outboard and were taken out to a dock which led to a falls called Devil's Throat. We had already been impressed to saturation, but this was even more spectacular since we were able to walk down the dock hanging on to wet railings and be almost within reach of the crashing falls. The dock trembled under our feet as tons of water roared down in front of our faces and left us soaked. Everywhere we went it was cool, clean and green. There were no crowds and no shops selling cheap souvenirs or fast food. Every new corner brought more deep, green jungle and roaring, white water.

Each evening I luxuriated in the giant tub — filling it to the brim, adding the complementary bubble bath and turning on the jets. Chuck was enjoying the shower equally with hot and cold faucets and no electric shower ring to adjust. When he turned on the hot, he got hot — in a steady full spray. And we dried off with giant, fluffy, white towels, instead of our thin rough ones.

Dinners in the dining room were served on tables with linen tablecloths and expensive stemware and every night there was entertainment. It was the best vacation either of us could remember. I couldn't decide if it was the comparison from our simple life in

Paraguay or if Iguazú really was the most gorgeous and magical place in the world. I used four rolls of film, trying to capture the beauty, but in case my efforts didn't do it justice, I also bought a pile of postcards, a new one for Delma and the rest to send back to the States.

On our last night, Chuck ordered an expensive Cabernet from Argentina and after the steward filled our goblets he raised his wine glass to mine, "Here's to a marvelous vacation." The glasses chimed together with the sound of a small, clear bell. Chuck gazed at me. "Well, are you ready to go home?"

Hearing the word home gave me a start. For a minute it was as though time had gone backwards and we were on a vacation from San Diego. We would get on a plane in the morning and return to the United States — and to our old house and to our jobs. Was that what I wanted? I didn't know. I looked back at him.

"And you?" I threw the question back. "Are you ready?"

He just smiled and shrugged. "We'll see."

21   A Long, Hot December

We managed to get back across the border without incident — like before, no one was interested in looking at our passports. And no one had missed us in Artigas either, so our weekend escape had been a complete success.

When I returned to the *cooperativa* the following Tuesday, I discovered that Christmas merchandise was on display. There were several boxes of ornaments, some Christmas themed wrapping paper, rolls of red and green ribbon and two, small, aluminum Christmas trees.

Ramón apologized for putting it out "so early" since it was only the first week of December, but he thought it might bring sales. I didn't want to let him know when his *Norte Americano* neighbors started the holiday merchandising game, but assured him it was not too early. I moved the trees to the front of the store with the papers and ornaments next to them.

Ramón said he wasn't expecting big sales from his small gift department, but that there would be an increase in grocery sales. Earlier he had told us that Christmas in Paraguay was more of a food holiday than a gift holiday. Actually, all celebrations were focused on food — big family dinners. Gift giving was too expensive. Adults never exchanged gifts except maybe to bring someone a special cake or a bottle of *cidra*, a sweet, slightly alcoholic apple juice. Children only received small gifts or candies and those were presented on the Day of Kings, January 6th.

Very few people had Christmas trees. Apparently only in the last decade had the idea of a Christmas tree been filtering down the Americas through television. The Paraguayan custom was to set up a manger scene, called a *posada*, outside in the yard. Some families made elaborate ones with plywood and others constructed a more simple affair or simply set up a small nativity scene inside their homes.

I had been pondering what to do for our tree. It would have been easy to cut a small, scraggly pine and bring it inside, but they were so full of bugs and dust I was reluctant to do so, especially when I went to such pains to keep out bugs and dust. And even if I hosed a tree down, it would dry out rather quickly in our 100 plus degree days. I finally hit on the idea of getting a large bare branch, propping it up with bricks and then decorating it with tissue paper green leaves and homemade ornaments. A hand-made artificial tree!

I found the perfect dead branch from one of our ailing fruit trees and propped it upright in a stacked brick enclosure. This was followed by a trip to the *cooperativa* for an assortment of colored papers, then I settled in for an afternoon of leaf making — small bits of green tissue paper tied in bows on the branches. By dinner I had what Chuck called "a pretty good Charlie Brown Christmas tree." The ornaments I planned to do more slowly. In Afghanistan we had made tin foil chains and painted blown-out eggs. We had even attempted popcorn chains, but I gave that up when fallen bits of popcorn invited even more cockroaches and rats than usual. But I had learned, after developing aching cheeks, that blown-out eggs didn't have to have tiny pin-prick holes in each end. No one saw the holes anyway. My Paraguayan eggs were going to have holes the size of a pencil.

In a week I had a pretty cute tree, if I said so myself. It even had gifts under it since my sister Linda's box had arrived. It had come right to the post office in Artigas and Ramón had picked it up for me. I was as delighted as a school child. I couldn't say why I was so excited about my sisters' presents, usually they weren't glamorous or expensive, but this year more than any other, I really, really wanted them. In years past we weren't together often at Christmas, in fact we had only spent a couple of Christmases together in the last twenty years. But this year, being so far away and so far from everything familiar, the gifts were my magic connection to family and the States. Rita had already mailed her small gifts to Mandy's parents and I knew they would arrive with them on Christmas day. I had asked for things like good Crayola crayons for the kindergarteners, quality socks and salad dressing mixes. All items I couldn't get in Artigas or Asunción. Artigas did have a nice workshop for leather goods though and I planned to get Chuck a new belt.

Around town various houses were now putting up their *posadas*, so Artigas was looking festive, although with the heat I still had a hard time thinking "Christmas."

But the heat had been good for the garden. Everything was sprouting vigorously, especially the cucumbers which already had little flowers. I worried some about the free-range chickens, knowing that if they found their way to the garden they would peck away with their voracious little beaks until nothing remained. The chickens belonged to the Barbosa's, so I hated to say too much. I knew they couldn't afford to keep the fence in good repair so I tried my best to block holes along the bottom with big stones. The chickens had been getting in anyway, but so far had limited themselves to pecking around the compost heap which I decided was a good thing. They ate bugs and added more fertilizer.

The dogs from the neighbors on the other side were a different matter. There were two of them, both brown, scraggly Paraguayan mutts, one slightly bigger and meaner looking than the other. They looked dreadful — skinny, with matted fur, numerous sores and when the light was right I could see fleas jumping from their backs. The dogs were always roaming about and had no trouble coming into the yard any time they chose despite our fence repair efforts. One day when I had some meat bones I considered giving them to the dogs.

"Feed them and they're yours," Chuck cautioned.

And then it dawned on me, "Why not?" They weren't hurting anything, they would eat all our scraps and maybe help keep the chickens out of the yard. I started throwing out any scraps I had after lunch and dinner. At first the dogs fought and snarled over them, then I wised up and flung the food out with both hands, throwing left and right. Once they learned they were both going to get some, the fighting between them stopped. It didn't take long for them to figure out when lunch and dinner was served. In a week Chuck could set his watch by them. The dogs began spending the night in the yard too. One night, someone must have been walking down the street because we heard our shared dogs race to the fence, barking furiously. Wonderful, we had watch dogs. This actually caused a problem for us when we were out past dark one night and returned home, only to find them charging us at our own gate! We had to talk to them some time to get them to recognize it was us — the bone providers! We took to referring to them as our half-dogs, since they were only half ours, not even that really, and gave them the original names of Uno and Dos. If we went somewhere, we had no responsibilities; they could just stay with their rightful owners. I was reluctant to get too close to them though; they were dirty, God knows what diseases they might carry and besides, I wasn't positive they wouldn't bite the hand that fed them.

Besides the crafty Christmas branch, my other artsy project had been painting walls in the kitchen. But not regular one color painting — I was creating a mural. This was all the consequence of having a bottle of wine to kick off the holiday season, or start the week or finish the week, can't remember now. What I do remember is that the cork crumbled apart half-way out of the bottle. There wasn't a way to pull it out any further and it didn't want to go back in. Chuck set the bottle firmly on the table in the kitchen, held the screwdriver on top of the broken cork, took the hammer and gave it a good whomp. Whoosh! Down went the cork and up spurted red wine — all over him, the table and the wall. Wine on him wasn't a problem and wine on the table was easily wiped off the oilcloth, but wine on the wall was another matter. The walls were painted light green with a water-based paint so when I wiped off the wine, the green paint came with it, leaving white splotches. I could have easily gotten more green paint and just painted over that section of wall, but it seemed a poor choice to have water-based paint in the kitchen in the first place.

I decided to use oil-based, glossy paint that could be washed. And, if I was going to that much trouble, I might as well have some fun with it. Kitty gave me her OK, and I set to work painting a large scene of sky and hills and trees. I can't describe what fun it was — like being a kid and told that yes, you can make crayon marks on the wall. It was a forbidden pleasure. Too bad I wasn't a better artist, but my "Grandma-Moses" -style painting looked quite striking. When I finished the wall behind the table, I started on the one behind the stove, painting a blue sea and strange looking fish. The stove actually had a lid on a hinge that acted as a splatter protector, but I decided that the oil-based paint behind it would be even better. And I was having too much fun to quit.

Before Christmas we were treated to a weekend visit from John and Julia Sarreal, a young Volunteer couple who were in a group that had arrived in Paraguay before us. Fortunately they happened to be passing through Artigas. We had such fun with them and they were terrific guests, doing so much work in the kitchen it was practically a vacation for me. John was second generation Filipino and he cooked up a fabulous Filipino dish of pork stew and rice. The stew was so good I decided to make it for our Christmas dinner.

I wished we had more young couples like them in our cycle, maybe that would have resulted in more friendships, but perhaps it was a moot point since we were now so isolated from everyone. Our group did have one *new* couple though — Izzy and Beth. They had come as singles, fell in love and had recently married. For a while they hid it from the Peace Corps, not knowing how to combine their work locations or what the policy would be, but then, it all worked out.

It was a bit of a letdown after John and Julia left and I found myself wandering around the house, melancholy and aimless. Logically, I had nothing to be depressed about: Christmas plans were coming along, the house was comfortable and we were way ahead of other Volunteers in our group. But, I just wasn't challenged and definitely not busy enough. I couldn't even paint any more, as I had painted all the available walls and even the bottom of the utility sink, using up the last drops of the enamel.

I finally decided I had to get busy doing something productive so I got out our laptop and opened the program file of my book, *The First Big Ride*. I hadn't done a thing on it since arriving, and other than my sister Rita's notice that one publisher might be interested, I hadn't thought about it either. I opened it to page one and started going over it again. In a few pages I was making small changes and happy that I was working on it again. Then suddenly, the screen went black.

"Crap," I said aloud.

This had happened before and was the first sign that it was too hot for the laptop to run. I hadn't backed up the small progress I had made, so now that was lost. There was nothing to do but wait until the computer cooled down, which wouldn't happen until the room temperature cooled down. That wouldn't happen until the sun went down and then not much. It was ungodly hot.

I went to the porch where we had our little thermometer. It read forty-one degrees Celsius in the shade which translated to about 105 Fahrenheit with suffocating humidity. Back in the house I took down our calendar, deciding to count how many days were left of our tour. Too many.

That night dinner didn't go well either. Chuck baked a chicken using an "oven bag" that we had bought in Asunción, but after roasting for one and half hours — with the kitchen as hot as the oven — it still wasn't done. After another forty-five minutes Chuck lifted the chicken out of the oven, but instead of holding the pan, he just lifted it out by the bag which ripped open, spilling rice, chicken and grease all over the oven and floor. I was instantly furious especially since I had told him to hold the pan not just the bag, and I said something like, "Oh, terrific."

Chuck yelled back telling me he didn't need that! A dark cloud hung over our heads as we ate the bits of salvaged chicken and went to bed without another word. It wasn't much better the next day. At noon I apologized and tiny fragments of conversation began to filter across the table. Chuck told me he had made some kind of vow to himself, but he wouldn't divulge it. No more cooking chicken in bags? I suspected it was something more serious.

Two nights later, out on the porch, he told me.

"I'm not spending another summer here. I just can't stand the heat and I'm not doing anything useful. Hell, I'm not doing anything at all much less what I want to be doing."

"But we are doing something useful," I protested. "The typing and computer work will really help these kids."

He just shook his head. "I want to terminate next December. Twelve more months and that's it."

I could see that my rebuttals weren't going to get me anywhere, especially since I wasn't 100% convinced myself. Yes, we were doing some useful work. But could a Paraguayan now take over our work? Yes. Were we doing anything to help the business of the town or *cooperativa*? No. Did it matter? That was the question. We had long ago figured out that helping the *cooperativa* increase sales only took money out of a competing merchant down the street. As Chuck had said, it was a zero sum game, with the money just going around in circles and no one improving. What the town desperately needed was more money from the outside. Spending our salaries there was probably our best contribution. We supported a laundress, bought vegetables, newspapers, groceries, paid rent and utility bills, all with outside money.

The Peace Corps always allows any Volunteer to go home any time they want. The only difference is if you leave before your official completion-of-service date, you do not get an open ended ticket home, just direct passage, so you can't travel on your way back. And, you don't get the priority listing for government jobs once back in the States, or availability for grants or special programs for master's degrees. None of those benefits were important to us now. Back in our Afghanistan days, those benefits were important, but leaving early had never been an issue with our steady teaching jobs at the Ministry.

I decided not to fret about it. It was still a long ways off and I knew that many things could happen that might change the situation. Once again, the best course for me was to "wait to worry."

22   A Tropical Christmas

Miracle of miracles. The play went well. It was a bit of a cliff hanger when "Mary" didn't appear until minutes before the play was to start — our third "Mary" by the way. And just before our Kings were to appear from the East, we discovered one was missing. I frantically went in search for Baltazar and found him outside in a tree! I was about hysterical, when I got him down and backstage seconds before his entrance. The costumes that Julia and Anna had made were very cute, and I think that they alone would have saved the show, but all the kids got their lines straight, the songs were shouted (can't really say sung) with gusto and the parents were all delighted.

This was on the 19th of December and both Julia and Anna wanted us to put the show on again on Christmas Eve. Chuck and I were flattered, but there were no buses running that day to San Pedro, and between the heat and carrying the guitar, getting there by bike wasn't even a consideration. Julia invited us to spend the night with her, but we really wanted to be home on Christmas Eve, and in our own house on Christmas morning. She kept saying it would be "*no problemo*" to have us, but despite our explanations, she really didn't understand our whole "Christmas morning" tradition. Paraguayans don't exchange gifts and their first Christmas

167

festivity is a big mid-afternoon meal. That plus a dance at midnight completes their Christmas day. But even without the gifts I had a lot of kitchen prep to be ready for Mandy and her parents. Julia finally acquiesced, but said they might present the performance without us, even though it wouldn't be *tan bueno* without Chuck's guitar.

Christmas Eve was a whole new experience. In a Catholic country I would have expected the whole town to troop off to Mass at midnight. But instead, Christmas Eve, called *Noche Buena* was celebrated like most Paraguayan holidays with lots of firecrackers and late night goings-on. On *Noche Buena* there was the rather nice tradition of families either walking around to their neighbors to wish them a *Feliz Navidad* or sitting on their front porches and receiving the neighbors, offering cookies or a drink or usually some *cidra*. And, like their dances or other big celebrations, the festivities didn't get started until one a.m. We decided we would be among those who sat on the porch, hopefully awake, to receive people. I baked dozens of macaroon cookies, which I had discovered were a big hit, to serve with boxed wine and *cidra*.

Then came the hard part for us, staying up! All the firecrackers exploding and neighboring boom boxes playing at full volume helped. We sat out in the backyard for a while admiring the night sky, finally finding Venus which was high in the sky, and Orion's Belt which was upside down and low in the Eastern sky. But my very favorite part of star-gazing was admiring the Southern Cross, the mariner's guidepost. We couldn't actually see that from the backyard, too many bushes, but by walking to the front road we could spot it easily. Turning north, the big dipper and northern star were missing — logical when I thought about it. When our necks were breaking from looking to the sky, we returned to the house and watched an hour of some ridiculous TV program.

Finally, the clock slowly ticked its way to 11:45 p.m., and we set all of our chairs on the front porch, hoping for early arrivals. No such luck. We sat for over an hour, listening to fire-crackers and dogs and roosters, and then just after one o'clock the entire Barbosa family came by, then Roberto and his family, followed by Ramón from the *cooperativa*. By then, our refreshments had dwindled and we were chock full of good Christmas wishes, so we turned off the lights and went to bed. We didn't hear any more clapping at our gate so if anyone else came by they could have assumed that the poor *Norte Americanos* didn't understand the tradition.

We had a perfect un-Christmasy morning. Having lived in San Diego for almost twenty years, we were used to not having snow, but not quite used to sweltering heat and waking to roosters crowing. Putting those differences aside, we made our morning coffee, I heated some special packaged cakes I purchased at the *cooperativa* and we settled down for our Christmas presents. Chuck loved his belt and he had gone to the same shop for my gift — a beautiful hand-tooled leather satchel I had wanted. My sister Linda's box was full of goodies I had requested: salad mixes, spices, more seeds for the garden, audio tapes and new socks for both of us. I was happy that Rita's presents would be coming later as it would spread out the whole Christmas day. I spent the rest of the morning making bread and a pie for our Christmas dinner while Chuck did our garbage burn, now his weekly chore.

Mandy and her folks came trudging up the road mid-afternoon. Her mother, an older, plumper version of Mandy, looked exhausted. Mandy had thought about getting a ride from a neighbor, but that hadn't worked out; the buses weren't running, so she had decided they could walk. I thought that was pretty ambitious in the heat especially with backpacks and I think her Mom would have agreed. Her Dad was quite lean and while hot and sweaty, didn't seem quite as done in as her Mom. We hurried them to the back yard to sit in the shade and I brought out ice drinks and cookies. They had been with Mandy a few days and we peppered them with questions on their travel to Paraguay, impressions of the country and of Mandy's house. They seemed delighted with everything. Once they recovered from their hike we took them into the house and showed off our Hanner Hilton with its guest room, T.V. and indoor toilet. They were equally delighted with our accommodations. After they got squared away I asked about the presents from my sister, Rita. They exchanged nervous glances.

"Well," her Dad hesitated. "We can't find them."

"You lost them?" I asked anxiously.

"I was sure we had packed them, but they aren't in the luggage and we have completely torn the bags apart."

"You forgot to pack them?" I asked, getting alarmed.

"I guess so," he answered dejectedly.

I was dumbfounded, and disappointed and angry. I had so been looking forward to Rita's box and she had gone to great pains to get the box to them — calling them, making sure the presents were light and small, and at their home in plenty of time, leaving them unwrapped at one end in case there was a customs issue. I knew she would be furious.

"But we brought you some goodies," her Dad said. "We thought that might help to make up for it." With that he dug out a sack full of cookies and Tootsie Rolls and nice marker pens — items I was sure had been meant for Mandy.

I tried to be gracious, but I was struggling. I went to the kitchen and busied myself, trying to get a grip. I knew the gifts were just small things anyway, hardly important and I knew that Mandy's parents didn't travel much, this might have been their first inter-national trip ever. They had probably packed with such excitement it was a wonder they remembered their own passports. I knew my reaction was totally unreasonable, but I still simmered. I reminded myself of the words of Mike Aylward, our old USAID friend from Afghanistan. "Intellectual understanding does not always mean emotional acceptance." By this time Mandy was in the kitchen, her usual bubbling self, helping me with whatever she could and I did my best to forget about the missing gifts. Chuck was upset, seeing me disappointed, so I pulled him aside and told him it was OK, it was no big deal. It WAS a big deal and he knew it, but we let it go.

The dinner was as good as I had hoped with fresh bread, salad, with cucumbers and green peppers from our own garden, and the pork stew and pie. Truly worthy of a Christmas dinner. We had promised Roberto we would attend the big Christmas dance at midnight, and Mandy and her parents were going to watch videos they had brought from the States. They were more than pleased to be left behind given that the dance didn't get underway until after midnight.

We would have preferred to stay home as well, but Roberto had been insistent: "*El mejor y mas grande fesitival del año. Tengan que venir!* [The best and biggest celebration of the year. You have to come!]"

So at 11:30 p.m. we unenthusiastically scrounged through our big duffel, found our better looking clothes, and put them on and felt decidedly out of place. We bid our guests goodnight and walked down to the main plaza.

Roberto was right about one thing — the entire town was there. We sat with him and his family, sipped the boxed wine we had brought and waited for the dancing. About 12:30 the band started warming up and by1:00 a.m. they were underway at a deafening volume. It ended all table conversation and we just smiled at everyone and managed to dance a couple of times. Even in the middle of the night though, it was too hot for dancing and we were sweating profusely when we returned to our table after the second dance. At 1:30 we begged off and went home. Not for a quiet night though. With our windows open the band might as well have been next door, the heavy bass practically shaking the dishes. I peeked in the open door to our guest room and saw that despite the racket and the heat, Mandy's folks were fast asleep. Mandy was on top of her sleeping bag on the floor sleepily watching the rest of *The Endless Summer*, an old surfing movie. Between the heat and the noise I tossed fitfully until about 4:00 a.m. when the band finally stopped.

After a late breakfast, our guests set off. My irritation over the gifts had subsided and now, as they headed out, I felt a little sorry for them. Mandy's Mom still looked tired.

We had the rest of the day to ourselves. I spent the day tidying the house, weeding the garden, and organizing for a trip to Asunción via pre-dawn *Fletcha* the next morning.

In early December we had received a special notice that the Peace Corps was having a session for all Volunteers during the week between Christmas and New Year's. Apparently everyone was in a state about the Y2K phenomenon and possible computer crash as the electronic digits advanced from 999 to 000 for the new millennium. I had read countess articles about it, mostly echoing concerns from the States that all the banks would go haywire, the elevators wouldn't open and the whole world would be plunged into darkness. We had started hearing about it years before while still working at Merrill, where computer records might have been reason for concern. But here? It made us laugh and Mandy thought it was particularly funny since she had no electricity at all. We weren't sure what was supposed to break down in our little rural hideaway. Nothing depended on computers and most other modern systems were already malfunctioning. In fact, I couldn't think of any place on earth that would be less affected than Artigas. But, assuming the roads weren't a river of mud and the buses were running, we planned to traipse to Asunción and prepare for the dangers. There were also had additional items on the agenda, including a discussion of an outbreak of dengue fever in the capital, so we couldn't quite justify not going.

As we organized for our trip to Asunción we packed long sleeved shirts, despite the heat, to protect ourselves from dengue-carrying mosquitoes. We already wore long pants as the Peace Corps didn't allow Volunteers to wear shorts in the city or at the Peace Corps office. It wasn't a problem for me, since women never wore shorts, and I didn't want to wear them in any case, but some of the guys griped about it. The newspaper reported some 15,000 cases of dengue so far, but it seemed to be concentrated in wetter parts of the city or in areas where there was garbage filled with rain water. So far, only two Volunteers had come down with the fever and they were both stationed in the city.

The first lecture at the meetings addressed our concerns about the disease. Dr. Avilia told us that the dengue mosquito comes out only at dawn and at dusk so we had to be covered or inside at that time. And of course, if we came down with fever and chills, we should see him immediately, or in our case, as immediately as we could being that we were seven hours away.

The next issue on the agenda dealt with where and what we should do if there was an emergency — for example, a military coup. Chuck and I would be notified through our contact in the *cooperativa*, Ramón, should such an event happened. And we were not go to Asunción, but to Encarnación, where all the Volunteers in our area would meet. From there the group would be sent to Argentina. A coup wasn't of much concern despite the continual strikes and rantings in the newspaper. According to the State Department, Paraguay was relatively stable and was expected to continue shuffling along indefinitely with their corruption and inept government.

The Peace Corps director finally did get around to talking about the Y2K, but he felt that the main issue might be problems with cash machines so we Volunteers were advised to have cash on hand.

Following the meeting we put in official requests for a vacation in January and were told it would be fine, just fill out the forms. After much deliberation, we had decided to fly to La Paz, Bolivia and then maybe take the train to Peru, depending on how much we could fit into our ten days. The biggest attraction in going north was that it would be cooler, and apparently, given the altitude of La Paz, it was always cool there.

We then went to one of the big malls, bought our airline tickets, spent an hour sending emails, then moved on to one of the large supermarkets to buy goodies and wine for our New Year's Eve celebration. John, our Volunteer friend in municipal services, was going to come back with us to experience Artigas's New Year's celebration. Roberto had promised big fireworks, loud music and more dancing.

The three of us walked to Roberto's about 11:00 p.m. with two bottles of real wine. Roberto's family seemed in high spirits with his two children chasing a new puppy and his shy wife, Maria, setting out small dishes of snacks. Kitty, our landlady was there along with another neighbor and various children. Roberto had brought out his small TV tuned to the local station which would do a countdown to midnight. We all joked about what would happen then — invasion of the body snatchers or just the TV shutting down? Roberto had wanted to have champagne so that at the stroke of midnight he could pop the cork. But, with no champagne to be had, he had his bottle of *sidra* with his hand on the cap.

"*Cuatro, Tres, Dos, Uno! Feliz Nueve Año!*" we all shouted and Roberto threw the bottle cap in the air. The children set off their small sizzling firecrackers while Roberto poured the *sidra* and we all toasted to the new year. I looked around to see if all appeared the same. It did. The TV still worked, the lights were still on and other than the explosions of neighbor's firecrackers and shouts, the night continued on as before.

About 1:00 a.m. Roberto said we should walk down and at least see the dance, but John decided to stay back and visit with Kitty. I couldn't tell if he really wanted to visit with her or just really didn't want to go to the dance. What Chuck and I really wanted to do was go home and go to bed, but we dutifully followed Roberto, then hung around the dance for an hour. Finally, we begged off, went home and tried to sleep through the deafening music.

John was not at the house when we had returned so we quizzed him in the morning about his "date," but he wouldn't comment other than to say Kitty was nice, which we took to mean it was not the beginning of a hot relationship. I don't think he had any inclination to start a relationship with a Paraguayan woman — which was generally the exact opposite of what the women wanted. For some, it was the American passport, for younger women, it was often the lighter skin. One Volunteer had told us that a grandmother offered to pay him to sleep with her granddaughter so they could have "lighter" children. With worldwide marketing they saw "white" as beautiful and everything else as second-class.

John headed home at noon, which was in the next province of Misiones. His town was located on the *ruta* so once he got off the twenty mile dirt road from Artigas, it was an easy ride. He still hadn't made any progress getting to work in the municipality, but had found a couple of women trying to start a library and had decided to concentrate his efforts there. It was at least keeping him busy. We spent the rest of the afternoon getting squared away for our departure the next morning. We would take the bus to Asunción, spend the night and then fly to Bolivia, for our big — and Peace Corps sanctioned — vacation.

23 Bolivian Misadventure

The vacation didn't start well.

At 5:00 a.m., when I put on my good khaki slacks they were uncomfortably tight and I had no other ones to wear. It was obvious I had been overdoing it with Brazilian cookies and Mennonite ice cream.

"We're going to walk a lot on this vacation," I told Chuck, struggling with the zipper.

Instead of waiting at Chacho's, the main bus stop, we decided to go up the road a few blocks in hopes of getting a better seat. Since the first of December, the buses had been packed as many Paraguayans were traveling to stay with relatives for the holidays. The extra walk was worthless. When the *Fletcha* stopped, it was already crammed with passengers, forcing us to stand for the first hour until we got on the bigger, slicker bus in Bogado. The air conditioning on that bus had broken so we were sweating and sticky, but at least we were sitting. We got off at the Multiplaza in Asunción to use the cash machine and the email, only to find both of them closed. We then proceeded to our beloved Hotel Paraguay, got our room and decided to take a nap before setting out again for the cash and email. We lay sweating under the fan until it finally dawned on us that the air conditioning wasn't working at all. We went back to the desk and they were most gracious about it, moving us to another room immediately. About four o'clock, with the sun less intense, we ventured out and finally met with success — emails, a working cash machine and dinner at a Mexican restaurant. The food wasn't Mexican as we knew it, but it had a different taste from our normal fare, the ambiance was cool and inviting and the wine was perfect.

I had made reservations at an inexpensive, family-run hotel in La Paz that looked more interesting than the big chain hotels. I had wanted local color and it even had advertised a shuttle to pick us up. Advertised or not, when we landed I was still surprised and pleased to see a fellow outside of customs holding a sign that read HANNER. Our luck seemed to be turning.

The first and best thing we noticed was the drop in temperature. It felt like the mid-sixties and we happily buttoned our jackets. The city was shaped like a bowl, with the airport on the top edge and the main city cradled in the bottom. As we drove down the switch-backs, it became slightly warmer and seemed less windy. And the architecture became grander, with nice looking houses and fancy landscaping. Even at the bowl's base though, the altitude was 11,900 feet and we had been warned to watch out for altitude sickness. "Don't drink too much," a Volunteer had told us, "or you'll have a headache like you can't believe. And take some of the cocoa tea they offer—it helps."

Our hotel was in the city center so straightaway we went out to explore. It was quite different from Asunción, with more modern buildings and wide sidewalks full of vendors and kiosks. Short Indian women hustled by in full bright skirts, with shawls over their shoulders fastened with large jewelry pins. To a one, they all wore black, felt, bowler hats on their heads and had long black braids hanging down their backs. I recalled having seen pictures of these women and the hats and wondered how the hats got to be so fashionable. It was fun to see native people instead of the bland mix in Paraguay where all true native Paraguayans had long ago disappeared.

We stopped for dinner at a small restaurant on a side street that didn't look as touristy as the others. In fact, it didn't look like anybody had discovered it as we were the only patrons. The waiter assured us that yes, it was open and I decided we must just be early, even thought it was already 7:00 o'clock.

"Maybe this is like Spain," I told Chuck, where dinner doesn't even get going until 10:00.

We were seated at a small corner table and the waiter brought us fresh hot bread while we studied the menu.

"Look Chuck," I said, "They've got fish."

"You remember the rule about fish?"

He was referring to our never-eat-fish-if-you-are-in-a-developing-country-not-directly-on-the-beach rule. It had started in Afghanistan, where they had warned us about fish in the high lakes, which looked clear and good, but were infected with a worm that once ingested, would grow to some thirty feet. And to reinforce the point, they had shown us one — preserved in formaldehyde, coiled around and around in a giant jar, making the jar appear solid white.

"This is what you'll get if you eat fish in Afghanistan," we were told.

We had all approached the jar to see just how gross the worm was and all simultaneously concluded that fish were not going to be a menu item. Of course there had never been a temptation to have them anyway because when they were available in the bazaar, they were already rotting and the stench carried for a block. So far in Paraguay I hadn't seen any fish available, but I reasoned La Paz was reasonably close to the ocean, a truck could deliver fish in one day.

"Different country, different fish," I proclaimed optimistically, but asked the waiter how fresh they were, just in case.

He told us that these fish were the best in Bolivia, caught yesterday, trucked in this morning.

"*Muy muy bueno*," he assured me.

"*Pescado para mi*," I told him confidently, while Chuck shot me the you'll-be-sorry look. He went for the ubiquitous grilled chicken.

When our plates arrived though, I looked longingly at his and decided he had made the better choice. His chicken was golden and glistened in a rich brown glaze and smelled of rosemary. My fish was distressingly pale, despite colorful attempts to garnish with canned peas, which were sprinkled liberally around the edges. There was no smell whatsoever. I took a few bites and while it wasn't bad, it wasn't good and the texture was mushy.

"I think this fish needed to swim harder," I said. But after a glass of wine I didn't care.

Our first project for the next morning was to find a new hotel. My "local color" cheapie wasn't so much local color as it was just a dump. The shower water had been tepid to cold, the toilet wouldn't flush and the double bed was an impossible sagging affair with springs that poked us all night long. In the morning we discovered the door knob didn't exactly open the door and it was only with careful jiggling that we were able to get out of there at all. I had only made a reservation for one night, not sure of our plans or if we might discover a cuter or quainter place. After a sleepless night, Chuck didn't want anything to do with cuter or quainter. We had noticed a very fancy high rise hotel just down the way on our walk the day before and Chuck decided that was the place.

"Look, it's our vacation. Let's stay in a really nice hotel."

So we did. Our room was on the ninth floor with a gorgeous view of the city, a bathroom to die for and a huge luxurious king-sized bed. Chuck refused to tell me what it cost, and I didn't care. I could hardly wait to come back in the evening.

We took a walk to the witches' market, an area up some steep side hills that featured old women selling amulets, herbs and god-knows-what to gullible tourists. I bought a tiny wooden Aztec statue and two tinier turtles that insured good health.

Right after we left the stand, I got a stomach cramp. I wondered briefly if they were bad-health turtles and the witchy vendor had sold me the cursed ones. But I was confident that if I walked around more the cramps would disappear, so I took a few deep breaths and kept walking. The cramps seemed to get worse. I finally confessed to Chuck I wasn't feeling well and just needed to sit down. We found a bench and I sat down, bent over and held my head in my hands. Chuck resisted saying, "I told you so," about the fish. I knew that once it was through my system, I'd be OK. But that wasn't going to happen quickly. As I sat there the cramping got worse and I felt nauseated too.

"It's no good," I confessed to Chuck. "I've got to go lie down. I'm sure I'll be alright in a bit." I was uplifted by the thought of returning to our upgraded hotel, but once there I felt so awful I couldn't even enjoy the big, comfortable bed.

"I think I have fish poisoning," I groaned to Chuck. "Can you die from that?"

We both thought no, but after an hour of me twisting and moaning in the bed, Chuck decided he would go in search of a pharmacy and find something.

"Surely, they will have something for stomach cramps or Pepto Bismol or something."

I waved him off, too nauseated to care. In an hour he was back, sweating, frustrated and empty-handed.

"Wouldn't you know it, everything and I mean everything, is closed from noon to 2:00."

I groaned weakly, never remembering feeling this bad with any of the rotten food I had eaten in Afghanistan.

"Maybe I should see a doctor. A hotel doctor maybe?"

"Wait," he said, brightening. "This is a Peace Corps country. I'll call them, maybe they can give us something."

He found the number in the directory and gave them a call. In a few minutes he was describing my symptoms to the American nurse on staff.

Yes, she was sure they might have something for me, but insisted that we both come by taxi as she wanted to check me out.

I didn't want to leave the bed, but I did, and we were there in twenty minutes.

The nurse was the only one in the office. Everyone else was off at some kind of conference. She listened patiently to my story of the previous night's fish dish and nodded sympathetically.

"Well," she said, "I'll give you a pill, but I want you to stay here and see how it goes for an hour or two."

Still feeling miserable, that was fine with me. I felt badly for Chuck just having to sit around, but he said he was OK, and would just read magazines. Two hours later nothing had changed. The pill, as far as I could tell, hadn't done anything and I felt like I had a major case of the flu coupled with cramps from hell. I was sure if whatever it was would just get through my system, I would be fine, but there was no action from my system in either direction. I squirmed around on the bed in every possible position trying to find relief and finally just lay on my back with my arms around my knees and rocked back and forth. The afternoon was interminable. Chuck paced the hall, read Spanish magazines and chatted with the nurse who appeared every half hour to check on my progress or lack thereof. Every time I told her that I hadn't left the bed, she seemed less pleased and at five o'clock she announced that I needed to go to the local clinic.

"Our doctor won't be here until much later and I want you to be checked out. It's just up the street, but we'll drive you."

"Is it really necessary? I'm sure that once it goes through my system. . .."

The nurse waved her hand, dismissing my protest. I asked her if another pill might be an easier solution and I got a firm negative. I felt she was really making a mountain out of a mole-hill, but there didn't seem to be any alternatives. I rolled off the bed, put on my tennis shoes and went with Chuck out to the car.

The clinic was close and they were expecting me. There was no paper work and they sent me immediately to an exam room and let Chuck come too. In minutes a youngish, thin man in a white lab coat came to the door.

"Señora Hanner?"

He waited for my response then entered and introduced himself as Dr. Cortez. He shook Chuck's hand, patted mine, and proceeded to poke and prod my stomach and listen to it with a stethoscope.

"Señora," he said kindly. "*Creo que necesitamos una radiographía de la abdomen.* [I think we need an x-ray of your abdomen.]"

It gave me a start. An x-ray? I didn't need an x-ray. I had food poisoning. I protested, thinking he hadn't heard about my fish dinner and repeated my story.

"*Pescado malo,*" I emphasized. "*Lo necescita ir a través de la sistema.* [It needs to go through my system.]"

I wasn't sure if he understood my Spanish so I made exaggerated sweeping motions with my hand, waving it from my throat to my abdomen. He listened very politely without interruption, then asked me again if I would, *por favor*, follow him down the hall for an x-ray. I sighed, then meekly obeyed, padding after him in my socks to the room marked *Radiographia*. It looked exactly like an x-ray room in the States, with a flat, padded table and a hulking x-ray machine pushed over to one side. I changed into the gown in the dressing cubicle and used the little stool to crawl up and lay down. He pulled on the machine until he was satisfied with the exact position then disappeared until I heard the customary buzz. He came back to my side.

"*Gracias, Senora Hanner,*" he thanked me. "*Usted puede regresar a su cuarto.* [You can return to your room.]"

I put my clothes back on and returned to my room, feeling the worse for the trip and thinking how unnecessary it all was. Probably costing a fortune, too. It was an hour before we saw him again, but this time he was accompanied by a large, portly doctor with curly, grey hair.

"Señora Hanner, Señor Hanner," he nodded in Chuck's direction, "*quisiera presentarles a Dr. Metterkofler, especialista digestiva.*"

I threw Chuck a worried look. Digestive specialist? I am poisoned, for sure, I thought. Doctor Metterkofler smiled, shook Chuck's hand then looked at me with clear blue eyes as he pressed his fingers all around my stomach. He listened with his stethoscope in various spots, then carefully took the earpieces out of his ears and folded the stethoscope into a large pocket on the side of his white smock. He sat down on the edge of my bed.

"Mrs. Hanner," he said in a perfect American accent. "Would you prefer I speak in English?"

"You speak English?" I asked, not believing my own ears.

"Pretty well, I think," and he laughed seeing my relief. "I grew up here as a boy, but left to go to college in the States. I went to medical school in Houston, Texas and did my intern work in Boston." He gave me a reassuring smile. "In fact I just got back from a clinic in Austin." He proceeded with easy chit-chat about Texas, and I tried to hide my growing anxiety. I related my fish dinner story once again.

"Do you think that's the problem?" I asked, trying to sound studious rather than worried.

"Well, we can't say what caused the problem, but you do have one. He paused and turned to Dr. Cortez who gave him a large white envelope. He pulled out a large, square x-ray and held it towards the light of the windows where I could see it. He looked at me gravely.

"See this?" he asked.

I could make out the images of a stomach and intestines, but the bottom part of the intestines were completely black, like someone had inked them in. Even to the unpracticed eye, it didn't look good; I suddenly felt afraid.

"This shows," Dr. Metterkofler continued, tapping his pencil against the black cloud, "that you have a total intestinal blockage, probably caused by a twist in the intestines."

My heart stopped. A twist? A total blockage? I was so stunned I couldn't speak. I swallowed and tried to comprehend what I had just heard.

My mind raced but I couldn't even think of an intelligent response. I finally asked weakly, "What causes that?"

He shook his head. "We don't know."

"Does it go away?" I asked in an even smaller voice.

"I wish it did, but it doesn't. I'm afraid you're going to need surgery as soon as we can set it up."

Surgery?! I couldn't believe what I was hearing. I threw a frantic glance at Chuck, my heart was banging against my ribs. I took a deep breath, trying to calm myself and suddenly I realized that the cramps were gone.

"Doctor," I said incredulously, "I'm not just saying this, but right now I feel really good." I lay perfectly still for a moment, just to be sure. "Great in fact!" I affirmed. "Amazing, really, the cramps are gone!" I wasn't lying or delusional; suddenly they were gone. I pulled myself up against the pillows and smiled hopefully.

"Yes, I know." Dr. Metterkofler said. "It's what happens. I just listened to your intestines and they are totally quiet, not a sound. This means that yes, you feel better. But the reason you do is because your intestines have stopped working altogether. They have been pushing against this block all day, which caused the cramps, but now they have given up, shut down."

I stared at him, unbelieving, still not wanting to comprehend that there was anything really the matter with me. I was desperate for an alternative solution.

"So if I didn't have surgery, what would happen?" I questioned, hoping for a better answer.

The doctor looked sympathetic.

"You'd feel fine for a day, until pressure finally made them burst. Then you'd be facing the risk of peritonitis and would need surgery immediately, or…"

"Doctor," Chuck interrupted anxiously. "Can't the Peace Corps send us back to the States? I could pay for the flights."

"We'll be consulting with the Peace Corps," Dr. Metterkofler assured us, "both the local doctor, who will be here shortly and Peace Corps medical back in Washington, but the problem we have here requires immediate surgery. The fastest you could get back to the States, given that the next flight out of here isn't until tomorrow morning, would be at least twenty-four hours. That's too late. You can't run the chance of having the intestines rupture. That is something we don't want to happen."

Chuck and I looked at each other in alarm.

Dr. Metterkofler looked down at his watch.

"I need to check on a few other patients. I'll be back later this evening to discuss the matter with Dr. Nelson, who will be back by then."

He gave us a small smile and left.

Chuck sat down on the edge of the bed and took my hand.

"It will be OK. Everything will work out."

He got up, paced the room nervously, then returned and sat down on the bed again.

"Everything will work out," he repeated, "it will be fine."

But neither of us was convinced.

24 Don't Worry

The Peace Corps doctor was a robust looking American, full of good cheer. He looked at the x-ray, listened to my silent intestines and read the chart that was hanging at the foot of my bed. I nervously rattled off my whole story and what the good German Doctor had reported.

"I'm sorry to say, he's absolutely right," he said sincerely. "You can't go anywhere. Right now you can have this surgery, they can straighten things out and you'll be fine."

"But surgery . . . here?" Chuck protested.

"Here happens to be a great place, but that's academic. This has to be taken care of in the next 24 hours. We can wait until morning though, which will give us time to call Peace Corps in Washington D.C. for final approval. They have to give the go-ahead to do surgery in-country. Obviously, they like to get Volunteers back to D.C. . . . when there is time."

I must have looked stricken.

"Don't worry, now," he said, trying to reassure me. "This is the private clinic where we send all Americans. We've had lots of surgeries, from appendectomies to cesareans, and the care is outstanding. Dr. Metterkofler has an excellent reputation and believes in doing the least amount of surgery possible. Quite frankly, you couldn't be in a better place or with a better doctor."

Chuck relaxed his death grip on my hand, and I felt a little better.

Dr. Metterkofler came back in, and the two doctors agreed on a time for the surgery. Finally, it was just Chuck and me. Chuck paced the room, crossing from my bed to the window, to the chair in the corner and back again.

"Should I call one of your sisters?" he asked, coming back around to the bed, looking more concerned than ever.

"No. They'll just worry and there is nothing they can do. And besides, I'll be out of this in a few days."

I wasn't even remotely sure of that but I tried to sound convincing. I didn't think having them worry about me would help anything. Chuck nodded glumly and finally sat down in the chair and stayed there until a nurse kindly suggested that maybe he should go back to the hotel and get some rest. He didn't want to leave, but there was nothing he could do sitting there all night.

"At least we've got a nice place for you to stay," I said.

He tried for a weak smile, then gave me a quick kiss and said he'd be back first thing in the morning. As soon as he left a nurse came in and gave me a shot *"para relajarse* [to relax]," she said.

I hoped it would take effect immediately, but it didn't. I stared at the ceiling and wondered how in the hell all this had come about. Was it something I ate before the fish? A birth defect? How could I, Miss Healthy, be lying in a clinic awaiting surgery in Bolivia? I still tried to convince myself that it was no big deal, but the facts were glaringly opposite. It was very quiet now and the lights in the hallway were turned down. I listened to the clock ticking and looked around the room in the semi-darkness. I closed my eyes and tried to envision something soothing and came up with a wooded scene, something from my childhood in Idaho.

Suddenly, I heard heavy footsteps. They came down the hall and stopped at my door. I looked over, and saw Dr. Metterkofler in the doorway.

"You have nothing to worry about," he said. He came to the

bed and through the covers, gave my toes a friendly shake. "You will be fine, just fine." Then he smiled and left.

This unexpected gesture brought tears to my eyes. I blinked them away, closed my eyes and did feel more relaxed. Any doctor who would take the time to come back and reassure me had to be one that took good care of his patients. I drifted off to sleep.

I was awakened about 6 a.m. having slept like a log. Nothing had changed with my intestines. The Peace Corps doctor came in and wanted to know if it was OK for Peace Corps in Washington to give my medical information to James Tinsley. I blinked. James Tinsley was my brother-in-law. He and Rita lived in D.C. Somehow they knew I was here.

"Yes, yes," I told the doctor, "and tell him too that I'm fine, not to worry."

When Chuck arrived, he sheepishly admitted that he had called them, but they weren't home and he had left a message. Chuck looked so miserable I couldn't be upset. He had bags under his eyes, rumpled hair and was wearing the same stained T-shirt from the day before. I wondered if he had slept at all. He hovered near me while they stuck needles in my arm and I found I was slowly losing interest in the whole process. As they started to wheel me away, he managed a last squeeze to my hand, then waved and gave me the thumbs up signal. A nurse rolled me through a set of double doors, stopped, then went through another set and stopped. I stared up at the ceiling. There were two long fluorescent tubes above me; one of them was out. Just swell, I thought. Surgery in the dark. I decided this was particularly funny and laughed out loud. Then I was rolling again through more doors. Now I looked up and saw the bright circle of lights, just like on the medical TV shows. This is better, I thought, and was asleep.

In a surgery instant I awoke in a dim room full of blinking machines and noted my left arm was tied down with an IV and there was a little plastic cap over one of my fingers. I put my free hand to my face and felt a thin tube leading to my nose. Oxygen, I guessed. A nurse was sitting in a chair nearby, there was a clock on the wall — I was obviously still alive. Relieved, I closed my eyes and went back to sleep.

The next time I awoke, Dr. Metterkofler and Chuck were at the foot of the bed.

"Hello sleepyhead," Dr. Metterkofler said. "How are you feeling?" He came around to my side, looked in my eyes then held my wrist and took my pulse. "Very good, very good," he muttered, and jotted the numbers down on my chart. He hung it at the end of the bed then came to my side and picked up my hand, holding it gently between his.

"I was just telling Chuck that you are going to be fine. The surgery went beautifully. Your intestines had formed a twist and had completely blocked your system. Fortunately there was little tissue damage and we were able to straighten out the twisted part without having to cut away any sections. They might have done that in the States, which would have complicated matters for you, but I didn't think you needed it. I stitched up that section so it won't be twisting again. Oh, and I took out your appendix while we were in there. We banged it around a bit and wouldn't want it to flare up now." He put my hand down and patted it once more. "Well, must make some other rounds. I'll be back to check on you in the morning."

Chuck thanked him profusely, then approached the bed and tenderly brushed my hair back. He kissed me on the forehead. I didn't know how I looked, but Chuck looked very tired. I wasn't sure that he hadn't gotten the worse end of the deal.

Later that afternoon I was moved back into my own room. Nurses checked on me hourly, coming into my room wearing their starched white uniforms, white nurses caps, which I hadn't seen in years, and blue sweaters. When they weren't available, they sent nurse's assistants, dressed in opposite uniforms of blue dresses, blue caps with white sweaters. I had a little bell to ring if I needed anything, but they popped in so often it was unnecessary. They would fluff my pillows, or brush my hair or do any tiny thing they thought might make me more comfortable. Before they would leave the room, they would stop at the foot of my bed and ask me, "*Con su permiso?* [With your permission?]" They wanted my permission to leave? Between their attentions and whatever was dripping into my arm, I felt like the Queen of Sheeba. I loved the clinic.

The next morning Chuck helped me get up and start my exercise walks, holding up my IV as we walked the length of the hall and back. I accidentally jerked out the IV when I got back in bed and rang the little bell. You would have thought a general alarm had sounded. Two nurses came rushing in, panic on their faces. The nurse couldn't seem to stick it back where it belonged and finally decided that her needle was too big. She sent the nurse assistant scurrying off to the supply room to find a thinner one while she patted my hand and asked about my family.

By the fourth day the tubes were all gone and my appetite was back. I was served a real breakfast of eggs and toast, which I devoured while I picked through articles of the newspaper. Dr. Metterkofler came in about ten o'clock and after a few pokes and prods announced that I was doing splendidly and that I could leave the next day, but I had to see him again in ten days.

Ten days! I wondered what the hotel bill would come to since I knew Chuck wouldn't want to move off to cheaper accommodations. But I needn't have worried. Shortly afterward I got a visit from the director of the Peace Corps in Bolivia. Her name was Meredith Smith and she already seemed to know everything about me and my operation. Apparently she had been on the phone with our Peace Corps Director in Paraguay. She also knew that we needed to stay an additional two weeks in La Paz.

"I insist that you come and stay with me," she told us. "I've got a big house, mostly empty since I'm single and I'd love to have you. And, it's just up the hill from here."

We weren't about to argue, so after a perfunctory, "Are you sure it won't be a bother," it was settled.

By mid-morning the next day Chuck already had the backpacks

at Director Smith's house and had planned to come back for me in a taxi. I decided to walk instead. I had been traipsing up and down the halls and even climbing slowly up and down the stairs, so I figured I could muster a few blocks. Chuck and I walked slowly up the hill to her place, a large, attractive house enclosed in a compound. She had a big dog and a niece visiting, but there was still room for all. I kept my distance from the dog though, as he liked to jump up on anyone walking by. That was the last thing I wanted with a belly full of stitches.

25   The Bermuda Triangle of Health

My sister Rita and her husband Jim were coming!
The morning after Chuck's hysterical phone call, Jim had gone directly to the Peace Corps office to find out for himself what was happening. That was when I passed on the information that "I was fine." Chuck had emailed them right after my surgery to confirm I really was fine; they didn't need to worry. They decided to come down anyway. Although I didn't need anybody at that point, it thrilled me to have them coming.

We both met them at the airport and had a wonderful reunion. The first couple of days went smoothly as we meandered through the tourist spots in La Paz, with me resting and sitting as needed. I was managing pretty well although sometimes I felt nauseated or extremely tired. But our troubles didn't really begin until we met them at their hotel on the third day.

Rita informed us that Jim was not doing too well.
"He had a terrible night and has a fever."
We looked over at him. He was sitting on the edge of the bed, fully dressed and ready to go, but he looked feverish and he was

mumbling, almost incoherently.

"I'm thinking we should call the hotel doctor," I said.

Rita and Chuck agreed and Jim just stared at us with glassy eyes. In about a half an hour the doctor knocked at our door. He didn't inspire confidence. He was small and thin with a pinched face and looked in ill health himself. His hair was greasy, his suit shiny and his shoes were scuffed — the picture of a traveling salesman who had seen better days. He took a stethoscope out of a battered bag, listened to Jim's heart and lungs, took his temperature and did all the regular thumping around his back.

He folded his stethoscope back into his bag and announced, *"Tiene pulmonia. Tiene que ir al hospital immediamente!"*

Pneumonia? Hospital? The three of us looked at each other and then at him and of course asked if he wouldn't just be OK with antibiotics. We got the lecture on high altitude pneumonia, or as he termed it, high altitude pulmonary edema, which apparently affects more than one visitor to La Paz. It boiled down to the fact that it could be very serious and we needed to get him to a hospital right away. Or actually a clinic like the one I had been in. This doctor's affiliation was not with the clinic I had been in, but another that he assured us was just as good, so we loaded Jim into a taxi and headed off. While we still didn't have the utmost confidence in the shabby little doctor, Jim did look awful and by this time was completely delirious. After a couple of hours it was confirmed by a second doctor that both lungs were affected and that Jim needed all sorts of antibiotics and a breathing tent. Since altitude was one of the problems I had asked if we couldn't take him somewhere lower.

"No, no," a nurse told us, *"El camino abajo es muy malo, peligroso. Se llama el camino de muerte.* [The road down is very bad, dangerous. It's called the road of death.]"

"The road of death!" Rita repeated and then decided that maybe the oxygen tent was a better option.

We found out later that the nurse wasn't kidding. Meredith confirmed that the road was a twisting, plummeting, no-guard-rail disaster, made worse by trucks and cars with bald tires or faulty brakes. The month before eight Israeli tourists had died when their jeep had skidded off the edge. And, once we got to the bottom, if we got there, she wasn't sure that the medical facility was any good.

We stayed close to the clinic for the next forty-eight hours until Jim was declared out of danger. At that point he felt pretty good and was joking with the nurses, reading magazines and wishing to be released. But the clinic doctor was insistent that he couldn't go until his lungs were perfectly clear and that it would be at least ten days.

Ten days! Ten more days! Was this a cosmic plot to keep us in Bolivia forever? Rita and Jim had planned to be home and back to work in five. We emailed Linda to contact his employers and his family. Linda sent an email back announcing all was taken care of, but should she come down to help?

"NO!" Rita and I both shouted when we read the letter.

"Whatever you do, DON'T COME HERE!" we emailed, "this place is the Bermuda Triangle of health."

Meanwhile I was getting stronger every day and wanted to see a little something of Bolivia besides La Paz. Jim assured Rita that he was perfectly fine and didn't need to have us hovering about so we decided to take a day's trip to Lake Titicaca, spend the night in Cocacabana, then return.

We found the central bus station where Mimi (the director's nickname, which we were now using) said we could catch a mini bus as they left on the hour. We got our tickets and seats and then noticed the driver kept taking money from people when there were no seats left.

It was going to be some packed ride I thought, until a well dressed Bolivian next to us stood up and demanded that the driver only allow the number of passengers for the number of seats. The driver tried to ignore him, but he persisted, announcing that he was a lawyer, he knew the laws and that the driver WOULD take the extra passengers off or he would be losing his license. When he sat down he turned to us and explained that Bolivians had to insist on the law — it was the only way to get the country on the right track. I almost felt sorry as an old lady and her son were forced off and their luggage thrown off the top of the bus, but on the other hand, I certainly didn't want to be the one smashed in my seat for the four hour plus trip. Rita and I whispered that we had lucked out — traveling with the Ralph Nader of Bolivia.

The scenery across the high Altiplano of the Bolivian Andes was green, grey and windswept and had an other-worldliness to it, made even more so by a rolling fog. Occasionally we would glimpse a few huts or a Bolivian Indian woman, with her long black braid down her back, walking along or a boy high up on a hill herding sheep. I felt like I was really in *National Geographic's* Bolivia. By the time we arrived at the lake, the clouds were building and we had little time to walk around the town of Cocacabana before large drops splattered on the cobblestones. We turned back to the hotel as the drops melded into a curtain of pouring rain that showed no signs of letting up.

By six o'clock it was still pouring and the one recommended restaurant in town was about five blocks away. I still wasn't in shape for running, but I hurried along, trying not to slow down Chuck and Rita. We arrived soaked, trailing water everywhere we stepped, but it didn't matter much as the place was rustic, with wooden plank floors and walls like an old western lodge. The waiter brought us a towel and we sat at one of the rough tables and studied the all-vegetarian menu. We didn't care and it wouldn't have mattered if we had — there was no chance of strolling about looking for better options. We all had varieties of bean soups and brown muffins and hoped the rain would let up, which it didn't.

By the next morning the weather had cleared, so we put on our damp clothes (the night on the radiator had only helped a little), and set out to explore the small town, the church and the shores of the famous Lake Titicaca. We had heard the old joke: The Titi part belonged to Bolivia and the Caca part was Peru's. I'm sure the joke would have been the exact opposite had we been staying on the Peruvian side.

There was a boat that would take tourists out to the islands, but the water was choppy and I was reluctant to subject my stitches to that much pounding. Instead, Rita and I picked up samples of fabulously marked rocks on the beach. They were smooth from eons of wave pounding and had unique markings, lines and circles and various patterns that looked like ancient imprints of fossils. Our sack was so full and heavy by the end of our walk that even we, dedicated rock lovers, had to jettison some of them.

Two days later my stitches were removed and I was declared fit to go home. Our vacation was long over, my medical leave was over and we needed to get back to Paraguay. Rita and Jim both assured us there was no reason for us to sit there five more days waiting for Jim's release.

"Well this is a fine turn of events," I told Jim. "You come to make sure I'm OK and now I'm leaving you in your hospital bed!"

Jim just laughed. "I'm fine really. Can't say why I even have to be in here for five more days."

He did seem to be well and Rita repeated the fact that it was just ridiculous for us to sit around for practically another week, but I still hated to leave them and cried most of the way to the airport.

26   House Challenges

We spent two days in Asunción. After picking up mail, a quick check-up for me by our Paraguayan Peace Corps doctor, and a shopping excursion for supplies, we headed home. Word had been sent to Ramón about my surgery — that meant everyone in town knew about it. We had discovered early on news in Artigas spread like wildfire and now everyone had an idea of what caused my twisted intestines. Delma thought it was because I was too thin, Roberto blamed it on altitude and Alejandro, the beef butcher, said it was surely the fish. But the whole town seemed happy to see us back with lots of waves and "*Bienvenidos*" as we walked about on our errands.

The house was in good order, but outside was a disaster. Arnaldo, Jorge's younger brother, had been in charge of watering the garden and my flowers, and it didn't appear much had been done.

In the front there were a few marigolds remaining along the porch, but the garden was pretty well gone. Most of the plants had been eaten down to the ground and only brown stubble poked up from the raised beds. I wondered if the chickens had eaten every-thing first and then Arnaldo had stopped watering or if he had just never watered in the first place. There were a few surviving green pepper plants with two small peppers. I was frustrated and wanted to march over and complain, but instead went inside and made an iced tea. After ranting to Chuck, I felt better and decided I wouldn't do anything. All I could accomplish was to cause bad feelings with our neighbors; it certainly wouldn't bring the garden back. Linda had sent me all kinds of seeds for Christmas, so I just decided to let the matter go and plant the new ones she had sent. And, should I leave again, I would definitely choose someone else for the watering detail.

The worst part of the yard though, didn't have anything to do with Arnaldo. The problem was with the entire back yard. All of the mangoes from the five big trees and the grapes outside the back door, had ripened, fallen and were now rotting in the grass, creating an unbelievable stench that in turn brought clouds of flies. Chuck and I started throwing the gooey mangoes over the fence for the omnipresent free-range pigs and chickens, but it was futile. The mangoes covered the entire back yard like fallen leaves. Even with the ravenous chickens of the Barbosas and a herd of pigs, eating away the supply would take forever. Never mind the task of throwing thousands of them over the fence while the stench and rot continued. Chuck and I had barely walked back in the house when we heard clapping at the gate and saw Cabana. I think he had just been waiting for us to walk around outside before proposing that he dig big holes and just bury them all. Sounded good to us.

On the sixth day after leaving La Paz, we got the anxiously awaited email from Rita and Jim that they were safely home, were well and that Jim was back to work. Chuck and I both felt a weight off our shoulders. I hadn't stopped thinking about them. Rita said that during her last days there, she walked all over La Paz and discovered better and cheaper markets for woven goods that we had admired earlier. Unlike Paraguay, which had little in the way of textiles or handicrafts, Bolivia was a gold mine for shoppers — alpaca sweaters, rugs, shawls, and all sorts of interesting woven materials. So, while not the best time in her life, her Bolivian stay was certainly not the worst. The only difficulty seemed to be when they went to settle the bill and found that the hotel doctor had tried to cheat them on his "consulting" fees, charging them for all sorts of daily things that hadn't existed. After Rita took him to task, he did lower his fee. Although the total bill was cheap by U.S. Standards (only about $2,000) Jim was quite happy he had taken out trip health insurance. I had no idea what my bill had come to since the Peace Corps had taken care of everything.

Chuck and I had talked about how fortunate that we had been in Bolivia with my twisted intestines, if you could even put the word fortunate together with twisted intestines. I had plenty of time in the hospital to visualize how the scene would have played in Artigas: for a day I would have felt awful, and would have said something like, "If it is like this tomorrow, we'll go to Asunción." Then, of course, I would have felt better, would have done nothing until the intestines burst, then would have been six or seven hours away from Asunción, assuming we could have found someone to drive us at breakneck speed. From what Dr. Mettekofler had told us, I probably would have died. I knew Chuck had played the same scene over and over in his mind and he now watched over me with great concern. Every time I went to the bathroom he wanted to know if everything was OK. When two days had passed and I hadn't had a bowel movement, we were both thinking something had gone awry and were thinking of catching the morning bus to Asunción. Happily, the issue was resolved the next morning.

"We can't keep worrying about this," I told Chuck. "What I had is over, I'm fine. We have to get back to normal." Chuck agreed but we were having a hard time with it. He accepted the fact that this Peace Corps assignment was originally his idea and from the beginning he had been more enthusiastic than I had been. Now, somehow, he was haunted by the idea that he could have lost me through this bizarre ailment.

It was still unbearably hot and we sweated through the sheets every night. School was still on holiday, families were gone and we weren't going to be able to restart our computer classes for three more weeks. Chuck gave a few guitar lessons and I worked on my book when the computer was running, but we were both bored.

The second week back I announced that I needed to start some kind of regular exercise. The surgery had been a rather dramatic diet and I had lost the extra weight (pants now were loose) and I didn't want it to creep back on. Even before Bolivia we had given up on long bicycle rides. The rutted roads were too jarring and too deep with dust, nor did I feel like jogging around the soccer fields. Roberto suggested we walk the abandoned railway tracks.

As Mayor Pete had told us when we arrived, Artigas had once been a thriving town on a rail line that ran from Argentina up to Asunción. Now the only workable portion was a few miles of track between Asunción and Aregua, where the train went back and forth several times a week, more as a ceremony than anything else. It apparently also justified paying a huge number of employees a salary, even though they did little or nothing.

The next morning, right after the coffee and paper we started at the end of town, walking northwest along the track. In a short distance we were at the old terminal where we stopped and poked around the empty station with its wind-blown bits of paper, broken windows and open doorways. It was a melancholy place, maybe because it was easy to imagine the hustle and bustle that once had been there.

Further along the track there was an abandoned rail car off to one side on a parallel track. Now, it appeared, a family was living inside. Laundry was hanging on a line between two bushes and a little girl sat in the pushed-open loading doorway, her feet dangling over the side. I supposed no one cared. It was a good shelter and someone might as well make use of it although it meant they were hauling water from some distance and using the bushes as a latrine.

We had walked about forty-five minutes when we came to a small gulley where the tracks had collapsed. Someone had handily laid a long plank across the gap. I eyed it dubiously, completely distrusting my ability to navigate across it, although I realized it was wider than my foot and if I just looked ahead there shouldn't be any problem. Yet . . . I didn't have the confidence to do it and it wasn't quite wide enough to crawl on.

Chuck felt the same. We could have scrambled down the side, across the gully and up the other side, but instead we came to the happy conclusion that it was the perfect turn-around spot. It was forty-five minutes from town so it made the walk an hour and a half, long enough anyway. It was already hot and we drank half our water and started back. The little girl was gone when we passed back by the railway car, but I had the distinct feeling we were watched. They probably feared we would tell them to get out or inform authorities. Like it would matter, but they didn't know that.

We had a break from the heat the next week with torrential rain. It was the same drill with the leaks in the house, but this time there were twice as many. All of my containers overflowed and small rivers ran through the living room. We tried to cover everything with plastic, or stack it together, but we only managed to cover the electronics leaving the tables and chairs to the drips.

"This is ridiculous," Chuck declared. "As soon as we can get to the road, I'm going to see if Kitty can't do something."

By late afternoon he made his way through the high grass banks above the road to Kitty's and complained as nicely as possible. Kitty didn't seem surprised and agreed it was time for a new roof, a tin one this time, and she would send Cabana over to measure for the tin sheets. Chuck returned, jubilant with the news, and in short order Cabana, handyman extraordinaire, was out front with his rickety ladder. He walked around the house sagely eyeing all angles then scrambled up on the roof and measured using nothing but some pieces of string. He announced that yes indeed, the roof was *muy malo* and that all parts were either *feo* [ugly], *podrido* [rotten] or simply *finito* [finished]. He said it would only take a week for

201

the sheets of tin to arrive, and then he would come and start. And, he cautioned, "*estaré un poquito polvo* [there will be a little dust]."

The morning Cabana and his sons came into view, pulling a small cart with large tin sheets precariously balanced on top, I decided that my best course of action was to stay out of the way. Heeding Cabana's advice about the dust, I had already covered all the electronics with our extra set of sheets, put the dishes away, used the plastic and newspapers I had to cover everything else and put remainders under the bed or table. There seemed little else I could contribute and with the first "wham" of the hammer, I was out the door. Chuck planned to hang around to supervise.

I took my time, meandering through the *cooperativa*, then on to Alejandro's butcher shop. I went home two hours later and was pleased to see a large stack of tiles in the yard. I came through the front door, then stopped.

A little dust? It looked as if a bomb had gone off. Dirt, debris and bits of broken tile covered every square inch and above were only the bare wooden beams and the blue, blue sky of Paraguay. Chuck waved at me excitedly from the back yard.

"Come see the beginnings of our new roof!" he called.

Dismayed at the rubble, I picked my way through the house to the back door and joined him outside. Part of the roof was now covered with shiny, bright, and very waterproof tin. Cabana looked down at me and waved.

"*Es bueno, no?*" he called.

"*Si, si,*" I replied, lacking conviction. I turned to Chuck. "You realize we have to clean and wash every single thing in the entire house, don't you?"

Chuck didn't see it as a big deal and told me not to worry as our house was small. He didn't think it was quite so small when we finally finished with the kitchen at 10 o'clock that night. Cabana and team had finished that section of the house by mid-afternoon so we ventured in and began carrying the big chunks of broken plaster and dirt out the back door. Once the floor was manageable we started with the cupboards and worked our way down, washing and wiping every surface and every dish. It was nice, though, that it wasn't my old San Diego kitchen. Here I only had six open shelves, two cupboards, one standing cupboard and a table.

That night we had half a house with a shiny tin roof and half with nothing at all. We lay under our mosquito netting, which was still hanging from the beams and gazed up at the night sky. It was a moonless night and the black sky was a panorama of a billion-trillion stars, cut across by the white band of the Milky Way. I remembered that long ago in Afghanistan I had seen such a night.

"Amazing that our ancestors enjoyed this sight every night," I whispered to Chuck. I turned my head to see if he was looking but he had fallen fast asleep.

The weather remained clear for two more weeks. The next storm came when Chuck and I were both home having afternoon tea. We heard the rain before we saw it, with big plunking sounds hitting the roof. Like a chorus of hammers, the noise built until it was deafening.

"Nothing's leaking," I yelled at Chuck.

"What? I can't hear you!"

"The tin roof isn't leaking!" I shouted again.

Neither of us had considered what a tin roof sounded like in a rainstorm. Chuck held up his hands in surrender and we both started laughing.

27   Music and Fish

A week after Cabana had finished the roof, he was clapping at our front door again.

"*Por favor,*" he began "*Puden asistir mi fiesta por el cumpleaño de mi hijo?* [Can you come to my son's birthday party?]"

It was to be held at his house that Friday night. We told him we would be honored and we would bring our box wine.

Cabana then motioned to Chuck, "*Y su guitarra! Habrá mucho musico y podemos tocar juntos.* [And his guitar! There will be much music and we can play together.]"

Chuck had no idea what instrument Cabana played, but come Friday night, we set off to his house, Chuck with his guitar and me with the wine.

Cabana's house was down the road from Kitty's and like many of Paraguay's poor, it was barely a shack. The party was set up outdoors with a long table and plastic chairs that had probably been brought by all the other invitees. Cabana saw us and came towards us with kisses for me and handshakes for Chuck and told us to come and sit and be welcome. He brought his wife and a couple of daughters over for introductions and they shyly gave me kisses and then stood back, not knowing what exactly to do.

I asked if I could help them with the dinner preparations and got emphatic NO's; I was the guest. After a few minutes though, the littlest girl, and the bravest one, shyly approached me and crawled up on my lap, making me feel a little useful.

Chuck busied himself with tuning his guitar and finally started in with a few songs. Right away someone wanted to play his guitar, so it was passed down the line for the Guaranie songs. Quite a few of Cabana's relatives could play, and even he played a bit, so they were all having great fun. Another guitar was produced and out came the instrument of Paraguay — the accordion! Chuck and I had often joked that all the accordions that kids used to have to play in the States had made their way down here. Paraguayans loved accordions. The men of the Cabana clan were stomping away with all sorts of songs, but as much as I tried to appreciate the music, the Guaranie polkas left me nonplussed. I could barely decipher a tune and it didn't even seem like they were all playing the same song except that they ended at the same time. A greater caterwauling couldn't be imagined, but everyone loved it. Every now and then they would pass the guitar back to Chuck and he would try to sing a song, but it was obvious that they preferred their own music. They finally hit on the idea that he could play their music with them and after trying to nail down what key it was in, Chuck gamely tried to chime in. He later asked me how he sounded and I just laughed.

"Sounded? It was so loud I couldn't hear you. You could have played Beethoven, the Beatles, anything would have blended into that . . . that," I searched for a word, "that cacophony!"

The wine and caña kept flowing and the group got happier and louder, yet no food was in sight. Cabana had told us that he had a big fish and it was roasting and at midnight it was still roasting. Chuck and I begged off with some reason or other about why we had to go. Cabana was sorry that we would miss the big feast, but given the fact that the musicians — including Cabana — were rapidly descending into a total state of inebriation, I didn't think we would be missed.

The next night on the porch though, Roberto told us it was a real shame we had missed the big fish dinner, as Paraguayan fish was really good. Really? I had been lamenting the fact that we couldn't get any and Roberto had assured us that the local streams were full of terrific fish.

"But how do we get them?" I asked.

"You have to know a fisherman," he told us. And as luck would have it, he knew all of them. "Next time I will have them bring you some."

Just thinking of a fresh stream trout made my mouth water. I had grown up in northern Idaho and had been brought up eating a type of fresh water salmon locally called blue-back. We would catch them by trolling in my Dad's aluminum boat, clean them on the dock and bring them home. Quickly fried and served with freshly squeezed lemon juice was beyond delicious. I always looked for fresh trout on menus, but was always disappointed. But now, maybe just maybe, if one of Roberto's friends brought the Paraguayan equivalent directly from the stream? I was hopeful.

It was the following week when upon hearing clapping at my door, I saw a strange fellow holding two fish on a line.

"*Por ustedes*," he told me smiling and refused all my attempts at paying for them. He handed me the line; I looked at the fish. I had been picturing speckled trout; these were the ugliest things I had ever laid eyes on. They were shiny and pitch black, with long whiskers and enormously long, ugly heads half the length of the body. I thanked him and tried to remain positive.

I took them into the kitchen and laid them on my cutting board. They looked like they came from the bottom of a dark swamp. With the long, thick whiskers they had to be in the catfish family and I reminded myself that I liked catfish, or most of it, anyway and not everything that looks bad is bad. Oysters and snails came to mind. These fish had already been cleaned so all I had to do was saw off the heads, dust them in flour and fry them. When Chuck came back from classes I told him we were going to have a special surprise for dinner. I presented the two fish with great flair. I had even gone out back for a couple of the orangy-lemons, quartered them and put them around the edges of the plate.

We both took our first bite. I stopped in mid-bite and looked at Chuck. A total look of disgust had crossed his face. Simultaneously, we spat them out on the plate.

"Oh, these are truly awful," I said reaching for my water glass.

"Horrors," was all that Chuck could say. He pushed back his chair and went to the bathroom where I could hear him rinsing out his mouth. "They taste like slimy dirt," he called back, then returned to the table, still grimacing. "And Roberto thinks these are good? Cripes."

I scraped all the fish back into the skillet, leaving our piles of rice and cabbage salad on the plate, hoping it hadn't been totally contaminated by the dirt-slime juices of the fish from hell. After dinner I took the skillet outside and threw the whole mess to the dogs. They rushed over as always, ready for left-overs, but in this case, just sniffed the fish then turned away. That was a new low. Uno and Dos would eat anything — anything but black mud-fish. I couldn't leave them there in the yard to rot, so I gingerly picked up all the pieces, put them in the skillet and walked to the back of the yard, which faced an empty field and gave them a mighty heave-ho. Either a strolling pig or the chickens would eat them, I thought. But considering the taste and my curiosity, I went back out the next morning to check. They were gone. Somebody or something had thought they were just fine.

When Roberto made his next nightly appearance we had to thank him again and I mustered a "they were good . . . but different." I think he guessed we didn't like them much since the conversation veered to how delicious the beef and pork were.

By the end of February we were finally able to start the computer typing classes again. While it didn't fill our entire day, it was a great relief to be doing something. We had another thirty excited students plus about five of our previous students who still wanted to practice on the two computers. We could only promise them that if one of the enrolled students didn't show up, and they were around, then they could use the computer until the next enrolled student came. This resulted in having these five hanging about on their way to and from school or all of Saturday mornings. It wasn't a problem though as we enjoyed their company since most of the time the new students had to practice by themselves and there wasn't much for us to do.

Chuck started again with his basketball group, but it had shrunk, probably due to the weather since it was still horribly hot in the late afternoon. A few boys came by including Jorge usually, or if he didn't come his brother showed up. Chuck wondered why they both didn't come, it would have made a better group and finally asked Jorge. Jorge replied, rather matter-of-factly, that only one of them came at a time because they only had one pair of tennis shoes and they took turns wearing them. Chuck and I pondered this distressing news.

"Well, if we buy them another pair of tennis shoes, what about the little sisters, whom I have never seen in shoes at all?" I asked. "And what about little Al, who only has plastic flip flops?"

We knew it could quickly become an out-of-control charity disaster, but it was hard to see the lack of things and not want to buy what they needed.

M andy came by the week after our new roof was in place and was treated to an afternoon rainstorm and our accompanying drumming concert. She could only laugh and tell us that her thatched roof was much quieter. She had come from Asunción and brought our mail along with the announcement that Peace Corps wanted us all to convene again for a workshop, but this time we were to bring our Paraguayan counterparts.

"And who is your counterpart?" I asked her. I already knew that the man who was supposed to be her contact had turned out to be a complete, chauvinistic stereotype and she spent as little time as possible with him.

She told me she was just bringing one of the women from her village. She had started many small projects with the women in her area, everything from making soap to having art classes for their children.

Our official counterpart was Ramón, but he didn't have the time to come and it wasn't like we were actually doing a project side-by-side with him anyway.

"Well, Ramón keeps sending us to the Education Committee, so maybe we can claim one of them," Chuck suggested.

We finally put the question to Ramón, and he suggested we ask Ramón Jara, the member of the *cooperativa* who had started us with the idea of the computers, and Hilda, one of the Kindergarten teachers. I thought the whole thing sounded so useless I was embarrassed to even ask that they take the time, but I was surprised when both of them seemed excited and pleased to go.

This meeting wasn't in Asunción, but in a province to the north of us called Caazapa. Ramón Jara had a car, so we got the treat of riding with him and Hilda instead of the bus, and were able to arrive early. It gave Ramón and Hilda a chance to meet and chat with other counterparts and we had time to visit with Volunteers from our group. All were curious to hear what exactly had happened to me in Bolivia. Or was it Chuck? Typical of gossip, the rumors were as twisted as my intestines had been — everything from appendicitis to dysentery befalling either one of us or both.

My story, however, was eclipsed by a young gal from another training group, who was recovering from a near disembowelment! One day she had foolishly taken a short-cut crossing a pasture she thought was empty. The next thing she knew she was sailing through the air. A bull had charged her, caught her up in his horns and thrown her. One horn had ripped across her abdomen, leaving a gash of some 12 inches from hip bone to hip bone. Another millimeter deeper and her intestines would have been on the field. As bad as it was she had managed to crawl to the edge of the field and yell for help and neighbors had come running. She was now mending and most willing to show off her scar, (rather impressive!) and remind us not to cross unknown pastures.

In the end, both Ramón and Hilda said they liked the meetings and told us they got new ideas. What did I know?

28 Manganades

The heat was breaking and it was high time to get my fall garden in order. We had been told that there was plenty of time between mid-March and June to plant and harvest. The spring garden (last fall) had produced very good cucumbers, green peppers and a few tomatoes, but the lettuce had been a disaster.

The problem wasn't that the little shoots didn't come up, but that they did, and the chickens soon discovered them. When I was home I ran out and scared them away. But I didn't do it by charging out waving my arms. Instead, I had collected a large stack of fallen mangoes in a pile by the back door, and when I saw a chicken approaching I ran out, picked up a mango and threw it, hard as I could, at the chicken. I rarely hit one, maybe never, but it did scare them away. My dark mangoes looked a bit like hand-grenades and throwing them made me feel like a special military operative, so I started calling them Manganades. Chuck suggested Grenangoes.

During our Bolivian excursion, every garden row had been de-voured. This time I had a better plan. In my long hours of chicken observation, I had concluded that chickens are very dumb. Someone once told me that turkeys were much dumber than chickens, but that remained to be seen. The chickens didn't come running over to my garden on a daily basis but only meandered over if that was the particular direction they were headed. They could fly, of course, but generally preferred to peck along, head down, eating the next thing in front of them. If that happened to be the first baby lettuce in a row, so much for the row!

The best solution would have been what Tim Barnes had done with his garden patch — build an entire chicken-wire fence around the whole thing and add a wire lid to keep out birds. But that seemed excessive and I kept looking for an easier alternative.

One afternoon as I was sitting in the back under the shade of the mangoes, I noticed that along one side of the fence we had left a couple of long PVC pipes, left over from the antennae experiments. The chickens, as they began to peck their way into our yard, walked around them. The next day, same thing. It occurred to me that perhaps they were too slippery for chickens to walk over and especially with two pipes together, since if they tried, their little claws would slip down between the two pipes and hold them. A "chicken cattle-guard"; that was my theory anyway. I went down to Kitty's and bought enough pipes to encircle the garden. After I had carefully planted peppers, tomatoes, cucumbers, carrots, potatoes and two rows of lettuce, I arranged the double row of pipes around the perimeter of the garden. It would be a month before I could see if my experiment was working, but I was pleased with myself anyway and bragged about it to Roberto on his next visit.

"*Porque no te compras la lechuga*? [Why don't you buy the lettuce?]" he asked.

"Buy the lettuce?" I looked at him like he was one of the aliens he was always talking about. He then went on to tell me that at this time of year, the farm at the eastern edge of town, the one with the pink house, sold lettuce.

"Real lettuce?" I questioned, knowing that their idea of bread wasn't really bread nor was their idea of a lemon a real lemon. But Roberto was decidedly sure. Even slightly offended that I thought a man from Argentina wouldn't know what lettuce was. I hadn't had a lettuce salad on my table since we had arrived and it sounded like heaven.

The next morning I set out right after breakfast and in ten minutes I was clapping at the gate of the pink house. I hadn't paid the place much attention as it wasn't on one of my normal routes. It was clearly a commercial effort though, with a huge garden, about the size of a city block, part of it covered with screening. After a minute, a small girl came skipping out.

"*Tiene lechuga*? [Do you have lettuce?]" I questioned.

She nodded.

"*Puedo comprar algo?* [Can I buy some?]" She merely nodded again, looking up at me cautiously with big brown eyes. I wasn't sure she understood Spanish, so I held up two fingers. "*Quiero dos.*" I told her. With that, she spun around on one heel and galloped off behind the house. In seconds she was back, holding two beautiful heads of butter lettuce, clumps of dirt still clinging to their stems. She held them out to me in one hand and held out the other with an open palm.

"*Ochocientos*," she said in a tiny voice. That was eight hundred guaranies, about twenty cents.

I made a big lettuce salad for lunch and another one for supper. Even if my chicken guard never worked, we would have lettuce for a couple of months.

A week after the lettuce news, Roberto came charging up to the porch, obviously excited. I wondered if there were more gastronomical delights in store for us.

"*Mira* [Look]," he exclaimed, waving a book. "*El secreto por la pérdida de peso.* [The secret for weight loss.]"

I was stunned. There in his hand was a copy of *Dr. Atkins Diet Revolution*, translated into Spanish. I felt I should write the good doctor and tell him that if his book had reached Artigas, his marketing team had now covered the entire world.

It wasn't as though Roberto needed to lose weight, he just was always working to stay trim. And he had a phobia of turning fat, like all the Norte Americanos he read about. He had given up on running with his stomach wrapped in cellophane; all that was

213

doing was causing a rash and making him sweat. It had been too hot to even run nude, in my opinion. Now, he was sure if he just ate protein, his weight would stay under control. I thought it would be an easier diet in Paraguay than in the States since few Paraguayan ate vegetables and the starch was mainly mandioca or the fat laden *chipa* rolls. No tempting fresh bread, baked potatoes or french fries. Chuck had tried the Atkins diet years before and found that yes, initially, he did lose weight but then his body seemed to adjust or maybe his portions got bigger, but the diet lost its effectiveness. Like all new ideas in Artigas, the book was passed around and soon I heard that Ramón's son was on the diet and one of the women from the Education Committee. I was back to my normal weight and I knew I could control that by just not eating all those Brazilian cookies.

Ramón told me that the Education Committee had a project for us and we should attend their weekly meeting. Chuck and I dutifully showed up and learned that they wanted to have a grade school art contest. They were trying to instill artistic development in their children, despite the lack of facilities, and thought this might make a start in awareness. There were three grade schools located in the community and we were to go with a member of the Education Committee to help pass out papers, pencils and crayons to the students. They would have an hour to draw their pictures, then we would collect them. After all the children had participated, the Education Committee would judge the drawings and hand out awards.

The students were asked to draw some type of outdoor scene. As an example, a house, a yard, or trees. The children all simultaneously chose to draw a house and a yard. And as I walked around one thing was obvious: someone, at sometime, had taught all the children to draw a house in exactly the same manner. A little square with a door with two square windows on either side and next to it, a tree that looked like a lollipop. I wondered who had taught this or maybe the picture was in a primary instruction book? It did seem odd that all the drawings were almost identical, regardless of the age of the student and even coming from different schools.

I also noticed that many of the children were drawing with their noses practically on their papers, a sign to me that they had poor eyesight and yet not one child anywhere in town wore glasses. In fact, with the exception of the nearly blind pork butcher, no one in town wore glasses. When I asked one of the teachers about it she said all the children had good eyesight. Later I asked Margarita, the town nurse, and she explained that like most things, there wasn't money for eye exams and that the children probably wouldn't wear them anyway since they didn't want to be different from the others. I wished I knew how to measure eyes or could arrange for an optometrist to come to the area. But again there was the money issue. When Chuck and I talked about it we also conceded that a dentist was equally important. There was a dentist in Artigas, but no one had the money for regular checkups and by the time the tooth hurt, it needed serious work. There was no money for that, and so teeth were just pulled.

We were wrapping up the art project when an amazing picture was drawn by a little boy about ten-or-eleven-years old. Instead of a box house, he had actually drawn a real looking house on a hill with a winding river and forest, all in perspective and then colored with pinks for a sky breaking at dawn. It was spectacular and it didn't take much judging to see that he would be the clear winner. He did win, of course and shyly accepted the blue ribbon. I could only wonder what his future would bring. Would he just be another poor farmer or would his art somehow take him further?

In keeping with the emphasis on arts education, I thought I'd try my theater idea again, but this time, with students. After my debacle with the adult community theater, one of the *cooperativa* board members had told me I should be working with the students, not the adults. They were the ones who would be receptive. So at the next education meeting after the art contest I announced that I

215

would try and start a drama club for teen-agers. They all thought it was a wonderful idea. I wasn't sure exactly what a drama club would do, but thought we could begin by just having fun and reading different roles in plays.

I put up some announcement posters in the *cooperativa* and at the high school and spoke with the high school principal about my project. Like the Education Committee, she thought it would be wonderful and I arranged with Ramón to hold the drama club meetings in the building where the kindergarten classes were held.

My next mission was to find a play written in Spanish. I thought this would be easy, thinking the high school library would have something. Then, of course, I discovered that there wasn't a high school library or a grade school library or any library. And zero plays anywhere.

One teacher managed to find me a battered copy of a play that at least had several parts for males and females. Ramón let me use the copier, but he didn't have enough paper or ink for me to run off the entire play book so I selected several promising pages. That took days as the copier was old and it broke down constantly. Plus, others came in to run copies, actual paying customers, so I had to cede to them. Finally, I had a small pile of scripts, three pages each and was ready for my drama students.

I had quite a nice sized group of both boys and girls at the first meeting. I wasn't sure if they were all there just to flirt with each other or if they cared about the drama part. Didn't matter though. They all seemed to enjoy reading the different parts and we just did that for an hour. The next week, we did the same, changing parts around. I wanted to do some kind of improvisation exercises, but it seemed beyond them. They were most happy with the script in hand. I realized though that I would soon have to get my hands on more material as the three pages of the silly little play they were reading was already a bit tedious. In another month we were due to go to Asunción again, so hoped I could string my weak material along until then.

Another issue was that the students didn't like the idea of actually doing the play or competing for parts or having anything to do with a performance. When I announced that the following week we would read to see who got which part, I was rewarded with no one showing up. I sat around for a half an hour, then decided that I would just shelve the whole thing until I could get some more plays.

M y other idea to start a Girl's Scout program wasn't getting too far either. I was tired of seeing the boys have all the fun and get all the exercise, while the girls, once they were teenagers, seemed to retreat into the house. There were some volunteers in country who worked with youth in the "inner-city" part of Asunción and I had tried to contact them while in Asunción, but never could connect.

Volunteers were helpful; our problem was communication. With no phones and no easy transportation, it was amazingly difficult to contact anyone. I didn't have much luck reaching the Girl Scouts leader either. She was out of the country for three months and it didn't appear anyone else could help me.

I wasn't sure what sports the girls would enjoy. When I had asked my girl typing students what they liked to do outside, all I got back were wrinkled up noses. It occurred to me I was making the classic "foreign aid" mistake — imposing what I thought they needed versus helping them with what they wanted or needed. Sort of like the Peace Corps idea of sending small business Volunteers to Artigas. I put the whole Girl Scout idea on the back burner.

29   Back to the USA

I had promised my Mom that I would come to see her in a year and it had been longer than that, since I hadn't been able to visit before we left for Paraguay. Mom had been worried about my health (my sisters had finally told her about my surgery), and I worried about hers and of course, had missed her terribly. We easily got permission from the Peace Corps for me to be gone. I wasn't sure if it was because of my illness in Bolivia or it would just be marked off against my future vacation time, but in any case, they said fine.

We took the bus to Asunción the day before, spent the night at the Hotel Paraguay and Chuck took me to the airport the following afternoon. Leaving Chuck and starting off by myself on such a long journey filled me with anxiety. I tried to analyze it. It wasn't as though I hadn't taken trips without him. In our Merrill days, I had often had business trips by myself and I was only going to be gone a week. And many times, I had traveled to see Mom by myself. But regardless, this time, I was still unreasonably nervous. Maybe it was the distance or the fact that we hadn't been apart at all in so long. In any case, tears were streaming down my cheeks with our final hug, like I was going off forever.

I didn't relax until I met Mom at the curb in Amarillo. She

seemed more frail and thinner than when I had last seen her and I was instantly filled with remorse at having left in the first place. It was wonderful to be at her side. We didn't plan to do much, mostly she wanted to sit and talk. Mornings were spent leisurely with the newspaper and coffee, then in the afternoon we did small projects and attempted to fill my list of things I wanted to buy and take back to Paraguay — things that weren't available anywhere in country, like size 14 tennis shoes for Chuck and an oven thermometer so I could at least vaguely calculate baking and roasting times. I marveled at the supermarket, having forgotten how big and bright they were and all the new products that had appeared in the last year. Evenings were spent watching videos or chatting with my aunts, who also lived in the same retirement building. The visit was rejuvenating for me.

Two days before I left, the phone rang and mother handed it to me. "It's for you," she said and we both shrugged, wondering who on earth would be calling me.

"Eloise Hanner?" the voice began, "This is Ronald Pitkin. I'm the publisher of Cumberland House Publishing. We love your book and want to publish it."

My brain was scrambling frantically, trying to register who this was and how he got this number, then suddenly I recalled that Rita had told me in Bolivia she had given a publisher Mom's number. Mr. Pitkin talked on about this and that, something about publishing my book in the fall, doing publicity and finished up by saying if I was agreeable, they would overnight a contract to me. Would that be OK?

"OK? YES YES YES!" I was ecstatic. I said yes to everything, then hung up the phone and wondered what on earth I was doing. How exactly was I going to publish a book while working in Paraguay? Was that possible? Travel back and forth to the States? Tell them I couldn't do any of the publicity? Ask them if they would wait another year, then publish it? Nothing looked good.

I went over the options with Mom, and I also told her how Chuck felt about his whole Paraguayan experience, which had now intensified since my Bolivian mishap. She sympathized with my dilemma, but couldn't help me. She wanted me to come back, but she didn't want me to be unhappy with my choice. She also thought it was a special opportunity to have my book published. My father had written short stories for years and never had any of them published, so Mom knew what a difficult and dicey business it was. I sent an email to Chuck announcing the news. I knew he wouldn't think it feasible to stay in Paraguay and promote the book.

The contract arrived the next day. I signed it and sent it back, still not sure how I could remain in Paraguay after it was published. Ideally I hoped I could have my cake and eat it too, but that remained to be seen.

Chuck was eagerly awaiting me in the airport in Asunción and grabbed me up in a big hug. He had gotten the email.

"I'm so proud of you!" he gushed. "A published author! They're going to publish your book!"

I told him how excited I was, but then poured out my dilemma about marketing the book and staying in Paraguay at the same time. I also confessed that I hadn't told the publisher I was supposed to be living in Paraguay for another year. Chuck just shook his head.

"Look, we can stay until fall, that will give us time for another typing class, maybe two more. It would be crazy not to go back for the book. Do you realize how difficult it is for most people to ever get a book published?"

I agreed, but had a heavy heart about the whole thing.

It felt good to be back with Chuck in our humble abode. During my one week absence there had been three startling events.

"First off," he told me, "the toilet tank fell off the wall!"

This had taken place in the middle of the night, scaring Chuck to death and sending a deluge of water and porcelain shards all over the bathroom floor. Kitty had already replaced the tank and

Cabana had put it up with stronger screws and brackets.

That had barely been swept up when unexpected number two appeared — a wind storm. This wasn't a windy day, but a tornado that roared through town, with a funnel of swirling red dust that ripped up trees and sent fence posts flying. At the time, Chuck had been at the *cooperativa*, and as customary, had left all the windows open for ventilation. By the time he made it back home dust and dirt had covered everything in the house. He had tried to shake and dust the surface of things, but when it came to the floor, it was just too deep. Dismayed, he had finally decided to bring the hose into the house and spray wash the floors, moving the furniture to one side of each room and then spraying the rest of the floor.

"It didn't work exactly," he confessed, and I tried to not think about the ensuing mud sludge he had probably created. However, in the subsequent days, he had managed to scrub it out the door and by the time I walked in, all looked pretty normal.

"And third," he continued, "army ants came through!" This happening wasn't actually at our house, but just to the north of us and they had passed through Mandy's house.

"It's wasn't quite as horrific as the movies make it out to be," he explained. "They don't exactly eat you in your bed, and you do have lots of advance notice. What they do do," he added, "is clean out every crevice and every dead bug and every spider web that ever was and leave your place quite clean. Mandy, apparently had been in Encarnación at the time and had come home to a very clean house. She was sorry to have missed the event.

30 Mangled Coup — No Problem

There was a coup attempt!

It was so feeble we didn't have to run down to Encarnación for safety. Nor did we get the special phone call through the *cooperativa* and only guessed that something might be amiss when the morning paper didn't show. By the next day it was the headline story and the topic of conversation for everyone. Apparently four tanks had rolled slowly down to parliament at midnight, or rather three did — one ran out of gas. Several shots were fired into the air then the tank drivers got out and surrendered. There was one photo in the paper of a "rebel" drinking *mate* with one of the soldiers. It was said that leaders in the government were behind the coup as they wished to be able to issue a "State of Exception" that would empower them to arrest anyone suspected of being part of the coup without due process — and thus be able arrest all of their enemies in the opposition party.

Paraguay hadn't had a decent government in, well . . . ever. The government was pretty well annihilated in 1865 when the dictator Francisco Lopez unwittingly decided to take on Brazil, Argentina and Uruguay all at the same time. What was left of the country limped from one leader to another until Alfredo Stroessner, who ruled as a dictator for some thirty years, was finally kicked out. The current president, Gonzáles Macchi was fast losing popularity and his whole party had recently resigned from congress, leaving him high and dry and ineffectual.

When we went to Asunción shortly thereafter for another Peace Corps assembly, the only effects from the coup that we noticed were tanks on various street corners and very bored looking soldiers standing around with AK-47s slung over their shoulders. Our first meeting featured a talk from one of the State Department officials who assured us there was no danger and that the assault rifles the soldiers were carrying weren't loaded.

The meetings were like always. Two days' worth of sessions and break-out groups for imparting information I felt could have been condensed into two hours.

What we did learn was that not many of the Volunteers in our group were satisfied with their assignments. A couple of our young guys were doing nothing. John was continuing his work with the library ladies. A few others in our group had small projects going, but many were still floundering. Doris, the other older Volunteer, had been plagued with problems and was now in Asunción, waiting to be relocated. She was also having dental problems and wasn't exactly happy with the treatment from the local dentist assigned by the Peace Corps. It sounded to me like she needed root canals and instead, they were just pulling her teeth.

On our afternoon dedicated to getting supplies, I went to every bookshop in the city searching for plays for the drama club. Nothing. Even literature in general was hard to find. Often the shops had some of the classics, like *Don Quixote* or a few of the popular mysteries, but most book stores were dedicated to school texts and non-fiction. One store owner thought he could get Shakespeare, but didn't have it in stock.

We came home in a pouring rain that soaked us thoroughly during the run from the bus stop to the house. The house was so snug and dry though, that the noise of the rain hitting the tin roof was music to our ears. The garden looked okay; all the rain staying in the trenches between the rows and pouring out to the street.

There did emerge a couple of problems, though.

Most immediate was dirty clothes, complicated by the fact that there were no dryers in Artigas. If the sun wasn't out there was no drying — so our Guarani laundry lady had not appeared. The next morning, I decided I would wash out a few items and hang them inside by the utility sink. I tipped our laundry basket over and picked through the jumble for a few undies to wash. What I didn't see in the dark corner was that the laundry was infested with fire ants — thousands of them. By the time I realized I was digging through an ant nest, I had bites all over both arms. Slapping them off my arms and cursing, I ran for the trusty bug spray and sprayed myself and most of the pile, making sure every last one of them was dead.

The treatment left the laundry — already smelling of sweat and mold — reeking with bug spray. I wondered what the laundry lady would think, but knew I would never know; I had never gotten any reaction from her. She never smiled, never said anything, and rarely made eye contact. I hadn't even been able to figure out her name. I thought it was probably due to her not being able to speak Spanish. Usually she brought her little girl with her who held out her hand for the money.

Along with ants in the laundry, we had other visitors — big spiders — which I dubbed the "Tarantula-Wanna-Bees." They were the same size, but not hairy. Not dangerous either, but scary enough in the middle of the night when Chuck almost stepped on one. That one was smashed in short order with his boot. Two others, which I found during the day, I was able to sweep outside because they didn't crawl too fast. I knew spiders ate other bugs, so I didn't really want to kill them, but didn't want them in my bedroom.

The rain stopped three days later, but it was an additional four days before the town got back to business. No school, no commerce, no transportation, for seven days. Life on hold all for the lack of paved roads. Artigas was like a rural settlement in the United States circa 1910. In that time, the two would have been almost equal — dirt roads, many homes without electricity and only the few rich with indoor plumbing. But, thanks to an inept government, Paraguay fell behind; in many ways it was still 1910.

Earlier I had been astonished to discover that all schools were closed the last Friday of every month so that teachers could go to the bank in San Marcos to pick up their salaries in cash. No one had a bank account, no one had a checking account, and the one bank in the county wasn't open on the weekends. This had come up at an education committee meeting and when I expressed incredulity, I was asked how teachers were paid in the United States. I told them *"por cheque"* which they understood, but were amazed when I went on to describe the concept of direct deposit.

Oh, how I wished we had been given the resources to work on a project of that magnitude.

In my search for something more useful to do at the *cooperativa*, I had come up with the idea of taking the *cooperativa* employees on a field trip to the real *supermercado* in Encarnación. I thought we could gather ideas on sales and advertisements in the windows, displays, organization, everything.

They were all quite excited about such an outing. Only a couple of them had been to the supermarket, and it was before they worked at the *cooperativa* so they weren't thinking of ideas to apply in Artigas. Alicia, the main manager hadn't been there in years, in fact she told me, she hadn't left town in over six years. Everyone was enthusiastic, maybe not so much for the supermarket trip as much as an opportunity to get out of town. We presented Ramón with our request for bus tickets for all of us to go the next Saturday after we closed. It really wasn't much money. A round trip ticket was only about $3.00, but there were eight of us, so $25. I was prepared to buy them myself if Ramón said no, but he was quite agreeable and thought it would be a good idea.

We left Saturday right after we closed the *cooperativa*. We ate *chipa* rolls and small empañadas on the bus and were in a very festive mood. I had given every person specific tasks to focus on once we arrived. They were to compare prices, note what was on sale and identify what displays and product arrangements they liked. Once we got there we spread out and roved up and down the aisles, taking notes.

It wasn't long before a stern looking manager approached Alicia and asked, "*Que estas haciendo?* [What are you doing?]"

Alicia brought the man to me, wide eyed, afraid we would be sent to jail. I explained our mission and that we were not competitors and only trying to improve our small *cooperativa* store. He seemed to relax, but still eyed us suspiciously the rest of the time we were in the store.

On Monday, we reviewed all of our information and had a number of good ideas, but as usual, there were obstacles to implementing them. Too much time, too much money, too much something. But, the excursion had jogged their thinking about marketing possibilities and I felt that was a step in the right direction.

31 Arts and Crafts

The first of May I received an email from the book publisher saying they planned to publish my book in the fall. They wanted some minor revisions and asked that I write an epilogue. I started working on revisions the next afternoon and after an hour, I took a break and went to the kitchen for a glass of water. When I returned to the project the whole computer screen was pitch black — no signs of life anywhere. I punched a few keys — nothing. I hadn't backed up the work I had done and losing the new changes was extremely distressing. Worse though— what would I do if the laptop was finished? I was pacing the floor by the time Chuck came in and he set to work immediately with his special re-start disks. It made me too anxious to watch for signs of progress so I was glad to go to the *cooperativa* for my turn at the typing classes.

When I got home he had the laptop going again. I re-wrote most of what I had done that morning, remembering the better part of it, but now I was paranoid and began to back-up my work every half-hour. For extra safety we decided to copy my manuscript on the computer at the *cooperativa*. We had heard from other Volunteers that laptops only lasted a year in Paraguay. Their small circuits just plugged up with the constant dust and humidity. We had always taken care to wrap it up each night and kept it stored away except when in use, but it hadn't helped. Or maybe it had; it was still working, after all.

There was plenty of time in my day for the writing as the typing classes only took half days and my kindergarten class participation had been cut to one day a week totaling about fifteen minutes. It really wasn't enough time to accomplish anything, even if I had the skills necessary to teach them, but I think the teachers liked to see what I would try next. Plus, I had brought them some supplies from the States: crayons, coloring books and hand puppets, so I think they wanted to keep me as a resource. I had been excited about the hand puppets, thinking that it would be a great way to teach simple language, but when I tried the first day, the students were frightened. The puppets were really cute, nice fuzzy moppets and I didn't do anything scary, just had one hand say "hello" to the other hand, then "how are you" and have the other hand answer "fine." One little boy actually started crying. Maybe they thought my hands were talking? I had no clue. The teachers assured me that the puppets would be great, just give it time. But they took the puppets and I never saw them again.

I was still attending the weekly soy cooking class on Saturdays and trying to show enthusiasm for it, especially since many of the farmers were now planting soy. Still searching for a contribution I could make, I finally hit upon the idea of teaching them a skill the Peace Corps had taught us: making drinking glasses out of old wine bottles. While it had nothing to do with soy, the teachers were also interested in re-cycling materials and promoting conservation. It was agreed that I could run the follow week's class and I told each girl to bring two old, washed, wine bottles. They had to be wine bottles, I emphasized, no other kind would work. Even though there wasn't a shop in Artigas that sold bottled wine, bottles were still around, brought in from Asunción for special occasions. Many were visible at the local dump that was simply a huge, growing pile of garbage in an empty lot at the edge of town.

Chuck promised to help me and the next Saturday we headed to "soy class" armed with rolls of masking tape, string, small twigs, a couple of buckets of ice, sand paper and wine bottles of our own. The girls all arrived with their bottles and I instructed them to decide how tall they wanted their glass to be and mark that with the top edge of a ring of masking tape.

"Now," I continued, "wrap more tape around over the top of the first until it is a centimeter thick."

They wrapped more tape then held out their bottles for inspection.

"*Buenisimo*," I told them "Now leave a small space, another centimeter and wrap again."

They did. Then Chuck paired the girls off and handed each pair one long piece of string tied on each end to a small twig which would act as handles. He showed them how to wrap the string twice around the bottle, fitting it inside the groove between the two wraps of masking tape. Then he had them sit in chairs facing each other about three feet apart. One girl would hold the bottle, while the other would saw the string back and forth. To the side of the girl with the bottle we had a bucket of ice water. Chuck told them that when he said "go" the string puller would begin and when he said "stop" the bottle holder was to plunge the bottle instantly in the cold water.

"Go," he shouted and the girl started pulling.

In about thirty seconds, Chuck commanded "Stop," and the bottle was submerged in the icy water. Craaaaack! It broke cleanly and perfectly at the line where the string was.

"*Ahora*," Chuck said, "just a little sanding around the edges and you are good to go."

The girls were delighted and attacked their bottles with enthusiasm. By the end of the afternoon every girl had one or two new glasses to take home and were very excited about collecting more bottles and making a whole set. Chuck and I were both pleased at how well it had gone and knew that there wouldn't be any empty wine bottles littering up Artigas for some time to come.

A contribution to the community, however small.

Chuck had two guitar students who had persevered. One was Al or Little Al as we called him. He really wasn't that little, just slightly small and about thirteen or fourteen years old. What made him look young was the fact that he was missing his two front teeth — already decayed and already pulled, giving him an endearing six-year-old appearance. He adored the guitar and also adored Chuck and was on our front porch frequently. He had also been one of our first and brightest computer students and now liked to come by and see if he could play games on our laptop. As the laptop was becoming less and less reliable, we had to turn him down, but he liked to come over anyway.

Jorge, our neighbor, was Chuck's other star pupil who practiced daily. We could hear him first thing every morning, practicing chords. After Thanksgiving when he had heard Chuck playing the guitar and singing, Jorge wanted to sing too, just playing wasn't enough. He wanted to play "American" songs and after Chuck played "Margaritaville," by Jimmy Buffett, that was it. He had to learn that song — in Spanish. Chuck set immediately to work, spending the next week translating the lyrics into Spanish.

"This is harder than I thought," he told me after the third night of working on it. "'Covered with oil' has to rhyme with 'beginning to boil,' and there's no way that I can make *cubierto con acieta* rhyme with *empezando a hervir*." After two more nights of erasing and rewriting, he had his own version. "It's not exact," he confessed. "I hope Jimmy won't be too upset, but it rhymes, more or less and keeps to the spirit of the song."

The *turistas* now ate *mariscos* [shellfish] with their *cuerpos bajo del sol* [bodies under the sun]. Jorge loved it; as far as he was concerned it was perfect. I listened to him practicing with Chuck for a couple of weeks before I said anything.

"Chuck," I started tentatively, one night after Jorge had gone.

"Jorge is really playing the song well, but . . ." I paused, wondering how to phrase it.

"But," Chuck concluded, "his singing is horrible."

"Well, yes, as a matter of fact, it is. Can you do anything?"

"Believe me, I'm trying. The kid has terrific technical playing skills, but his voice is all over the place. I swear he just can't hear any differences between the notes. Can't tune the guitar either, is lost without my electric tuner. This week I'm even giving him scales to try and sing."

They worked the next two lessons singing to basic chords and notes. From the kitchen I could hear Chuck singing do-re-mi, then Jorge repeating, but not even coming close. Chuck finally gave up and just decided they would sing "Margaritaville" over and over and maybe with time, he would hear it better. But he didn't. He did have enthusiasm though. Every morning at dawn we could hear him warbling *"Milles de touristas, comen los maricos,"* from his yard, accompanied by the barking dogs. My favorite part was after the line, *buscando por mi vaso de sal* [looking for my jigger of salt], Jorge would yell out in English, "OH YEAH!" then continue in Spanish.

Jorge had a special goal in mind — to debut with his guitar on his birthday. On the big night, we arrived with two boxes of wine and our chairs. We sat under his family's big acacia tree, much like we had the very first time we had been introduced almost a year before. The smaller children chased each other around while we and the older relatives sipped our box wine. Their long wooden dining table had been moved outdoors and Delma and her daughters loaded it down with the customary roasted beef, boiled mandioca and mayonnaise-potato salad. As usual when I tried to help, I was shooed back to my chair. We were finally called to the table and Rudy made a toast to his son, first in Guaranie, then in Spanish for our benefit. After birthday cake had been cut, passed around and praised mightily, Jorge brought out his guitar. I threw a nervous glance at Chuck, but before I could get eye contact, Jorge had launched vigorously into "Margaritaville." As I feared, he sang from flat to sharp rarely matching his guitar notes. I watched the faces of his relatives: nothing but big smiles followed by loud applause. Then Jorge played a sing-along Guaranie song and all the relatives joined it. The truth was suddenly revealed. The entire family was tone deaf. As far as they were concerned, Jorge was the greatest. After about a half-an-hour, Jorge passed the guitar to a relative who sang another Guaranie song, then passed it to another relative down the line of chairs. It was clear that as awful as they sounded to me, they all loved making music. We finally excused ourselves and headed home with our chairs.

"How can they all be tone deaf?" I asked Chuck. "Or is it that what sounds off-key to us is on-key for Guaranie music? Like the discordant sound of Chinese music?"

"I don't have the slightest idea," he said, shaking his head. "I'm only delighted that they liked Jorge's music and that he was a hit."

I thought about the music the next morning and reflected on how cultural it is. When we had graduated from our Peace Corps training they had played the Paraguayan National Anthem. At the time, it seemed pretty awful. It didn't have a beat and I couldn't hear any melody at all. Most national anthems have a real martial beat to them, but this one just rambled all over the place. I couldn't decide if that was the way it was supposed to sound or maybe the recording had just been terrible. Now, reflecting back on Cabana's party, I decided it was how they liked their music. I recalled back in Afghanistan Chuck and some others had put together a selection of American folk music for an Afghan musical night. A second group was to do a rock and roll number and the Afghans were to play their music. We found the Afghan music awful, and the Afghans didn't like our folk music at all. In fact the only real hit of that evening was the electric guitar.

32   Simple Pleasures

My book was getting harder to ignore. I was assigned a specific editor named Mary, and she wanted me to list all of the marketing ideas I had and what I planned to do to promote the book. Chuck and I brainstormed and made lists of ideas, but all of them involved using the Internet — hours and hours on the Internet. Problematic, to say the least.

Mary also wrote she was sending me the entire physical manuscript for me to check and send back. Regular mail to either Artigas or our Peace Corps box in Asunción took weeks, so Mary planned to use the international express company of DHL, which did deliver in Paraguay, but only as far as Encarnación. She said she would have them call us when the package arrived. I didn't want to tell her that we didn't have a telephone and that going to get it would take an entire day. Certainly, it was my problem, not hers. After she gave us the date she was sending it, Chuck and I waited five days then called the DHL office in Encarnación. It was there. Chuck decided he would take the bus the next day, get it and some groceries and be back by late afternoon. I would cover his classes.

The next morning we woke to pouring rain. At dawn we walked to Chaco's for the first bus and waited under the dripping eves, but no bus arrived. At 7:30 I trotted back home, made more coffee and carried a cup back to Chuck. Chacho told us that he thought the bus would come, but didn't know when. I waited with Chuck another hour, then had to go get ready for the computer classes. I had a break at eleven and ran down to Chacho's to see if Chuck was still standing there. Happily, he was gone. Chacho said the bus had come around 10:30a.m. I was relieved, but I knew it would be a very long day for him and I couldn't expect him for dinner. He finally came in around 9:00p.m., tired but triumphant.

"The manuscript," he announced proudly, pulling a big fat DHL package from his backpack. "And wine! And cheese and bread!"

We had discovered a bakery in Encarnación that made wonderful yeast breads, and Chuck had been able to buy a French loaf, and some real cheddar cheese at the big *supermercado*. We made a meal of it right then and toasted to the arrival of the manuscript.

In a week I was ready to send it back, but this time it wasn't raining enabling Chuck to return by late afternoon.

O n the dry weekends, we kept up with our exercise of railroad-track walking. I wanted to keep my post-surgery size and Chuck was competing with Roberto, who was claiming great success with Dr. Atkins.

One morning when we got to our turn-around ditch, we scrambled down and up the other side, just to see what was out there. After walking about a mile we spied an old 1940's — Chuck's best guess — Packard in a field, long abandoned. That got our imaginations going. Who would have had the money to buy such a car? How did it get there? Was it one of Paraguay's corrupt politicians or a fleeing Nazi? The Nazi bit was not that far-fetched as we had heard stories that many Nazis who were fleeing post-war Germany came this way after landing in Buenos Aires. Argentina was naturally the destination of choice, but I suspect many might have had to flee further, and central Paraguay would have been completely off the radar. Still is. The year before we arrived, a

German farm in central Paraguay was burned to the ground, with high suspicions of an old Nazi connection. At least the people who burned the place down thought so.

The next rainstorm brought out our Scrabble board. We had watched every possible video in town and were tired of trying to read under our one hanging light bulb in the living room. We dug the game out of our duffel and set it up on a little table on the front porch.

"I think we should play it in Spanish," I told Chuck. "It would help our Spanish and give it a little twist."

"What about the Spanish letters?" Chuck asked. "Like accents, the double L and the CH and the squiggle for the en-yea?"

I thought for a minute. "Well, I think we can forget the accents and the double L's can just be two L's, same for the CH — just use a C and an H. We can mark up a few of the N's." I checked the box and we found that there were six N's, so we would change three of them to N's with squiggles. And we could use the Spanish dictionary all the time.

We were struggling along when Roberto strolled up to the gate. He was intrigued with the game and I let him have my spot. It didn't take him long to catch on. He would check his letter points and eye the board like a master.

"*Me gusto mucho este juego!* [I love this game!]" he exclaimed, as he laid down "*zarpa*" on a triple word play for forty-eight points. Chuck and I quickly looked up *zarpa*: claw. In the next hour we learned such vocabulary gems as *yegua* [mare], *jebe* [rubber plant] and *sarrio* [a Pyrenean mountain goat].

"*Puedo venir manana y jugar mas?* [Can I come tomorrow and play more?]" he asked, delighted to have trounced both of us with one hundred point leads.

"*Por supuesto*, [Sure,]" we told him, feeling that we could do better the second night.

But we didn't. More strange Spanish words appeared with combinations of Z's and J's and Q's.

Chuck had forgotten that it was the night for Jorge's guitar lesson, so when he came up to the porch, I brought out another chair and he joined in. Since Spanish was technically a second language for him, he wasn't quite as good as Roberto, but still beat the pants off of us, and was delighted to think he could beat the *Norte Americanos* at their own game. In defense I was going to bring up the fact that it was an English game and we were playing it in Spanish, but decided to just let it go.

Jorge came back the next night with his brother and after they beat Chuck they played against each other. Word of such an innovative past-time spread, of course and two days later Ramón was asking about the game. We decided to loan it out and try and buy a Spanish version on our next trip to Asunción.

I was most pleased with my garden and my chicken-guards! By the end of May I had a full crop of peppers, cucumbers, and some lettuce. Mandy had given me seeds for a shade plant and told me to plant them along the west end of the garden. They grew quickly and tall and as the garden was developing, the bushes provided shade from the hot afternoon sun. She had planted a similar row along the west side of her little house, lowering her inside summer temperatures by a substantial degree.

Once the weather cooled, the bushes died off, but by then, they weren't needed any more. My cilantro had done well and the lettuce too, but it was attacked by worms so I didn't get many heads. Both Kitty and Delma kept asking for a cucumber or two, which I gladly supplied, but I found it a bit curious that neither of them put a garden in their own yards. When I asked Roberto about it, he said many people thought it was too much work. Especially, I considered, since Paraguay really wasn't a vegetable eating country.

Ramón had a real interest in gardening though and was especially keen to get some sweet corn seeds since he had tasted North American table corn and loved it. Like Spain, the only corn Paraguayans knew was the tasteless stuff used for cattle feed. Another treat I gave Ramón was an introduction to pecans. I had brought a package home from the States and gave some to him to sample. He couldn't believe how good they were. I had no idea if it was difficult to grow a pecan tree, but thought I'd ask Mandy if there were seeds available. I thought that it might be an easy project, unlike many of the Peace Corps agricultural proposals that took acres of land and possible lost revenue. Here they could plant some seeds in the back yard and if they grew, fine. If not, no loss. Paraguay's climate would be very similar to Georgia's where pecans flourished.

In addition to a flourishing garden, our yard was looking quite trim thanks to our new lawn-tender, Jorge. After the initial months of having Cabana and sons whack agonizingly through the grass with their machetes, Jorge had stopped by to say that he could cut our lawn with a real lawn mowing machine. I hated to take the job from Cabana, but I also hated seeing them working like slaves, not to mention worrying about them cutting their toes off. Besides, I was intrigued — a real lawn mower? I had never seen such a thing in Artigas, or anywhere in Paraguay for that matter.

The next day Jorge clapped at the gate, ready with his mower. If there was such a thing as a cute lawn mower, this was it. It was a tiny motor, mounted on a small piece of plywood. Under the plywood was a single blade that swung around in a circle. Notches were cut in the four corners of the plywood and little hand carved wooden wheels had been attached to metal bars underneath. But the best part was the enormously long electrical cord, at least fifty yards in length, spliced and mended beyond count — every couple of inches displaying an abundant bulge of electrical tape. By plugging it into the outlet we had by the front door, he could cover the front yard, and when he was ready to mow the back, we moved the cord to the kitchen and ran it out the back door. Jorge could make it to the first mango tree and we didn't cut the grass beyond that anyway.

Chuck and I followed Jorge raking and throwing the grass over the fence to a cow, who thought it was quite a treat. At first there was one cow, then two and finally a small herd had gathered. The whole project took about two hours, versus the four hours with Cabana and crew. And this amazing little mower cut the grass evenly, unlike the patchy work from the machetes.

I still felt badly about taking the work away from Cabana, but Jorge also needed the money. Everyone needed the money.

33 The Decision

Paraguay's Independence Day was coming — May 15th, which Artigas celebrated by having a parade of all the school children. Independence from Spain had been declared in 1811 making Paraguay the second independent country in the New World after the United States. We had asked Roberto what the parade was like and he just shrugged and suggested that we might enjoy going to see our students march by.

This sounded like a good idea so on Saturday morning, Chuck and I stood on the corner next to the *cooperativa*, awaiting the parade. On the opposite corner were three boys, two with snare drums and one with a bass drum. This was the parade band. The teachers felt it would be unfair for the band to actually be in the parade as only the students in front of them or behind them would hear the beat. Instead, they positioned the drummers on the corner so when the students marched by they would all be able to hear the music. After a number of students passed by, we decided that we were drummed-out and strolled home.

By now, my book was hanging over my head like the sword of Damocles. Every time I got a notice about the progress of the book, I was torn between delight and anguish. We had learned that the book would be published in August and it was being considered for a book fair in October. If my book was chosen, they would send me there for a signing. Mary told me that once my book was out, she would have six months to work with me, then she had to move on to new projects. It made sense. If you weren't Stephen King, they had to publicize new books and new possibilities of blockbusters. I didn't believe my book would become a bestseller, but still, I felt I had to do everything I could to try and help it along. So, basically I had from August to January to market with their support. If we left at the end of August I thought we could fit in one more computer class and I would still have five months of assisted marketing. Chuck and I hashed out all of our options one more time. I knew I would always be conflicted about the decision, but everything pointed to an August departure. So that was it. We planned to make all the announcements in July.

Of course the other big question was where in the heck would we go in the States? We had sold the house, the cars, and there wasn't a compelling reason to return to California at all. In fact, the idea of trying to reestablish in San Diego wasn't even appealing. On our walks down the railroad tracks, Chuck and I discussed options.

"As long as we're starting over, we might as well go to a tax-free state. How about Nevada?" Chuck said.

"Yuck," was my only reply.

We had been to Las Vegas twice and both times I had hated it. I was too much of a tightwad to enjoy gambling, it was too hot and windy and the casinos seemed sleazy, despite the bright lights. I swore I wouldn't return even if they paid me.

"Wyoming?" Chuck said, and we both shook our heads together. Too cold. "Texas, maybe, Florida?"

I didn't know much about Florida. I did know a little about Texas. My parents had come from there and as a child I had been to Amarillo several times. Now, of course, Mom lived in Amarillo with her sisters. That town didn't seem too appealing, but we had read that Austin was a good spot — lots of music and a University that gave it an intellectual bent. Plus, it sounded like my sister Rita and her husband would be moving to the San Antonio area. A few more walks and Austin became our number one choice. The plan was to rent a furnished apartment for a few months, which would give me time to work on the book and at the same time, we could see how Texas living suited us.

I harvested the last of my garden produce in June. By then we were having the occasional cold spells that killed off the vegetables and left us chilly in the house. For this "winter" though, we had purchased a little, portable, electric heater we could at least drag around to keep our feet warm. I also used our old Afghan trick, of covering the windows with sheets of thick plastic, tacking them around the outside window sills. I couldn't do it with all the windows as we needed some circulation, but I covered the main ones in the living room and second bedroom. I was still amazed that the Paraguayans did nothing to protect themselves from the cold. I thought it seemed a simple measure to have a Franklin stove put in the house with a stove pipe like we had in Afghanistan where it had kept us toasty with freezing temperatures and snow. When I asked Delma about putting in a stove she just shrugged and smiled.

"It's not so cold here," she told me as we stood outside wrapped in heavy jackets, hats and gloves. "And it's only for a short time." She was right, it wasn't life-threatening cold, just cold. But there was no relief — no place one could go to warm up. Stores were cold, the *cooperativa* was cold, buses were cold. The only salvation was under the covers.

We were due back in Asunción for another Peace Corps meeting in late June. Roberto was disappointed that we were going to miss Artigas's San Juan Festival. It's great fun, he assured me. I recalled the fire balls, burning Judas and walking on the coals from Pindolo and thought I could do without it.

Besides, this particular meeting had special significance for me: I had to have a colonoscopy! They wanted to check, it was explained to me, that all was OK in my colon. I told the Peace Corps nurse Julie that all was gurgling as it should (Chuck put his ear to my stomach almost daily just to be sure) and I felt super and things were "going" fine so maybe I could take a pass? But she said "No," they wanted to make sure. And, she assured me, I wouldn't feel a thing, they would put me to sleep and it would be easy — except the day before, of course.

We got our customary rooms at the Hotel Paraguay and I stopped by the Peace Corps office to get all my necessary powders and pills. The next morning I started my fast, taking only coffee for breakfast and looking longingly at Chuck's scrambled eggs and real bread rolls. I wondered how this examination would differ from one in the States and also wondered if it was safe, then decided it wasn't worth the time to fret about it. It couldn't be any less safe than the surgery in Bolivia. It would have been nice to be at home though, not in a hotel and especially not in a hotel where you couldn't flush the toilet paper. It embarrassed me to think what the maid would think of my collection basket the next day. But, the day passed and although I was up half the night, the morning light finally slanted through the edges of our room's heavy curtains.

To make it easier for me, Julia the nurse, picked me up and drove me to the clinic so I wouldn't have to mess with taxis and buses and the possibility of getting lost, or the possibility of just skipping out on the whole thing. We waited together in a plain — bordering on shabby — waiting room and after a half an hour, I was called in. I really can't say I remember much after that. I dimly remember being driven back to the hotel and hearing that my colon was just fine.

"Tell Chuck it's fine," I mumbled, then went back into my zombie state and slept the rest of the day.

I learned later that patients in the States usually wake up and after a half an hour, are good to go. Maybe they really conked me out, but I wasn't complaining.

We had two social occasions for July. The first was a visit from Mandy for the 4th of July. It was a pretty low-key affair. I tried to make a facsimile of hot dogs using chipa rolls for bread and pork sausage for the hot dogs. I had mustard from the *cooperativa* and had carried home some little ketchup packages from a Burger King in Asunción. Mandy, being a vegetarian, filled her roll with tomatoes and onions. I had put some little red and blue stickers on our napkins and we had a special iced tea from a mix I had bought in Asunción. The three of us raised a toast to the American Revolution and munched down a few Brazilian cookies. It was at least as good as last year's "Happy Pak" from Mc Donald's.

The next weekend we had three guests, all from the municipal side of our group — outside of John, they were our favorite people — Izzy and Beth, the newly-married couple, and a single Volunteer named Kathleen. They were touring parts of the country to compare municipal governments and could spend two nights with us. They arrived with backpacks full of wine and goodies and on Saturday all of us cooked up a storm. It kept us warm and helped us celebrate both Izzy's and my birthday — his was the 13th of July and mine was the 14th. For the birthday lunch we baked a huge pork roast, tossed a cabbage salad, made bread and stuck candles into our Mennonite ice cream.

We were barely clearing the dishes when Ramón clapped at the gate. Somehow, he had discovered it was my birthday and informed us there was a big birthday lunch for all of us down at the *cooperativa*. We all looked at each other thinking, another meal, now? But there it was. We couldn't refuse; we had to have a second lunch. So we managed, even had some of their special cake, then lumbered back home hoping we wouldn't explode. Dinner that night was mostly wine, which made our games of charades funnier and funnier. I couldn't remember when I had laughed so much. Sunday morning Izzy, Beth and Kathleen were off and I hated seeing them go. Their visit reminded me of stories from the old West where visitors were always welcome and were encouraged to stay as long as possible.

After their visit the cold weather arrived with a vengeance in mid-July. It had been cold, but now the cold went for a record. We had seven consecutive days of night temperatures between twenty-seven and thirty-two and the high daily temperature had only been forty-one. According to what we read in the paper this broke records going back twenty-seven years. This called for more drastic measures in the Hanner household. We basically moved into the kitchen and blocked off the kitchen from the rest of the house with our spare sheet nailed across the doorway. Now the little electric heater had a fighting chance of warming up that smaller space and we could get heat from the stove and oven. We moved two chairs into the kitchen, ate at the kitchen table for dinner then made a bee-line for the bedroom and dove into our freezing bed. Showers were moved to "high noon" when the bathroom was least glacial. The hot water ring couldn't compete with the extra cold, so the shower only got to lukewarm. That, plus the frigid room and the icy floor led us to decide that we really didn't need a shower every day; it wasn't like we were sweating much.

Roberto came clapping at our fence and we invited him into our little somewhat-warm kitchen. He thought we had a pretty good solution; his house was just freezing. Wine warmed us up — at least our spirits — and we entertained him with stories of winters with snow. How people have to shovel their driveways and their roofs. How dangerous it is to drive on ice. After a while we practically felt balmy.

34 Hidden Talent

The time had finally come to tell Ramón about the book and about leaving Artigas. Chuck and I decided to announce it together so we both went to Ramón's tiny office in the back of the *cooperativa*. I knocked and he called us in, looking up in surprise to see us both.

"*Tenemos malas noticias* [We have bad news]," I began, then told him the whole story of my book, and how it had progressed to the publishing stage, years ahead of what I had expected. After listening he nodded glumly.

"*Yo habria ido el mismo* [I would have done the same]," he told me. He then went on to say that I shouldn't turn down the opportunity and that he understood completely, but, of course was most disappointed that we were going to leave them. It was a relief to tell him and his understanding helped lighten my feelings of guilt.

We knew the news would spread around town in a day. It didn't take that long. Roberto was on our steps that evening, crestfallen about our departure.

"*Ahora, quién va a charlar conmigo acerca de extraterrestres?* [Now, who is going to chat with me about aliens?]"

He did wish us well and wanted to talk all about books and publishing and how famous I would become. I had to explain that

I wouldn't become famous, that lots of people published books, but he wasn't hearing any of it. As far as he was concerned, I was going to be the most famous person he had ever known.

We went to Asunción the next weekend with a long to-do list. First and foremost we had to go to the Peace Corp director's office and tell him we needed to go back to the States. I had been dreading it, but he was most understanding, almost like he was expecting the news. It was a huge relief to have all the anxiety and months of worrying about it over with. We also told our field director and nurse Julie and other staff members we knew well. Everyone's reaction was the same: happy for us, but sad to see us go.

Our second big project was to make Certificates of Completion for our computer students. We had done this with our previous classes and it was a big hit. Peace Corps had special certificate paper that we could print with our program information and the students' names and then sign and date them. Not only did they look nice, but they gave the students proof they had computer experience.

We made another visit, this one to Pindolo to see Digna and her family. She had insisted we come for lunch and we agreed to come out the day before we went back to Artigas. Both she and her husband Victor were there along with their children Little Victor and Diana, but her sister was gone for the day. It was lovely and she used the tablecloth we had bought for her. She was sad to hear that we would be leaving, but happy for us too.

When we mentioned that we were expecting to have difficulty getting the bicycles back to the Peace Corps with all of our luggage, Victor Señor piped up, "*No problemo. Nos a llevarles a Asunción en mi camión.* [No problem. We will take you to Asuncion in my truck.]" He added that he still didn't have any trucking jobs and it would be a good excursion for them. It was a great idea for us and solved a huge problem. I told Digna that in exchange I would give her all my kitchen dishes, utensils and pots and pans. She protested, saying I didn't need to give her anything, but I persisted, hastening to explain I didn't have much and it wasn't fancy. But everything in her kitchen had seen years of service and I don't think she had one dish that wasn't chipped or cracked. Her pans were dented and stained beyond redemption. I had had first-hand experience with them, having done the dishes and had scrubbed them unmercifully with no results. She was delighted. We agreed on an approximate date, but I planned to call as the time neared to firm it up.

As we walked back to the bus stop Chuck and I talked about what a surprise it was that Victor Señor had spoken up so enthusiastically.

"I thought he didn't like us at all." I said.

"Maybe it was just that his Spanish was so poor he was embarrassed to speak to us, or he's excited to see us go," Chuck said with a chuckle.

We laughed at the thought of his truck coming, as it was the cab portion of a giant eighteen-wheeler. I had never seen anything that large come into town.

Our first task when we returned to Artigas was finding a fair way to give everything away without hurting anyone's feelings. Everyone needed everything, so it wasn't like we could just give to the needy. Neighbors had already started with their requests. Roberto had been eyeing our large bed since he was the same size as Chuck. Cabana wanted our tools, Kitty wanted the other furniture, Alicia wanted the refrigerator. It went on and on. I started making lists and comparative values.

We finished our last computer typing class and were able to give the students their attractive Peace Corps certificates. We encouraged Ramón to continue with the typing classes as our first students could easily teach the others on a part-time basis. We had two students in particular who said they could teach a couple of afternoons a week. Ramón wasn't terribly enthusiastic though. He thought the class just wouldn't have enough momentum without us. I agreed that it wouldn't be quite as intensive as our classes, but it would keep the program going and I made a schedule for the classes anyway, hoping that it would fall into place.

As part of our farewell celebrations — which seemed continuous — we wanted to have a big party at our home and invite Kitty and her extended family that included Roberto, his wife and daughter. We had attended so many *asados* at their home, it hardly equaled it out, but was a gesture.

I had decided to make a huge spaghetti dinner. Everyone always liked it and it was something unusual for them. Especially the mushrooms in the sauce, which were practically unknown.

Our dinner was a big success with more people than plates, but I had learned that it didn't matter. I served up spaghetti in anything I could find and sent one child back home to bring his own bowl. Grownups sat in chairs at the table and in the kitchen and kids sat on the edges of things or on the floor. With children coming and going it was hard to figure out how many I did have, but it was about double the actual number I had invited.

Two days later the *cooperativa* had a special lunch for us and many of the employees brought us special little gifts. Alicia had bought me a cute little ceramic figure and told me that I had to keep it so I could keep her in my memory. Two other women, Yoli and Blanca, brought me items they had crocheted. After lunch we sat and chatted with Ramón. Normally, our conversations were brief as he always had to get back to work, but this time, it was Saturday and everything was closed. We talked about the business of the *cooperativa* and said we wished we could have helped more. Chuck got into the discussion of how Artigas needed outside money coming in to make things grow and Ramón agreed entirely.

"Too bad you don't have some kind of handicraft to export," I said.

"But we do," Ramón said.

I looked at him. "What handicrafts?" thinking that he misunderstood the meaning of my Spanish word *artesanales*.

"Los croché," he said.

"Crochet?"

He reaffirmed that and said we had to see all the wonderful crochet products made by women in Artigas. He stood up and announced we would go pay a visit to Oscar's mother, who lived just up the street and had lots of crochet. Chuck and I exchanged a here-we-go glance, but dutifully followed. Momma Oscar was home, of course, and more than happy to have us come in, share some tea (she guessed *mate* wasn't our drink) and view her crochet work.

It was a bit like stepping back in your grandmother's house, with crocheted doilies on the backs and arms of every chair, on the end tables, under the lamps, crocheted pillows on the couch and a crocheted table runner on the dining table.

I didn't know the first thing about crochet, but they did look well made and I praised her for her workmanship. Ramón beamed.

"*Puedes venderlos en los Estados Unidos?* [Can you sell them in the United States?]"

I hesitated and explained that crochet wasn't all that popular any more.

"But we have different kinds," he insisted. Mamma Oscar nodded vigorously and said she'd be right back, she was going to run to a neighbor's and bring back some of her crochet.

She was out the door despite my feeble, "*No es necesario.*" She came bursting back through the door in a remarkably short time given the fact that she was a bit stout for running anywhere, even next door. Her arms were stacked high with crochet. She laid the pile on the coffee table and started holding up the pieces, one by one. In the pile were cute vests, hand bags and interesting window shades — definitely more marketable than table doilies.

"You could sell them, right?" Ramón asked.

"Well, maybe," I said. I looked at Chuck and shrugged. We agreed to talk about it and let him know tomorrow.

After discussing the possibilities Chuck and I thought there had to be some kind of market. At a local store maybe or the Internet.

If we could get it going, it might be a real source of incoming revenue for the town, which was desperately needed. Neither one of us had been thinking of getting into the import business, but we went back to Ramón the next day and said we'd give it a try. We would take back a small selection and see how it went. Ramón was more than delighted; now he couldn't wait for us to leave. We made an initial pile of items to take back and coded them with numbers and sizes so it would be easy for me to reorder them.

I had been hoping to keep our luggage to a minimum on the trip home, but with the extra crochet, that was now an impossibility. The next morning, while I was stewing over how to fit in the crochet, Ramón clapped at our gate.

"*Un regalo para ustedes,* [A gift for you,]" he told us. "*De Aritgas.* [From Artigas.]"

He handed me a large package. I motioned him inside and called for Chuck so we could open it together. It was big and heavy and carefully wrapped in paper and twine. I slowly untied it and opened the paper to find a beautiful crocheted bedspread, big enough for a double bed. I was flabbergasted and couldn't thank him enough.

"I will put it on my bed forever," I told him sincerely. It was far too expensive a gift for us. I couldn't even think how long it took someone to crochet it, especially given the fact that few women had time to do such activities during the day and were only crocheting at night, under very weak lights.

If I had a packing challenge before, it now had worsened. My worn duffel, that we had planned to give away, was called back into service. We layered the bedspread inside with other crochet, folded the bag over and tried to zip it up. The zipper completely broke apart. There was no saving the zipper and no way to buy another bag either. I finally hit on the idea of sewing the bag shut with dental floss. I wasn't sure how that would go in customs, but didn't see another good way to do it. I did have a stout needle but no thimble, so spent the entire afternoon pushing the needle through two layers of canvas with a small rock.

By the next day we had our whole stack of luggage ready to go. We had given away the stove and Alicia was buying the refrigerator at half price with a loan from the *cooperativa*. We had decided we couldn't just give it away as it was so much more expensive than the other things that it would be grossly unfair. Chuck's guitar was going to Jorge and miscellaneous items were going in every which direction.

The day before our departure we said good-bye to about everyone. We knew we would see Kitty again to take back our key, but tried to get a final good-bye in with everyone else. Little Al, Chuck's guitar student came by with tears in his eyes, so sad to see us leave. He wanted to know if we could take him with us. We promised Roberto we would try and come back, maybe for his daughter's *quinceañero* [15th birthday celebration]. The Barbosa's were depressed as well, saying what good neighbors we had been and how important it was to have good neighbors. They were cheered somewhat by Jorge getting Chuck's guitar and by some small items I had given Delma. Cabana came by for the tools we had promised him and brought us a huge sweet potato from his garden, thinking we could eat it on our way. It still had the dirt clinging to it. Many people did envision our trip as a very long bus ride. The woman who cut my hair wanted to know just how many days the bus ride would take. When I told her we were taking a plane, she looked at me with amazement. Like Alicia, she rarely left town and a long trip for her was the bus to Asunción. Since airplanes didn't fly over Artigas, she had never actually seen a plane in the sky, but she had, she assured me, seen them on television.

Victor's big truck roared into town late in the afternoon and, as I expected, it drew a crowd. Digna and the kids were all in the huge front cab and the whole family piled out, giving us big hugs and the customary two-cheek Paraguayan kisses. I explained to Digna that we would have to clear out the kitchen and clean as we went. I wasn't sure about dinner or the sleeping arrangements, but it all seemed to fall into place. We bought a couple of Chacho's chickens, some empañadas and that seemed to do the trick. Digna and her husband slept in the truck and the kids were in the spare bed. Or I think they were. We were exhausted and went to bed before they had all turned in for the night.

We went to work with a flurry the next morning — loading things, cleaning shelves, mopping, sweeping and by noon the house was spic and span and empty except for furniture left for Kitty and Roberto. Chuck walked down, gave Kitty our key, walked back and Digna, Victor, Chuck and I got in the front of the cab, with Little Victor and Diana in the back.

The truck slowly pulled away from the house and turned right, out to the main street. As we passed the train tracks, I took one last look backwards.

Chuck squeezed my hand. "We're on our way now," he whispered in my ear.

Epilogue

My book, *The First Big Ride, A Woman's Journey*, didn't become a best seller nor did I become famous. I was happy though with my decision to come back to the U.S. to put time in the marketing with book talks and work on the Internet. The book was selected for the Northwest Book Conference in Portland, Oregon where I traveled for a book signing.

We initially landed in Austin, but found after a short time that the city really didn't suit us. We moved on to Arkansas and by November discovered that it got too cold there — colder than Paraguay!

My sister, Linda, suggested Sarasota, based on something she had read, so that became our next stop. Sarasota seemed to have many of the things we liked: a beach, places for cycling and an active arts scene, so after a month we made an offer on a house and, to our surprise, we got it. That was a bit scary, but we figured we would only stay until we could find something better. That was thirteen years ago.

We sold crocheted products from Artigas for ten years. I had two stores that I worked with, one in San Antonio and the other in Sarasota. The Sarasota store, The Artisans World Marketplace, run by Sandy Ramsey, was by far the larger outlet and Sandy's help over the years was outstanding. Crochet sales never developed into the large-scale business we had envisioned for Artigas, mainly due to the exorbitant shipping costs involved. I lost money on every shipment, but it was a slow loss and thanks again to a grant from Sandy, we were able to keep it going for the ladies of Artigas until 2010. Sandy may still have a few items for sale.

I am still in touch with Ramón, in fact I spent the winter of 2010 sending him car parts for his Ford.

I went on to write another book, a play and now, of course, offer this account of our time in Paraguay. Chuck and I travel a great deal, bicycle, play tennis and enjoy life in Sarasota.

I still have the Artigas crocheted bedspread on my bed.

Acknowledgments

A special thanks for my sister, Linda Carlton, for her extensive editing and grammar review, to Leita Kaldi for her continued support and information on Peace Corps Writers and to Marian Haley Beil at Peace Corps Writers for her excellent book design, editing and assistance.

Made in the USA
San Bernardino, CA
11 August 2014